math

FOR THE PROFESSIONAL KITCHEN

This book is printed on acid-free paper. ∞

The Culinary Institute of America
President   Dr. Tim Ryan '77
Vice President, Dean of Culinary Education   Mark Erickson '77
Senior Director, Educational Enterprises   Susan Cussen
Director of Publishing   Nathalie Fischer
Editorial Project Manager   Lisa Lahey '00
Editorial Assistant   Shelly Malgee '08

Published by John Wiley & Sons, Inc., Hoboken, New Jersey
Published simultaneously in Canada

All material from *The Book of Yields* by Francis T. Lynch copyright © 2008 by John Wiley & Sons, Inc. Reprinted with permission of John Wiley & Sons, Inc.

Limit of Liability/Disclaimer of Warranty: While the publisher and author have used their best efforts in preparing this book, they make no representations or warranties with respect to the accuracy or completeness of the contents of this book and specifically disclaim any implied warranties of merchantability or fitness for a particular purpose. No warranty may be created or extended by sales representatives or written sales materials. The advice and strategies contained herein may not be suitable for your situation. You should consult with a professional where appropriate. Neither the publisher nor author shall be liable for any loss of profit or any other commercial damages, including but not limited to special, incidental, consequential, or other damages.

For general information on our other products and services or for technical support, please contact our Customer Care Department within the United States at (800) 762-2974, outside the United States at (317) 572-3993 or fax (317) 572-4002.

Wiley also publishes its books in a variety of electronic formats. Some content that appears in print may not be available in electronic books. For more information about Wiley products, visit our web site at www.wiley.com.

LIBRARY OF CONGRESS CATALOGING-IN-PUBLICATION DATA

Dreesen, Laura.
  Math for the professional kitchen / the Culinary Institute of America ; Laura Dreesen, Michael Nothnagel, and Susan Wysocki.
     p. cm.
  Includes bibliographical references and index.
  ISBN 978-0-470-50896-1 (pbk.)
  1. Cookery—Mathematics. I. Nothnagel, Michael. II. Wysocki, Susan. III. Culinary Institute of America. IV. Title.
  TX652.D73 2011
  641.501'51—dc22
                                        2010013124

PRINTED IN THE UNITED STATES OF AMERICA

10 9 8 7 6

math

FOR THE PROFESSIONAL KITCHEN

Laura Dreesen, Michael Nothnagel, and Susan Wysocki
THE CULINARY INSTITUTE OF AMERICA

WILEY

JOHN WILEY & SONS, INC.

contents

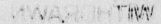

acknowledgments

Our gratitude:

Shelly Malgee

Keith Ferris

Lisa Lahey

Nathalie Fischer

Pamela Chirls

Bonnie Bogush

Chef Michael Pardus

Chef Thomas Schneller

Student Assistants:

Brooke Maynard

Daniel Clark

Carissa Sutter

Renée Leber

foreword

Why are we doing math? I came here to cook.

—ANONYMOUS CULINARY STUDENT

If this is what you are thinking, I'd like you to consider the following:

How many cups in a gallon?

How many grams in an ounce?

What does it mean to make a 1:1 simple syrup or a 5:3 bread dough?

If I need 50 pounds of peeled onions, how many pounds of unpeeled onions should I buy?

Why is it better to weigh ingredients than to measure by volume?

If my bonus is tied to food cost percentage, what does that mean, and will I get a bonus?

Proper application of math in the kitchen *will* impact how you cook and how long you stay in business. If you measure incorrectly, miscalculate the ratio, or end up with a lower than expected yield, driving food costs up, you could potentially put yourself out of the cooking business.

So, you came here to cook? To be successful in the industry, you'd best start with the math!

Here's a true story. When opening a new place, a smart restaurateur will keep some cash in reserve to help cover the first year's growing pains. With one property I ran, we were lucky. At the end of the first year we were actually a bit in the black—the investors hadn't had to touch the reserve fund, and it accumulated interest instead. The investors called the management team in, explained the surplus, and then gave each of us an all-expenses-paid vacation as a reward for being good stewards.

Good luck with your careers. Cook well, with integrity and intelligence.

Chef Michael Pardus
Professor, The Culinary Institute of America
Hyde Park, New York
September 2011

introduction

Carpe diem does not mean "fish of the day."

—ANONYMOUS

Doing mathematics is a lot like cooking. Of course, there are a lot of differences, too. For example, it's hard to chop something with a calculator, and taking notes on the back of a frying pan isn't as easy as it might sound. Here are some similarities between doing math and cooking:

- **YOU BEGIN WITH GIVEN INFORMATION. A math problem gives you known quantities, conditions, and other facts that you need to get started. A recipe provides a total yield, ingredient amounts, and sometimes a list of specialized equipment.**

- **YOU FOLLOW A STEP-BY-STEP PROCEDURE. In math, you do calculations until you arrive at a solution. When using a recipe, you follow the specified method until you end up with a finished product.**

- **SOMETIMES YOU CAN DO THINGS YOUR WAY; SOMETIMES YOU CAN'T. Often in math, there are multiple ways to get to the same answer. In other cases, the "rules" of math say the calculations need to be done in a specific order. Recipes sometimes give you flexibility with ingredients or quantities; other times you have to follow the recipe to the letter or it won't work correctly.**

- **YOU NEED TO MAKE SURE YOUR RESULT IS WHAT YOU WANT. In math, checking to see if your answer is reasonable and is labeled properly is always a good idea. Likewise, it is essential that you test your finished product in a kitchen to make sure everything is cooked properly and tastes good.**

Our goal is to show you mathematical procedures that are frequently used in professional kitchens and bakeshops. We have strived to explain these procedures in a succinct, understandable way without oversimplifying them. As with many topics in mathematics, the proof of the pudding is in the eating: it is your job to take these concepts and successfully apply them. As you progress through your culinary or baking career, you will build upon the ideas discussed in this book. You may even encounter procedures that work better for you than those we describe.

Learning how to do mathematics is an essential part of being a professional chef or baker. It may not always be apparent, but being a successful member of the hospitality industry means having a working knowledge of math, science, business, and art, among many other subjects. Expanding your knowledge in all of these areas will help you to *carpe diem* every time you enter your kitchen.

Laura Dreesen, Michael Nothnagel, and Susan Wysocki
Hyde Park, N.Y.
July 2011

math
FOR THE PROFESSIONAL KITCHEN

1

Units of Measure and Unit Conversions

KEY TERMS

weight

volume

U.S. customary system

metric system/Système International d'Unités (SI)

avoirdupois

equivalent

mixed measurement

unit conversion

tare

KEY QUESTIONS

What types of measurements are used in a professional kitchen?

When measuring a substance by weight, what property are you measuring?

When measuring a substance by volume, what property are you measuring?

What standard U.S. and SI units are weight measures? Which are volume measures?

What are you doing when you convert units of measure?

Why do foodservice professionals need to convert units of measure?

1.1 Measurements Used in the Professional Kitchen

When measuring ingredients in the kitchen, you measure by **weight** (gravitational pull) or by **volume** (a defined amount of space). The focuses of this chapter are (1) the formal standards by which ingredients are measured in the professional kitchen and (2) converting quantities from one unit of measure to another.

There are two commonly used systems of measurement: the **U.S. customary system** and the **metric system.** The metric system, which is formally known as the **Système International d'Unités (SI),** is the most prevalent standard across the globe. Both SI and U.S. customary unit standards will be discussed in this text. Care has been taken to pare down the amount of information to manageable quantities for the emergent professional. Over time you will expand your knowledge base past the contents of this resource.

MEASURING BY WEIGHT

Standard weight measurements are defined legally. Weight measures based on the U.S. customary 16-ounce pound are called **avoirdupois** measures. The metric gram has been defined as being the weight of 1 cubic centimeter of water, and the kilogram is defined as the weight of 1000 cubic centimeters, or 1 liter, of space filled with water.

MEASURES OF WEIGHT	WEIGHT MEASURE	ABBREVIATION
METRIC SYSTEM	gram	g
	kilogram	kg
U.S. CUSTOMARY SYSTEM	pound	# or lb
	ounce	oz

Written in order from the smallest to the largest unit of weight:

gram

ounce

pound

kilogram

The standard weight **equivalents,** or relationships between the weight measures, are shown below. These relationships are constant.

28.35 g	=	1 oz					
453.6 g	=	16 oz	=	1 #	=	0.4536 kg	
1000 g	=	35.27 oz	=	2.205 #	=	1 kg	

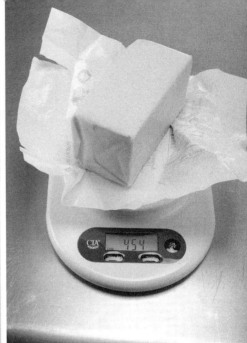

Equivalent weights. Left: Butter weighed in pounds on a spring scale. Right: The same butter weighed in grams on a digital scale.

Each row in the chart contains equivalent quantities. For instance, the second row tells us that if 453.6 grams of a substance is placed on a digital scale, the scale could read 16 ounces, 1 pound, or 0.4536 kilograms. The quantity on the scale did not change, but the weight was expressed using different units of measure. Similarly, if 1000 grams of a substance was placed on a digital scale, the scale could read 35.27 ounces, 2.205 pounds, or 1 kilogram. You can also use **mixed measurements** (measurements using more than one unit) to specify a quantity. For example, 21 ounces could be written as 1 pound 5 ounces.

To measure weight you can use a traditional spring scale, a digital scale, or a balance scale.

For professional kitchen use, a digital scale accurate to within 1 gram or 1/100 of an ounce is adequate for just about any need. Many kitchens use scales weighing in intervals of 5 grams or 1/8 ounce, which are less accurate but also less expensive. Your choice of scale depends upon the needs of your particular kitchen.

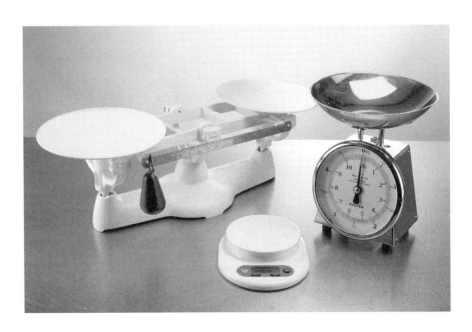

Types of scales. Left to right: balance scale, digital scale, spring scale.

MEASURING BY VOLUME

Measuring an ingredient by volume means that you are filling a certain quantity of space with an ingredient. Volume measures are legally defined in the U.S. customary system, and there are liquid volume and dry volume measures. The liquid and dry volume measures are two separate sets of volume measurements, and corresponding units are different sizes. The volume units used in the professional kitchen are based on the liquid volume scale with the exception of the peck and bushel, which are U.S. customary dry volume measures. (For more information about liquid and dry volume measurements, see Appendix I.)

The milliliter is defined as 1 cubic centimeter of space, or the amount of space that 1 gram of water occupies. The liter is defined as 1000 cubic centimeters of space or 1000 milliliters of volume. This can also be looked at as the amount of space that 1 kilogram of water occupies.

MEASURES OF VOLUME	VOLUME MEASURE	ABBREVIATION
METRIC SYSTEM	milliliter	mL or ml
	liter	L
U.S. CUSTOMARY SYSTEM	teaspoon	tsp or t
	tablespoon	tbl or T
	fluid ounce	fl oz
	cup	C
	pint	pt
	quart	qt
	gallon	G or gal

Written in order from the smallest to the largest unit of volume:

milliliter

teaspoon

tablespoon

fluid ounce

cup

pint

quart

liter

gallon

The standard volume equivalents or relationships between the volume measures are shown below. Once again, these relationships are constant.

							1 T	=	3 t	=	0.5 fl oz			
							2 T			=	1 fl oz	=	29.59 mL	
					1 C	=	16 T	=	48 t	=	8 fl oz			
		1 pt	=	2 C						=	16 fl oz			
	1 qt	=	2 pt	=	4 C					=	32 fl oz			
											33.8 fl oz	=	1000 mL	= 1 L
1 G	=	4 qt	=	8 pt	=	16 C				=	128 fl oz			

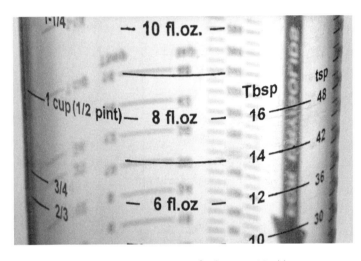

Equivalent volumes. One cup, ½ pint, 8 fluid ounces, 16 tablespoons, and 48 teaspoons are all equivalent volumes. Note: This measuring device is correctly marked in fluid ounces. Many volume measuring devices are marked in ounces, which could potentially be confusing. A person using such a device must know it means fluid ounces by volume.

Equivalents can be found by moving across rows in the chart above. For instance, the first row shows us that 1 tablespoon is equivalent to both 3 teaspoons and 0.5 fluid ounce. This means that if you measured 3 teaspoons and poured the contents into a tablespoon, the tablespoon would be exactly full. You can move across the second row and see that 2 tablespoons is equivalent to both 1 fluid ounce and 29.59 milliliters.

It will help your efficiency to have weight equivalents and volume equivalents memorized. Equivalents are used in the process of converting units of measure, which is a necessary part of a foodservice professional's duties. Converting units of measure is addressed in the next section.

1.1 PRACTICE PROBLEMS

For questions 1–9, use your knowledge of standard unit equivalents to help you answer the questions.

1. Which object would most likely weigh 1 gram?

   (A) a peanut

   (C) a shallot

   (B) a strawberry

   (D) an artichoke

2. Which U.S. customary unit is approximately equivalent to 1 liter?

   (A) 1 pint

   (C) 1 quart

   (B) 1 cup

   (D) 1 gallon

3. One pound of butter is most closely equivalent to which of the following metric measures?

   (A) ¼ kilogram   (B) ½ kilogram

   (C) ¾ kilogram   (D) 1 kilogram

4. One gallon is equivalent to which of the following quantities?

   (A) 4 pints   (B) 2 liters

   (C) 16 cups   (D) 8 pounds

5. If a standard wine bottle holds ¾ of a liter, approximately how many fluid ounces does the bottle hold?

   (A) 13 fluid ounces   (B) 16 fluid ounces

   (C) 25 fluid ounces   (D) 32 fluid ounces

6. During dinner service, your chef says to you, "I need 5 cups of chicken stock!" In the walk-in refrigerator, you find four containers of stock. Without leaving your chef short on stock, which container holds an amount that is closest to the quantity that your chef needs?

   (A) 1 quart   (B) 1½ quarts

   (C) 2 quarts   (D) 2½ quarts

7. Your grocery list for a banquet menu includes 1 kilogram of semolina flour. Which of the following bag sizes is closest to the quantity that you need for the recipe, without leaving you short on flour?

   (A) 1 pound   (B) 1½ pounds

   (C) 2 pounds   (D) 2½ pounds

8. Without using any references, fill in the missing numbers in the ten standard equivalents below:

   a. 1 quart = _____ cups

   b. 1 kilogram = _____ grams

   c. 1 gallon = _____ quarts

   d. 1 tablespoon = _____ teaspoons

   e. 1 cup = _____ fluid ounces

   f. 1 pint = _____ cups

   g. 1 pound = _____ grams

   h. 1 liter = _____ fluid ounces

   i. 1 cup = _____ tablespoons

   j. 1 kilogram = _____ pounds

9. Match the quantity in the first column with its approximate equivalent in the second column.

a. 1 pound
b. 2 teaspoons
c. 225 grams
d. 16 fluid ounces
e. ⅓ ounce
f. 280 grams

i. ½ liter
ii. ½ pound
iii. ½ kilogram
iv. 10 grams
v. 10 milliliters
vi. 10 ounces

10. For the recipe below, rewrite the given ingredient quantities as approximately equivalent quantities expressed in the unit in the "revised quantity" column.

Example:

INGREDIENT	RECIPE QUANTITY	REVISED QUANTITY
Heavy cream	1 qt	approx. 1 L

Filling for Pecan Diamonds
Makes 100 pieces

(Adapted from The Professional Chef *[8th ed.] by The Culinary Institute of America)*

INGREDIENT	RECIPE QUANTITY	REVISED QUANTITY
Butter, cubed	1 #	kg
Brown sugar, light	1 #	kg
Sugar, granulated	4 oz	g
Honey	12 oz	g
Heavy cream	4 fl oz	mL
Pecans	2 #	kg

1.2 Converting Units of Measure Within Weight or Within Volume

Unit conversion is the process of expressing a given quantity in a different unit of measure. You can also look at unit conversions as measuring an ingredient quantity two different ways. For example, 3 pounds of flour weighed in ounces would be 48 ounces of flour. By converting the units, you are calculating the equivalent weight rather than finding the equivalent weight by measuring the ingredient again with the scale set to ounces instead of pounds.

Foodservice professionals frequently convert units of measure to accomplish tasks and goals in a professional kitchen. At times the converting is done mentally as a quick estimation. A more formal procedure is done at other times: while interpreting and standardizing recipes, purchasing and portioning product, and costing recipes.

As a foodservice professional, you might need to convert units of measure to:

- **accurately measure ⅛ gallon**

- **convert 36 teaspoons to a more easily measured unit**

- **convert recipe quantities from U.S. customary to metric measurements**

- **estimate the number of portions you will make from a given recipe**

Equivalent volumes. By using a quart container to measure 1 cup, you can see that 1 cup is equivalent to ¼ quart.

Converting units for ease of measurement. Using a gallon container (especially a metal one, like that shown here) to measure ⅛ gallon could be difficult. Converting ⅛ gallon to 2 cups and using a pint container may make more sense.

In the subsequent examples, we will most often use standard equivalents from the abridged chart that follows. Our goal is to use different combinations of equivalents to give you a broad picture of the unit conversion process. You may choose to use different equivalents; in many cases, you will calculate a slightly different quantity.

COMMONLY USED VOLUME EQUIVALENTS			COMMONLY USED WEIGHT EQUIVALENTS	
1 T = 3 t	1 C = 16 T	1 G = 4 qt	1 oz = 28.35 g	1 kg = 2.205 #
1 T = 0.5 fl oz	1 pt = 2 C	1 L = 33.8 fl oz	1 # = 16 oz	1 kg = 1000 g
1 fl oz = 29.59 mL	1 qt = 2 pt	1 L = 1000 mL	1 # = 453.6 g	
1 C = 8 fl oz	1 qt = 4 C			

THE BRIDGE METHOD

A simple technique for converting units of measure easily and accurately is called dimensional analysis. It is also known as the bridge or unity fraction method. Professionals in the sciences, such as physicists, doctors, and chemists, also utilize this method.

The bridge method is one way of organizing the information used to convert a measured quantity. The procedure has seven steps:

1. Rewrite the quantity you want to convert without any fractions or mixed units of measure.

2. Identify the type of unit conversion (e.g., weight to weight, volume to volume, or between weight and volume).

3. Draw arrows to indicate the target unit to which you are converting as well as the sequence of units you will use to get to your target unit.

4. Write the original quantity as a fraction with a denominator of 1. Copy the unit from the numerator of the first fraction to the denominator of a second fraction.

5. Determine an equivalent that includes this unit and the next unit in your sequence diagram.

6. Repeat steps 4 and 5 until the final unit you are converting into is located in the numerator of the final fraction.

7. Multiply the fractions in your bridge to calculate your answer.

EXAMPLE 1.2.1 CONVERTING TO AN EASILY MEASURED UNIT

A catering function requires you to scale a recipe to a smaller number of portions. You end up with ⅛ gallon of milk as a recipe quantity. You decide that the equipment you will be taking on-site can more easily measure this amount in cups. How many cups are contained in ⅛ gallon?

We need to rewrite ⅛ gallon as a number of cups. We'll use the bridge method to convert this quantity into cups.

STEP 1: Rewrite the quantity you want to convert without any fractions or mixed units of measure.

⅛ G = 0.125 G

STEP 2: Identify the type of unit conversion.

This is a volume-to-volume unit conversion.

STEP 3: Draw arrows to indicate the target unit to which you are converting as well and as the sequence of units you will use to get to your target unit.

In this instance, the conversion is from gallons to cups. We could convert directly from gallons to cups (1 G = 16 C), but for purposes of this example, we will use quarts as an intermediary unit.

gallons ⟶ quarts ⟶ cups

STEP 4: Write the original quantity as a fraction. Put the quantity in the numerator and one (1) in the denominator. Copy the unit from the numerator of the first fraction to the denominator of the second fraction.

G ⟶ qt ⟶ C

$$\frac{0.125\,G}{1} \times \frac{}{G}$$

STEP 5: Determine an equivalent that includes this unit and the next unit in your sequence diagram. Since the next unit in our arrow chart is quarts, we write "qt" in the numerator, and insert the appropriate numerical relationship between quarts and gallons.

G ⟶ qt ⟶ C

$$\frac{0.125\,G}{1} \times \frac{4\,qt}{1\,G}$$

(If you evaluated the conversion at this point, the answer would be in quarts.)

STEP 6: Repeat steps 4 and 5 until the final unit you are converting into is located in the numerator of the final fraction. Our next (and desired) unit is cups, so we need one more fraction containing the relationship between quarts and cups.

G ⟶ qt ⟶ C

$$\frac{0.125\,G}{1} \times \frac{4\,qt}{1\,G} \times \frac{4\,C}{1\,qt} \longleftarrow \text{our desired unit}$$

STEP 7: Multiply the fractions in the bridge to calculate your answer. All the units except for cups should cancel, since each appears in one numerator and one denominator.

$$\frac{0.125\,\cancel{G}}{1} \times \frac{4\,\cancel{qt}}{1\,\cancel{G}} \times \frac{4\,C}{1\,\cancel{qt}} = \frac{2}{1}\,C = 2\,C$$

As you may remember, if a fraction's numerator and denominator have the same value, the fraction is equal to 1. Given that the fractions in our bridge above, except for our initial fraction, are unit equivalents, they have the value of 1. Thus you are multiplying the original quantity by 1 and are not changing the initial quantity at all. You are merely rewriting the quantity in a different unit of measure.

EXAMPLE 1.2.2 CONVERTING TO AN EASILY MEASURED UNIT

After scaling a home recipe for large-scale production, you end up with 36 teaspoons of baking soda. Rewrite this quantity in a larger unit of volume so it can be more efficiently measured.

As in the last example, we'll use the bridge method to do the conversion.

STEP 1: Since 36 teaspoons doesn't contain a fraction or a mixed unit of measure, we're ready to convert.

STEP 2: This is a volume-to-volume unit conversion.

STEP 3: It seems like cups would be a good unit in which to measure our ingredient, so we'll convert teaspoons to cups. You could convert directly from teaspoons to cups (1 C = 48 t), but for purposes of this example, tablespoons are used as an intermediary unit.

teaspoons ⟶ tablespoons ⟶ cups

STEP 4: Copy the unit from the numerator of the first fraction into the denominator of the next fraction.

t ⟶ T ⟶ C

$$\frac{36\,t}{1} \times \frac{}{t}$$

STEP 5: Since tablespoons is the next unit in this case, you write "T" in the numerator, and insert the appropriate numerical relationship between tablespoons and teaspoons.

t ⟶ T ⟶ C

$$\frac{36\,t}{1} \times \frac{1\,T}{3\,t}$$

STEP 6: Our next (and desired) unit is cups, so we need one more fraction containing the relationship between tablespoons and cups.

$$\frac{36\,t}{1} \times \frac{1\,T}{3\,t} \times \frac{1\,C}{16\,T} \longleftarrow \text{our desired unit}$$

STEP 7: Calculate the answer.

$$\frac{36\,t}{1} \times \frac{1\,T}{3\,t} \times \frac{1\,C}{16\,T} = \frac{36}{48}\,C = 0.75\,C$$

EXAMPLE 1.2.3 CONVERTING TO METRIC UNITS

During a menu development meeting, your executive chef asks you to convert 3 # 5 oz of beets, 1 # 10 oz of onions, 4 fl oz of olive oil, and ⅔ oz of salt to metric units. **What metric quantities are these recipe amounts equivalent to?**

Since there is a sizable quantity of each of the vegetables, a logical metric unit to convert them to is kilograms. The olive oil and salt are relatively small quantities, so the logical metric units to convert to are milliliters and grams, respectively.

Beets: 3 # 5 oz = 53 oz, or 3.3125 #
Onions: 1 # 10 oz = 26 oz, or 1.625 #
Salt: ²/₃ oz = 0.6666 oz

First, eliminate the mixed measurements given for the beets and the onions, and convert ²/₃ into a decimal.

Beets: oz ⟶ # ⟶ kg

$$\frac{53\ oz}{1} \times \frac{1\ \#}{16\ oz} \times \frac{1\ kg}{2.205\ \#} = \frac{53}{35.28}\ kg = 1.5022\ kg$$

Use standard unit equivalents to convert the ingredient quantities into metric units.

Onions: # ⟶ kg

$$\frac{1.625\ \#}{1} \times \frac{1\ kg}{2.205\ \#} = \frac{1.625}{2.205}\ kg = 0.7369\ kg$$

Olive oil: fl oz ⟶ L ⟶ mL

$$\frac{4\ fl\ oz}{1} \times \frac{1\ L}{33.8\ fl\ oz} \times \frac{1,000\ mL}{1\ L} = \frac{4,000}{33.8}\ mL = 118.3431\ mL$$

Salt: oz ⟶ g

$$\frac{0.6666\ oz}{1} \times \frac{28.35\ g}{1\ oz} = \frac{18.8981}{1}\ g = 18.8981\ g$$

The choice to start with the ounce weight of the beets and the pound weight of the onions was to demonstrate different ways to convert units. You could just as easily have used the other unit to start those two calculations.

Our conversion examples thus far have used only standard equivalents; however, nonstandard unit equivalents may be used as well. In the following two examples, we will use 1 serving = 3 ounces and 1 bottle = 750 milliliters as equivalents. These are examples of nonstandard equivalents, since serving sizes and bottle capacities are not all the same.

EXAMPLE 1.2.4 PORTIONING

A recipe for potato latkes makes 1 kilogram of batter. How many 3-ounce servings will you get from one batch?

kilograms ⟶ pounds ⟶ ounces ⟶ servings

Determine the order of units needed to convert kilograms into servings. Use 1 serving = 3 ounces as an equivalent.

$$\frac{1\ kg}{1} \times \frac{2.205\ \#}{1\ kg} \times \frac{16\ oz}{1\ \#} \times \frac{1\ serving}{3\ oz} = \frac{35.28}{3}\ servings = 11.76\ servings$$

Use standard unit equivalents to convert the quantity of batter into a number of servings.

EXAMPLE 1.2.5 PORTIONING

You have 12 bottles of champagne in inventory. If each bottle contains 750 milliliters, how many servings of 4 fluid ounces can you pour from the case?

bottles ⟶ milliliters ⟶ fluid ounces ⟶ servings

Determine the order of units needed to convert bottles into servings. The given information gives us two equivalents to use: 1 bottle = 750 milliliters and 1 serving = 4 fluid ounces.

$$\frac{12\,btl}{1}\times\frac{750\,mL}{1\,btl}\times\frac{33.8\,fl\,oz}{1{,}000\,mL}\times\frac{1\,serving}{4\,fl\,oz}=\frac{304200}{4000}\,servings=76.05\,servings$$

There are two common equivalents between fluid ounces and milliliters.

$$\frac{12\,btl}{1}\times\frac{750\,mL}{1\,btl}\times\frac{1\,fl\,oz}{29.59\,mL}\times\frac{1\,serving}{4\,fl\,oz}=\frac{9000}{118.36}\,servings=76.04\,servings$$

You will note that the answers above do not match exactly because two different equivalents between milliliters and fluid ounces were used. Keep in mind that many unit equivalents contain rounded numbers, so using different combinations of unit equivalents may result in slight variations between answers. For the most part, you need not be too concerned about these small differences. In Appendix I there is more information about exact equivalents.

1.2 PRACTICE PROBLEMS

Use your knowledge of equivalents to answer the following questions. Your answers may vary slightly from those given in the back of the book depending on which equivalents you use. Round all answers to the nearest hundredth (2 decimal places).

1. A scaled recipe calls for 12 teaspoons of baking powder. How many cups of baking powder would you need to measure for this recipe?

2. A recipe for crème brûlée calls for 960 milliliters of heavy cream. If you have 1 pint in the walk-in refrigerator, do you have enough heavy cream to make the recipe?

3.   A recipe calls for 430 milliliters of white wine. How many cups would you need to use?

4.   At an upcoming catering event, you will be serving 6 fluid ounces of gazpacho to each of 110 people. How many gallons of soup will you need to make?

5.   You are making cheese tuiles, each of which requires ½ ounce of imported Parmesan cheese. How many kilograms of Parmesan cheese would you need to make 1200 tuiles?

6. Your recipe for oatmeal raisin cookies calls for 3 pounds 3 ounces of rolled oats. Assuming you had enough of the other ingredients, how many times can you make the recipe using a 25-pound bag of rolled oats?

7. A recipe for bread dough yields 7½ kilograms of dough. If you divide the dough into 275-gram loaves, how many loaves will you be able to make from the recipe?

8. You are planning to serve salmon with béarnaise sauce to 64 people at a banquet. Each serving requires 1½ fluid ounces of béarnaise sauce. How many quarts of béarnaise sauce do you need to make?

9. For a banquet, you will be serving 1 taco to each of 50 people. You have 12½ pounds of prepared turkey taco filling. If you want to divide this filling equally between the tacos, how many ounces of taco meat should you add to each taco shell?

10. Convert each given recipe yield to an appropriate unit of measure based on the given serving size. Then, use that serving size to determine the number of portions that can be made. (Round answers *down* to a whole number of servings.)

	RECIPE YIELD	UNIT CONVERSION	SERVING SIZE	NUMBER OF SERVINGS
a.	1½ gallons		4 fl oz	
b.	2 gallons		½ C	
c.	1 pound 10 ounces		¾ oz	
d.	2 quarts		2 T	
e.	1 pint		⅓ C	
f.	1½ liters		3 fl oz	
g.	1 liter		50 mL	
h.	375 milliliters		1 fl oz	
i.	2½ kilograms		6 oz	
j.	1¾ kilograms		118 g	
k.	2¾ pounds		50 g	
l.	3 pounds		4 oz	
m.	5 kilograms		250 g	

11. For each ingredient in the recipe below, convert the given quantity so it is expressed in the unit in the "revised quantity" column. Round your revised quantities to the nearest hundredth of a kilogram (2 decimal places) or to the nearest gram.

Cottage Dill Rolls
Makes 24 dozen rolls

(Adapted from The Professional Chef *[8th ed.] by The Culinary Institute of America)*

INGREDIENT	RECIPE QUANTITY	REVISED QUANTITY
Water	3 #	kg
Yeast	1¼ #	g
Flour, bread	21 #	kg
Cottage cheese, low-fat	12 #	kg
Sugar, granulated	1 # 2 oz	kg
Onions, minced	6 oz	g
Butter	1½ #	kg
Salt	6 oz	g
Dill, chopped	4 oz	g
Baking soda	4 oz	g
Eggs, large	1½ #	kg
Horseradish	¾ oz	g

12. For each ingredient in the recipe below, convert the given quantity so it is expressed in the unit in the "revised quantity" column. Round your revised quantities to the hundredths place (2 decimal places).

Rustic Raisin Bread

Makes 4 small loaves

(Adapted from The Professional Chef *[8th ed.] by The Culinary Institute of America)*

INGREDIENT	RECIPE QUANTITY	REVISED QUANTITY
Flour, bread	2.83 kg	#
Yeast, instant dry	43 g	oz
Milk, whole	2.4 L	G
Honey	85 g	oz
Salt	57 g	oz
Raisins	1.47 kg	#
Butter	113 g	#
Egg yolks	1 ea	ea

13. For each ingredient in the recipe below, convert the given quantity so it is expressed in the unit in the "revised quantity" column. Truncate your revised quantities at the ten-thousandths place (4 decimal places).

Trout Amandine

Makes 60 servings

(Adapted from The Professional Chef *[8th ed.] by The Culinary Institute of America)*

INGREDIENT	RECIPE QUANTITY	REVISED QUANTITY
Milk	3 pt	G
Flour, all-purpose (1 bag = 25 #)	18 oz	bag
Oil	12 fl oz	qt
Butter	60 oz	#
Almonds, slivered	24 oz	#
Trout filets	60 filets (6 oz ea)	#
Lemon juice	3¾ C	qt
Parsley, dried (1 jar = 3 oz)	4 oz	jar

14. For each ingredient in the recipe below, convert the given quantity so it is expressed in the unit in the "revised quantity" column. Truncate your revised quantities at the ten-thousandths place (4 decimal places).

Lemon Meringue Pie

Makes fifteen 9-inch pies

(Adapted from The Professional Chef *[8th ed.] by The Culinary Institute of America)*

INGREDIENT	RECIPE QUANTITY	REVISED QUANTITY
Water	5¾ L	G
Sugar (1 bag = 5 #)	2¾ kg	bag
Salt (1 box = 26 oz)	42 g	box
Lemon juice	900 mL	pt
Lemon zest	84 g	oz
Cornstarch (1 box = 1 #)	510 g	box
Egg yolks	24 ea	dozen
Butter	340 g	#

1.3 Converting Between Weight and Volume

Standardizing recipes for quality control purposes, ordering, and planning in your professional kitchen can get a bit more complicated when recipes measure dry ingredients by volume. For the sake of accuracy and product consistency, you will sometimes need to convert between volume and weight.

The recipe below is from a cookbook written for a home cook, and many of the ingredients are measured by volume.

Cheddar Corn Fritters

Makes 6 to 8 fritters

(Adapted from Vegetables *by The Culinary Institute of America)*

¾ C all-purpose flour

3 T granulated sugar

2 t chili powder

2 C fresh corn niblets

3 T diced red or green pepper

2 large eggs

½ C grated cheddar

½ C water

2 T butter

2 T vegetable oil

2 t salt, table grind

If you were to use this recipe in a professional kitchen, you might want to rewrite the recipe to measure all ingredients by weight (for accuracy, for ease of use, or due to available equipment). To do so, you need information in addition to standard unit equivalents, because you are now converting units of volume to units of weight.

Take our first ingredient, all-purpose (AP) flour. Our recipe calls for ¾ cup, but our chef would like all dry ingredients measured by the pound. Thus, you would need to convert ¾ cups of AP flour to pounds. You might be thinking, "That's easy. One cup weighs 8 ounces, and three-quarters of that would be 6 ounces. Divide 6 ounces by sixteen to convert it to pounds, so you need to use 0.375 pounds of flour to make this recipe."

If this is what you were thinking, think it over one more time. If you **tared,** or zeroed, a scale with a 1-cup measuring tool on it, then measured 1 cup of flour and put the full cup of flour on the scale, the scale would read approximately 4.6 ounces in weight. Where is the logic in the above paragraph flawed? One cup is 8 fluid ounces of space, but a cup of an ingredient does not necessarily weigh 8 ounces. *Do not assume that 1 fluid ounce of an ingredient weighs 1 ounce. A fluid ounce is a quantity of space, and an ounce is a quantity of weight!*

In order to revise these recipe quantities (which are, with the exception of eggs, written by volume), you need to know the weight of some volume of each ingredient. That is, you need an equivalent to set the relationship between weight and volume for that ingredient. You can get equivalents like these by weighing the ingredients yourself, or you can get approximations from resources such as *The Book of Yields* by Francis T. Lynch, as we have done throughout this text. (Appendix V contains information from *The Book of Yields*.)

The following are volume-to-weight equivalents from *The Book of Yields*. These will be used in Example 1.3.1 to convert the quantities in our recipe for Cheddar Corn Fritters to their weight equivalents.

All-purpose flour	1 cup = 4.6 ounces
Granulated sugar	1 cup = 7.10 ounces
Chili powder	1 tablespoon = 0.235 ounces
Corn niblets	1 cup = 5.75 ounces
Green pepper, diced	1 cup = 3.2 ounces
Cheddar, grated	1 pint = ½ pound
Butter	2 cups = 1 pound
Salt, table grind	1.6 cups = 1 pound

Effect of density on weight. Each container holds 1 cup of an ingredient (left to right: corn kernels, water, chili powder), yet the weights are all different because the density of each ingredient is different.

Take some time to review these equivalents. For the sake of this example, various options of available volume-to-weight information have been used. If utilizing one type of volume-to-weight equivalent makes the conversion process easier, use the information that is easiest for your mind to visualize. For example, many utilize the weight-per-cup equivalent consistently, which makes the unit conversions more familiar. Listen to your internal sense of logic about these relationships.

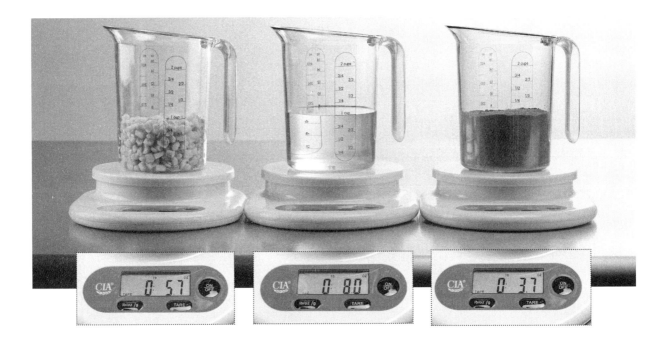

What factors affect the weight of a specific volume of substance? Think about your answer to this question as we convert the recipe quantities below.

EXAMPLE 1.3.1 CONVERTING RECIPE QUANTITIES

For each ingredient in the Cheddar Corn Fritters recipe, convert the given recipe quantity so it is expressed in the specified unit. Truncate all quantities after four decimal places.

Cheddar Corn Fritters

Makes 6 to 8 fritters

(Adapted from Vegetables *by The Culinary Institute of America)*

INGREDIENT	RECIPE QUANTITY	CONVERT RECIPE QUANTITY INTO THIS UNIT	REVISED RECIPE QUANTITY
Flour, all-purpose	¾ C	pounds	$\dfrac{0.75\,C}{1} \times \dfrac{4.6\,oz}{1\,C} \times \dfrac{1\#}{16\,oz} = \dfrac{3.45}{16}\# = \mathbf{0.2156\,\#}$
Sugar, granulated	3 T	ounces	$\dfrac{3\,T}{1} \times \dfrac{1\,C}{16\,T} \times \dfrac{7.10\,oz}{1\,C} = \dfrac{21.3}{16}\,oz = \mathbf{1.3312\,oz}$
Chili powder	2 t	ounces	$\dfrac{2\,t}{1} \times \dfrac{1\,T}{3\,t} \times \dfrac{0.235\,oz}{1\,T} = \dfrac{0.47}{3}\,oz = \mathbf{0.1566\,oz}$
Corn niblets, fresh	2 C	pounds	$\dfrac{2\,C}{1} \times \dfrac{5.75\,oz}{1\,C} \times \dfrac{1\#}{16\,oz} = \dfrac{11.5}{16}\# = \mathbf{0.7187\,\#}$
Pepper, red or green, diced	3 T	ounces	$\dfrac{3\,T}{1} \times \dfrac{1\,C}{16\,T} \times \dfrac{3.2\,oz}{1\,C} = \dfrac{9.6}{16}\,oz = \mathbf{0.6\,oz}$
Eggs, large	2 ea	each	**2 ea**
Cheddar, grated	½ C	pounds	$\dfrac{0.5\,C}{1} \times \dfrac{1\,pt}{2\,C} \times \dfrac{0.5\#}{1\,pt} = \dfrac{0.25}{2}\# = \mathbf{0.125\,\#}$
Water	½ C	cups	**½ C**
Butter	2 T	pounds	$\dfrac{2\,T}{1} \times \dfrac{1\,C}{16\,T} \times \dfrac{1\#}{2\,C} = \dfrac{2}{32}\# = \mathbf{0.0625\,\#}$
Vegetable oil	2 T	tablespoons	**2 T**
Salt, table grind	2 t	ounces	$\dfrac{2\,t}{1} \times \dfrac{1\,C}{48\,t} \times \dfrac{16\,oz}{1.6\,C} = \dfrac{32}{76.8}\,oz = \mathbf{0.4166\,oz}$

So, what factors affect the weight of a substance when measured by volume? The most common factors are:

- **THE INGREDIENT USED.** Different ingredients have different densities. All-purpose flour weighs 4.6 ounces per cup, corn weighs 5.75 ounces per cup, and chili powder weighs 3.76 ounces per cup.

Effect of preparation method on weight. One cup of shredded cheddar (left) weighs less than 1 cup of diced cheddar (right).

■ **COMPACTION. If we sifted all-purpose flour before weighing it, a cup would weigh 4 ounces. Compare this to unsifted flour, which weighs 4.6 ounces per cup. Unpacked brown sugar weighs 5.10 ounces per cup, but when it's packed, brown sugar weighs 7.75 ounces per cup.**

■ **PREPARATION METHOD. Shredded cheddar cheese weighs 4 ounces per cup, diced cheddar weighs 4.65 ounces per cup, and melted cheddar cheese weighs 8.6 ounces per cup.**

When working with volume-to-weight equivalents for recipe interpretation and adaptation into a professional production kitchen, be sure that you take these factors into consideration. It is very easy to make the assumption that 1 fluid ounce equals 1 ounce in weight, which will not always be true.

Take a moment before you begin each conversion to identify the type of conversion you are doing. If you are converting from a weight measure to another weight measure or from a volume measure to another volume measure, then all you need are standard unit equivalents. If, however, you are converting from a weight measure to a volume measure or from a volume measure to a weight measure, then you need more information. You need to weigh a certain volume of that ingredient, or you need a resource (such as *The Book of Yields*) with volume-to-weight approximations. If your ingredient is, for any reason, not consistent with the information listed in your resource, you should take your own measurement with your own product. Additionally, it is advisable to find and use volume-to-weight equivalents of your own when you need to plan for the use of an expensive or atypical ingredient, or when the preparation method varies greatly from that in your resource.

In sum, the most accurate method to measure ingredients by is weight. Typically, in a professional kitchen, dry ingredients are measured by weight and liquid ingredients are measured by volume, but some kitchens prefer to measure everything by weight. It is up to the chef to determine the best way to measure each ingredient. We have calculated our recipe quantities to different levels of accuracy to demonstrate different procedures. Ultimately, the equipment you use to measure your ingredients will determine how accurate your recipe quantities need to be. Accurate measurement will help with product consistency, planning, and ordering. Be sure to test any recipes converted from volume to weight measures and adjust them as necessary to finalize.

PRACTICE PROBLEMS

Use the information from *The Book of Yields* in Appendix V as necessary to answer the following questions. Your answers may vary slightly from those given in the back of the book depending on which equivalents you use. Round your answers to the nearest hundredth, unless otherwise specified.

1. For each ingredient in the recipe below, convert the given quantity so it is expressed in the unit in the "revised quantity" column. Round your revised quantities to the nearest hundredth of a unit.

Italian-Style Spinach
Makes 50 servings

(Adapted from Cooking at Home with the CIA *by The Culinary Institute of America)*

INGREDIENT	RECIPE QUANTITY	REVISED QUANTITY
Olive oil (1 C = 7.7 oz)	5 T	C
Pancetta, thinly sliced (1 # = 32 slices)	15 oz	#
Onion, ¼" dice (1 C = 4.45 oz)	2½ C	#
Garlic cloves (12 cloves = 2.1 oz)	15 cloves	oz
Spinach (1 C = 1.5 oz)	6¼ G	#
Salt, table grind (1 T = 0.645 oz)	4 T	oz
Black pepper, cracked (1 T = 0.25 oz)	3 T plus 1 t	oz
Parmesan, grated fresh (1 C = 3 oz)	3¾ C	#
Nutmeg, ground (1 T = 0.235 oz)	2½ t	oz

2. For each ingredient in the recipe below, convert the given quantity so it is expressed in the unit in the "revised quantity" column. Round your revised quantities to the nearest gram or milliliter, or to the nearest hundredth of a kilogram.

Sweet Polenta Cake

Makes two 8-inch cakes

(Adapted from Baking at Home with the CIA *by The Culinary Institute of America)*

INGREDIENT	RECIPE QUANTITY	REVISED QUANTITY
Flour, all-purpose (1 # = 3.48 C)	1½ C	kg
Baking powder (1 C = 6.9 oz)	2 t	g
Salt, table grind (1 T = 0.645 oz)	1 t	g
Eggs, large, shelled (1 ea = 1.777 oz)	6 ea	g
Egg yolks, large (1 ea = 0.586 oz)	12 ea	g
Vanilla extract (1 C = 8.3 oz)	1 t	mL
Butter (1 # = 2 C)	2 C	kg
Sugar, granulated (1 C = 7.1 oz)	2 C	kg
Cornmeal, fine (1 # = 2.5 C)	1 C	kg

3. Fill in the missing information in the chart below.

INGREDIENT	VOLUME-TO-WEIGHT EQUIVALENT	NUMBER OF OUNCES IN 1 CUP	NUMBER OF FLUID OUNCES IN 1 CUP
a. Rosemary, chopped fresh	1 T = 0.15 oz	$\dfrac{1\,C}{1}\times\dfrac{16\,T}{1\,C}\times\dfrac{0.15\,oz}{1\,T}=2.4\,oz$	8 fl oz
b. Flour, spelt	1 pt = 7.8 oz		
c. Pecans, chopped	3.8 C = 1 #		
d. Nutmeg, ground	4.25 T = 1 oz		

4. Fill in the missing information in the chart below.

INGREDIENT	VOLUME-TO-WEIGHT EQUIVALENT	NUMBER OF CUPS THAT 8 OUNCES WOULD FILL	NUMBER OF CUPS THAT 8 FLUID OUNCES WOULD FILL
a. Honey	1 C = 12 oz	$\dfrac{8\,oz}{1}\times\dfrac{1\,C}{12\,oz}=\dfrac{2}{3}C$	1 C
b. Lime juice	1 C = _____ oz		
c. Carrots, 1/3" dice	1 C = _____ oz		
d. Chile flakes, red	1 C = _____ oz		

5.   A recipe calls for 1 cup of ground almonds. How many ounces of ground almonds should you use for this recipe if 1 pint of ground almonds weighs 0.42 pounds?

6.   A recipe calls for 1½ pounds of honey. How many cups of honey should you measure for this recipe if 1 cup of honey weighs 12 ounces?

7.   A recipe for blueberry smoothies calls for 6 cups of yogurt. How many quarts of yogurt do you need to use if 1 cup of yogurt weighs 8.6 ounces?

8. A recipe calls for 2½ quarts of high-gluten flour. If high-gluten flour weighs 5 ounces per cup, how many pounds of flour should you use for this recipe?

9. A recipe for individual chocolate hazelnut tarts calls for ½ cup of hazelnuts per tart. If 1 cup of hazelnuts weighs 4 ounces, will a 5-kilogram bag of hazelnuts be sufficient to make 75 tarts?

10. Your recipe for risotto cakes calls for 1 cup of risotto per 3 servings. If 1 cup of risotto weighs 6¼ ounces, how many pounds of risotto would you need to use for 555 servings?

11. You are writing a cookbook for the home cook. One of the recipes you are testing calls for 14 ounces of shredded cheddar cheese. How many cups of shredded cheddar cheese should the revised recipe call for if shredded cheddar cheese weighs 8 ounces per pint?

12. What, if any, is the difference in the ounce weights of 2 cups of unsifted powdered sugar and 2 cups of sifted powdered sugar?

13. A recipe for focaccia calls for 6 ounces of olive oil. If olive oil weighs 7.7 ounces per cup, how many full recipes could you make using a 5-liter bottle of oil?

14. How much will ¼ cup of nutmeg weigh in grams?

15. A carrot cake recipe calls for 2¾ pints of grated carrot. How many pounds of grated carrot do you need for this recipe?

16. How many ounces should 200 milliliters of lemon juice weigh?

17. A recipe calls for 3 pounds of whole grape tomatoes. How many pints of grape tomatoes do you need?

18. A recipe calls for ¾ cup of molasses. The sous chef making this recipe decides it would be easier to measure the molasses by weight, and adds 6 ounces to the mixing bowl.

a. Explain the incorrect assumption that this sous chef made.

b. If the molasses is weighed for this recipe, how much does the sous chef really need?

19. An extern is working with a recipe that calls for 2 tablespoons of curry powder. Remembering that measuring by weight is often more accurate than measuring by volume, he measures 1 ounce of curry powder and mixes it into the recipe.

a. Explain the mistake that this extern made.

b. Correctly determine the weight of 2 tablespoons of curry powder.

20. Standardize the recipe below for production in a bakery that uses a digital scale accurate to $\frac{1}{100}$ of a pound. For each ingredient, convert the given quantity into an equivalent quantity rounded to the nearest hundredth of a pound. Use the information from *The Book of Yields* in Appendix V as necessary.

Sour Cream Shortcake Biscuits

Makes 72 biscuits

(Adapted from The Herbfarm Cookbook *by Jerry Traunfeld)*

INGREDIENT	RECIPE QUANTITY	REVISED QUANTITY
Flour, all-purpose	6 qt	#
Baking powder	¼ C	#
Baking soda	2 T	#
Salt, kosher flake	1 T	#
Sugar, granulated	4½ C	#
Butter, unsalted	3 C	#
Sour cream	3 qt	#
Milk, whole (4%)	3 C	#

21. For each ingredient in the recipe below, convert the given quantity so it is expressed in the unit in the "revised quantity" column. Use the information from *The Book of Yields* in Appendix V as necessary. Round your revised quantities to the nearest gram or milliliter.

Orange Soufflé

Makes 8 servings

(Adapted from Cooking at Home with the CIA *by The Culinary Institute of America)*

INGREDIENT	RECIPE QUANTITY	REVISED QUANTITY
Butter	2 T	g
Sugar, granulated	½ C plus 2 T	g
Egg yolks, large	4 ea	g
Flour, all-purpose	¼ C	g
Salt, kosher flake	1 t	g
Milk, whole (4%)	1¾ C	mL
Vanilla extract	1 t	mL
Orange juice	¼ C	mL
Orange zest (1 T = 0.165 oz)	1 T	g
Egg whites, large	10 ea	g
Sugar, powdered (unsifted)	1 T plus 1 t	g

Recipe Scaling

KEY TERMS

recipe yield

scaling factor

constraining ingredient

standardized recipe

subrecipe

KEY QUESTIONS

If I need a yield or number of servings that's different from what my recipe calls for, how can I adjust my recipe?

How do you standardize a recipe?

As a chef, you will need to be able to understand both recipe quantities and **recipe yield** (the total usable product expected from a recipe). Recipe writers can write and increase or decrease recipes to yield as many or as few servings as desired, and those servings can be any necessary size. The process of scaling a recipe begins by calculating the number that will appropriately adjust your recipe, which is called the **scaling factor** (also known as a recipe conversion factor).

2.1 Calculating a Scaling Factor

Most often, scaling a recipe is based on the need to make a different amount of product than the recipe currently yields. Sometimes, however, it is based on the quantity of one of the recipe ingredients you have on hand.

USING RECIPE YIELDS TO CALCULATE A SCALING FACTOR

You will see recipe yields written many different ways. Usually the yield is written at the top of a recipe near the recipe title. Below are some examples of recipe yield information:

CHICKEN SOUP Yield: 1¼ gallons	GUACAMOLE Yield: sixteen 2-ounce portions
BLUEBERRY MUFFINS Yield: 3 dozen	CRANBERRY-MINT MARTINIS Makes four 4-fluid-ounce servings

To calculate a scaling factor using recipe yields, divide your desired yield by the current recipe yield:

Scaling factor = desired yield ÷ current recipe yield

Keep in mind that this number will not always be a whole number: for example, you can make a recipe that is 3½ times or 0.6 times as large as the original recipe.

A scaling factor can be thought of—and written as—a percentage. Using a scaling factor of 3½ means the scaled recipe yield will be 350% of the original recipe yield, and using a scaling factor of 0.6 means the scaled recipe will make 60% of the original recipe's yield.

EXAMPLE 2.1.1 CALCULATING A SCALING FACTOR

You are catering an event and need 1½ gallons of chicken soup. What scaling factor will adjust a recipe for chicken soup that yields 1¼ gallons?

If you made this recipe twice, you would make a whole gallon of soup more than you need! This may be fine if you have another catering event or a restaurant that will use the remaining product. Even in a restaurant where leftover product is used, overproduction can impact food costs and, ultimately, profit. Calculating a scaling factor (and not rounding it to a whole number) will allow you to produce the exact yield you need.

$$\begin{aligned}\text{Scaling factor} &= \text{desired yield} \div \text{current recipe yield}\\ &= 1.5\,\text{G} \div 1.25\,\text{G}\\ &= 1.2\end{aligned}$$

Divide the desired yield by the current recipe yield.

This scaling factor means that to make exactly what we need for our event, our scaled recipe needs to yield 1.2 times as much as the original recipe. (As you will see in the next sections, this also means that the ingredient quantities we need to use will be 1.2 times as large as the quantities in the original recipe.)

Another way to find a scaling factor is to treat the recipe yield as a kind of unit conversion. For the previous example, we can use 1 recipe = 1.25 gallons as a unit equivalent:

$$\frac{1.5\,\text{G}}{1} \times \frac{1\,\text{recipe}}{1.25\,\text{G}} = 1.2\,\text{recipes}$$

Convert gallons to recipes using the recipe yield as part of a unit conversion.

Again, this shows that your scaled recipe needs to be 1.2 times as large as the original recipe to produce 1½ gallons of chicken soup.

EXAMPLE 2.1.2 CALCULATING A SCALING FACTOR

If you expect to serve fourteen 8-ounce family-style portions of guacamole, what scaling factor will adjust a recipe that yields sixteen 2-ounce portions?

$$\begin{aligned}\text{Recipe yield} &= 16\,\text{portions} \times 2\,\text{oz per portion} = 32\,\text{oz}\\ \text{Desired yield} &= 14\,\text{portions} \times 8\,\text{oz per portion} = 112\,\text{oz}\end{aligned}$$

Determine the total yield of the original recipe and the total desired yield.

$$\begin{aligned}\text{Scaling factor} &= \text{desired yield} \div \text{current recipe yield}\\ &= 112\,\text{oz} \div 32\,\text{oz}\\ &= 3.5\end{aligned}$$

Divide the desired yield by the current recipe yield.

Alternatively, use 1 recipe = 32 ounces as a unit equivalent:

$$\frac{112\,\text{ounces}}{1} \times \frac{1\,\text{recipe}}{32\,\text{ounces}} = 3.5\,\text{recipes}$$

EXAMPLE 2.1.3 CALCULATING A SCALING FACTOR

Your original recipe for blueberry muffins yields 3 dozen muffins. What scaling factor will adjust the recipe to produce the 27 blueberry muffins you expect to sell in your bakery tomorrow?

To get an accurate comparison between yields, convert both yields so they are expressed in the same unit. One option is to convert the desired yield into dozens:

$$\frac{27\,\text{muffins}}{1} \times \frac{1\,\text{dozen}}{12\,\text{muffins}} = 2.25\,\text{dozen}$$

Convert the desired yield into a number of dozens.

$$\begin{aligned}\text{Scaling factor} &= \text{desired yield} \div \text{current recipe yield}\\ &= 2.25\,\text{dozen} \div 3\,\text{dozen}\\ &= 0.75\end{aligned}$$

Divide the desired yield by the current recipe yield.

Alternatively, you could convert the recipe yield into individual muffins:

$$\frac{3\,\text{dozen}}{1} \times \frac{12\,\text{muffins}}{1\,\text{dozen}} = 36\,\text{muffins}$$

Convert the recipe yield into a number of muffins.

$$\begin{aligned}\text{Scaling factor} &= \text{desired yield} \div \text{current recipe yield} \\ &= 27\,\text{muffins} \div 36\,\text{muffins} \\ &= 0.75\end{aligned}$$

Divide the desired yield by the current recipe yield.

Using 1 recipe = 3 dozen as a unit equivalent:

$$\frac{27\,\text{muffins}}{1} \times \frac{1\,\text{dozen}}{12\,\text{muffins}} \times \frac{1\,\text{recipe}}{3\,\text{dozen}} = 0.75\,\text{recipe}$$

EXAMPLE 2.1.4 CALCULATING A SCALING FACTOR

Your recipe for cranberry-mint martinis makes four servings of 4 fluid ounces each. What scaling factor will adjust the recipe to yield the 4½ liters of cranberry-mint martinis you will serve at your next catering event?

The current yield of our recipe is 16 fluid ounces (4 servings of 4 fluid ounces each). We need to convert our yields into the same unit of measure. Using fluid ounces as the common unit is one choice:

Convert the desired yield into a number of fluid ounces.

$$\begin{aligned}\text{Scaling factor} &= \text{desired yield} \div \text{current recipe yield} \\ &= 152.1\,\text{fl oz} \div 16\,\text{fl oz} \\ &= 9.50625\end{aligned}$$

Divide the desired yield by the current recipe yield.

In this book, we will round scaling factors to the nearest hundredth. Therefore, we would use a scaling factor of 9.51 to adjust our martini recipe.

Or you could use liters as the common unit:

$$\frac{16\,\text{fl oz}}{1} \times \frac{1\,\text{L}}{33.8\,\text{fl oz}} = 0.47334\,\text{L}$$

Convert the recipe yield into a number of liters.

$$\begin{aligned}\text{Scaling factor} &= \text{desired yield} \div \text{current recipe yield} \\ &= 4.5\,\text{L} \div 0.4734\,\text{L} \\ &= 9.51\end{aligned}$$

Divide the desired yield by the current recipe yield.

Using 1 recipe = 16 fluid ounces as a unit equivalent:

$$\frac{4.5\,\text{L}}{1} \times \frac{33.8\,\text{fl oz}}{1\,\text{L}} \times \frac{1\,\text{recipe}}{16\,\text{fl oz}} = 9.51\,\text{recipes}$$

USING INGREDIENT QUANTITIES TO CALCULATE A SCALING FACTOR

So far, all of our scaling calculations have made one assumption: you have the ingredient quantities needed to make the scaled recipe. But what if you don't? Perhaps you are getting low on butternut squash but would like to use the squash and make as much soup as possible. This is an example of a **constraining ingredient.** In this case, the desired recipe yield will not determine the scaling factor; the available ingredient quantity will.

$$\text{Scaling factor} = \text{constraining ingredient quantity} \div \text{recipe ingredient quantity}$$

EXAMPLE 2.1.5 CALCULATING A SCALING FACTOR

Your recipe for corn chowder calls for 1½ pounds of fresh corn kernels. You have 3 pounds 10 ounces of corn kernels left over from a previous day's production. What scaling factor should you use to adjust your chowder recipe to use all this corn?

3 # 10 oz = 3.625 #	Convert the mixed measurement into pounds.
Scaling factor = constraining quantity ÷ recipe quantity	Divide the constraining quantity by the recipe quantity.
= 3.625 # ÷ 1.5 #	
= 2.42	

EXAMPLE 2.1.6 CALCULATING A SCALING FACTOR

Your muesli recipe calls for 3 kilograms of rolled oats. In your dry storage area, you have a container with 6 quarts of rolled oats. What percent of your recipe can you make?

Since our recipe quantity is a weight and our constraining quantity is a volume, we need to look up a volume-to-weight equivalent for rolled oats. According to *The Book of Yields*, 1 cup of rolled oats weighs 3 ounces:

$\dfrac{6\,qt}{1} \times \dfrac{4\,C}{1\,qt} \times \dfrac{3\,oz}{1\,C} \times \dfrac{1\,\#}{16\,oz} \times \dfrac{1\,kg}{2.205\,\#} = 2.0408\,kg$	Convert the constraining quantity into kilograms.
Scaling factor = constraining quantity ÷ recipe quantity	Divide the constraining quantity by the recipe quantity.
= 2.0408 kg ÷ 3 kg	
= 0.68	

Rewriting the scaling factor as a percent shows us we can make approximately 68% of our recipe. We chose to convert the constraining quantity into weight, but you could convert 3 kilograms (the original recipe quantity) into quarts (8.82 quarts, to be precise), then calculate the scaling factor by dividing 6 quarts by 8.82 quarts.

PRACTICE PROBLEMS

Use the information from *The Book of Yields* in Appendix V as necessary to help you answer the following questions. Round decimal answers to the nearest hundredth.

1. When decreasing a recipe, the scaling factor would be

    (A) greater than 1
    (B) less than 1
    (C) a negative number
    (D) impossible to predict

2. When you increase a recipe, why is the scaling factor always greater than 1?

3. If you are making 0.72 of a recipe, what percentage of the recipe are you making?

4. If you are making a recipe 2½ times, what percentage of the recipe are you making?

5. While scaling a recipe, you determine that you need to use a scaling factor of 3.4. Why wouldn't you round this factor up to 4 or down to 3 to make the calculation of the new recipe quantities easier?

For questions 6–10, calculate the scaling factor that will adjust the recipe to produce the desired yield.

	RECIPE YIELD	DESIRED YIELD
6.	1½ # hummus	5¼ # hummus
7.	3 qt Manhattan clam chowder	4½ C Manhattan clam chowder
8.	Twenty-four 6-oz crab cakes	Three hundred 2-oz crab cakes
9.	10 # pie dough	Two hundred fifty 2-oz tart shells
10.	1 # mayonnaise	2 qt mayonnaise

For questions 11–15, calculate the scaling factor that will allow you to make as much of the recipe as possible using the given constraining ingredient quantity.

	RECIPE INGREDIENT QUANTITY	CONSTRAINING INGREDIENT QUANTITY
11.	1 dozen eggs	5 eggs
12.	600 g all-purpose flour	2 # all-purpose flour
13.	2 # whole milk	3 qt whole milk
14.	3 C olive oil	1½ L olive oil
15.	3 T ground nutmeg	1 oz ground nutmeg

16. Your chef brings you 3 pounds of eggplant to make ratatouille. If your recipe calls for 7 pounds of eggplant, what scaling factor should you apply to your recipe to make as much ratatouille as you can with the 3 pounds of eggplant?

17. Your restaurant's recipe for Mediterranean-Style Seafood Terrine yields 32 ounces. If you need 750 ounces of terrine, what scaling factor should you use to adjust the recipe?

18. Your local farmer delivers 12 pounds of tomatoes to your restaurant. You are planning to make tomato sauce, and your recipe for tomato sauce calls for 30 pounds of tomatoes. What scaling factor should you use to adjust your recipe?

19. Your recipe for fudge brownies calls for 8 squares of semisweet chocolate. If you only have 2½ squares on hand, what scaling factor will appropriately adjust the recipe for this amount of chocolate?

20. A recipe for Barbecued Chicken Pizza with Tomato Salsa makes ten 8-slice pizzas. For a 60-person banquet, you estimate that each person will eat 3 slices. What scaling factor do you need to use to adjust the pizza recipe for the banquet?

21. For daily production in your bakeshop, you estimate that you will need 7 dozen cookies, each weighing 1½ ounces. The recipe you would like to use yields 2 dozen 2-ounce cookies. What scaling factor should you use to adjust this recipe?

22. A recipe for a sweet-and-sour glaze yields 2½ quarts. For service each day, you need to make 2 tablespoons of sauce for each of 25 servings of sweet-and-sour chicken. What scaling factor should you use to adjust your sauce recipe for your daily requirement?

23. This evening in your restaurant, you will need thirty-five 250-milliliter servings of white bean soup. Your recipe makes 2 liters of soup. What scaling factor will adjust the recipe to the amount you need for this evening?

24. Your recipe for falafel makes 6 pounds and calls for 1 quart of raw garbanzo beans. You have 3 pounds of raw garbanzo beans that you would like to use. What scaling factor will appropriately adjust your recipe?

25. Your recipe for caramelized leek and goat cheese tarts make 8 tarts and calls for 12 ounces of raw chopped leeks. You will need 50 tarts for a party you are catering, but you only have 3 pounds of chopped leeks on hand. Do you have enough leeks to make the 50 tarts?

2.2 Scaling Recipes Based on a Desired Yield

Once you calculate a scaling factor, multiply the original ingredient quantities by that factor to determine the quantity of each ingredient that is needed to make the desired yield.

EXAMPLE 2.2.1 SCALING A RECIPE BASED ON A DESIRED YIELD

Our recipe for butternut squash soup makes 1 gallon. In our restaurant, we serve 6-fluid-ounce portions of soup. If we expect 47 soup orders this evening in our restaurant, how much of each ingredient will we need to measure?

Butternut Squash Soup

Yields 1 gallon

2 fl oz olive oil

4 oz shallots

2 # butternut squash

3½ qt vegetable stock

½ oz cumin

$$\text{Scaling factor} = \text{desired yield} \div \text{current recipe yield}$$
$$= (47 \times 6 \text{ fl oz}) \div 128 \text{ fl oz}$$
$$= 2.20$$

Determine the scaling factor. Determine the total desired yield, and convert 1 gallon into fluid ounces.

$$\frac{47 \text{ orders}}{1} \times \frac{6 \text{ fl oz}}{1 \text{ order}} \times \frac{1 \text{ C}}{8 \text{ fl oz}} \times \frac{1 \text{ G}}{16 \text{ C}} \times \frac{1 \text{ recipe}}{1 \text{ G}} = 2.20 \text{ recipes}$$

Alternatively, use the unit conversion method to determine the scaling factor.

Now multiply each original recipe ingredient quantity by the scaling factor:

Butternut Squash Soup

	Yields 1 gallon		Yields 2.2 gallons
INGREDIENT	**RECIPE QUANTITY**	**SCALING FACTOR**	**SCALED RECIPE QUANTITY**
Olive oil	2 fl oz	× 2.20	= 4.4 fl oz (or 4½ fl oz)
Shallots	4 oz	× 2.20	= 8.8 oz (or 9 oz)
Butternut squash	2 #	× 2.20	= 4.4 # (or 4 # 6 oz)
Vegetable stock	3½ qt	× 2.20	= 7.7 qt (or 1 G + 3¾ qt)
Cumin	½ oz	× 2.20	= 1.1 oz (or 1 oz)

You may need to adjust scaled quantities so they are easily measurable. Our easily measurable quantities are written in parentheses in the scaled recipe quantity column above. What constitutes an easily measurable quantity is subjective and will depend on the available measuring tools and your measuring preferences. Also, you will need to use your skills as a chef to maintain the integrity of the original recipe. For example, scaled quantities of certain seasonings may need to be adjusted during recipe testing.

You can also calculate a revised recipe yield using the scaling factor. By multiplying the original yield of 1 gallon by 2.2 (the scaling factor), you can calculate that the scaled recipe should make 2.2 gallons of butternut squash soup.

2.2 PRACTICE PROBLEMS

Use the information from *The Book of Yields* in Appendix V as necessary to help you answer the following questions. Round decimal answers to the nearest hundredth.

1. A recipe for Southern-style potato salad yields 15 portions. For a barbecue you are catering, you will need 120 portions of potato salad.

   a. Are you increasing or decreasing the recipe?

   b. What scaling factor will appropriately adjust the recipe?

   c. The original recipe calls for 4 ounces of diced green pepper. How many pounds of diced green pepper would you need for the scaled recipe?

2. A recipe for crème anglaise yields 2 quarts. For a plated dessert you will need 25 portions of 1 fluid ounce each.

a. Are you increasing or decreasing the recipe?

b. What scaling factor will appropriately adjust the recipe?

c. The original recipe calls for ½ pound of sugar. How many ounces of sugar would you need for the scaled recipe?

3. Your recipe for chocolate chip cookie dough yields 5 pounds of dough. For an event you are catering you need 6 dozen cookies, each of which uses 2 ounces of dough.

    a. Are you increasing or decreasing the recipe?

    b. What scaling factor will appropriately adjust the recipe?

    c. The original recipe calls for 3 tablespoons of vanilla. How many cups of vanilla would you need for the scaled recipe?

4. A recipe for curried lentil soup yields 3 gallons. For a luncheon you are catering you will need 12 servings of 8 fluid ounces each.

    a. Are you increasing or decreasing the recipe?

b. What scaling factor will appropriately adjust the recipe?

c. The original recipe calls for ¾ pound of diced celery. How many ounces of diced celery would you need for the scaled recipe?

5. Your recipe for corn and jícama salad makes 1 gallon. You will need 1½ pints for today's dinner service.

a. Are you increasing or decreasing the recipe?

b. What scaling factor will appropriately adjust the recipe?

c. Your original recipe calls for ¾ cup of chopped cilantro. How many tablespoons of cilantro do you need for the scaled recipe?

6. You have found a recipe for fruit salsa in a cooking magazine that yields six 3-ounce servings. You would like to convert the recipe to make 10 pounds.

a. Are you increasing or decreasing the recipe?

b. What scaling factor will appropriately adjust the recipe?

c. The original recipe calls for ½ cup of granulated sugar. How many pounds of sugar do you need for the scaled recipe?

7. Your award-winning recipe for Asian-style marinade makes 2 liters. You are going to package the marinade for resale and would like to convert the recipe to produce four dozen bottles of 6 fluid ounces each.

a. Are you increasing or decreasing the recipe?

b. What scaling factor will appropriately adjust the recipe?

c. The original recipe calls for ¼ liter of sherry. How many fluid ounces of sherry do you need for the scaled recipe?

8. A recipe for fresh mango chutney yields 16 portions of 150 milliliters each. You would like to make 120 portions of ¼ cup each.

a. Are you increasing or decreasing the recipe?

b. What scaling factor will appropriately adjust the recipe?

c. The original recipe calls for 150 milliliters of fresh lime juice. How many ounces of lime juice would you need for the scaled recipe?

9. A recipe for limeade calls for 10 limes, ¼ cup of sugar, 1 quart of water, and 1 sprig of mint, and yields eight 4-fluid-ounce servings. How many limes would you need to make fifteen ¾-cup servings of limeade?

10. Your recipe for chocolate mousse makes 1 gallon and calls for 400 grams of chopped bittersweet chocolate. You will be making two dozen 3-inch cakes for a pastry order, and you want to use ½ cup of mousse per cake. If you want to make only enough mousse for this order, how many ounces of chocolate should you use in the scaled recipe?

11. Your recipe for Potatoes Duchesse calls for 15 pounds of peeled potatoes and yields 50 portions, each weighing 5 ounces. How many pounds of peeled potatoes do you need to serve thirty 3-ounce portions during the dinner service?

12. You will be catering a private party for 12 people. You decide to make 1½-ounce cranberry-orange muffins, and you estimate that each person at the party will have three muffins each. Your recipe makes 15 pounds of dough and calls for 4 pounds of cranberries. How many ounces of cranberries will you need for the muffins for this party?

13. Your recipe for Quiche Lorraine makes eight quiches, which you cut into 6 slices for lunch service. For a cocktail reception, a serving will be one-eighth of a quiche, and you need 400 slices. If your recipe calls for 4 pounds of bacon, how much bacon will you need for the quiches for this reception?

2.3 Scaling Recipes Based on a Constraining Ingredient

If you calculate a scaling factor using ingredient quantities, the next step is the same as with recipe yields: multiply the original recipe quantities by the scaling factor.

EXAMPLE 2.3.1 SCALING A RECIPE BASED ON A CONSTRAINING INGREDIENT

If you had 1¼ pounds of clean, cubed squash, how many times could you make the Butternut Squash Soup recipe? How much of the other ingredients would you need? Approximately how much would the scaled recipe yield?

$$\text{Scaling factor} = \text{constraining quantity} \div \text{recipe quantity}$$
$$= 1.25\,\# \div 2\,\#$$
$$= 0.625$$

Determine the scaling factor.

$$\frac{1.25\,\#\,\text{squash}}{1} \times \frac{1\,\text{recipe}}{2\,\#\,\text{squash}} = 0.625\,\text{recipe}$$

Alternatively, use the unit conversion method to determine the scaling factor.

Since 0.625 gallons (the scaled recipe yield) is exactly equivalent to 2½ quarts, we will not round our scaling factor to 0.63 in this case.

Now multiply each original recipe ingredient quantity and the original recipe yield by the scaling factor:

Butternut Squash Soup

	Yields 1 gallon		Yields 2½ quarts
INGREDIENT	**RECIPE QUANTITY**	**SCALING FACTOR**	**SCALED RECIPE QUANTITY**
Olive oil	2 fl oz	× 0.625	= 1¼ fl oz
Shallots	4 oz	× 0.625	= 2½ oz
Butternut squash	2 #	× 0.625	= 1.25 #
Vegetable stock	3½ qt	× 0.625	= 2.1875 qt (or 2 qt + ¾ C)
Cumin	½ oz	× 0.625	= 0.3125 oz (or ⅓ oz)

Once again, you may need to adjust the scaled quantities so they are easily measurable. Our easily measurable quantities are written in parentheses in the scaled recipe quantity column above.

PRACTICE PROBLEMS

Use the information from *The Book of Yields* in Appendix V as necessary to help you answer the following questions. Round decimal answers to the nearest hundredth.

1. Your recipe for caramelized apples calls for 8 seasonal apples. A local orchard donated a bushel of apples to your restaurant, and you have 25 apples left over from this bushel.

    a. If you make caramelized apples using the 25 apples, are you increasing or decreasing the recipe?

    b. What scaling factor will appropriately adjust the recipe?

    c. The original recipe also calls for 7 ounces of sugar. How many ounces of sugar would you need for the scaled recipe?

2. Your recipe for rémoulade sauce calls for 3½ cups of mayonnaise. You have an open jar of mayonnaise that needs to be used up. In the jar is 1¾ cups of mayonnaise.

   a. If you make as much rémoulade sauce as you can with the 1¾ cups of mayonnaise remaining in the jar, are you increasing or decreasing the recipe?

   b. What scaling factor will appropriately adjust the recipe?

   c. The original recipe also calls for 3 tablespoons of chopped tarragon. How many tablespoons of tarragon would you need for the scaled recipe?

3. Your recipe for Greek salad calls for 4 pounds of chopped lettuce. Because of an ordering error, you have 2½ pounds of chopped lettuce to use for this recipe.

   a. If you make as much Greek salad as you can with the 2½ pounds of chopped lettuce, are you increasing or decreasing the recipe?

b. What scaling factor will appropriately adjust the recipe?

c. The original recipe also calls for 30 tomato wedges. How many tomato wedges would you need for the scaled recipe?

4. Your recipe for pumpkin bread calls for 3 pounds of pumpkin purée. While making the purée, the sous chef read the recipe wrong, so you have 5 pounds of purée to use up.

a. If you use all 5 pounds of purée to make pumpkin bread, are you increasing or decreasing the recipe?

b. What scaling factor will appropriately adjust the recipe?

c. The original recipe also calls for 3 teaspoons of baking powder. How many ounces of baking powder would you need for the scaled recipe?

5. Your recipe for white bean stew calls for 2 pounds of cooked white beans. Your extern cooked too many beans for another recipe, so you now have 3 cups of cooked white beans left over.

a. If you use the 3 cups of cooked beans to make white bean stew, are you increasing or decreasing the recipe?

b. What scaling factor will appropriately adjust the recipe?

c. The original recipe also calls for 6 ounces of chopped onions. How much chopped onion would you need for the scaled recipe?

6. A recipe for buttermilk fried chicken calls for 1 pint of buttermilk and 4 ounces of Dijon mustard. If you use only 1 cup of buttermilk, how much mustard should you use?

7. A recipe for crème caramel requires 16 eggs and 40 milliliters of vanilla. If you only use 1 tablespoon of vanilla to make this recipe, how many eggs should you use?

8. A recipe for French lentil soup calls for 900 grams of lentils and 5¾ liters of chicken stock. If you use 1 kilogram of lentils, how many liters of chicken stock do you need?

9. A recipe for gazpacho calls for 500 milliliters of red wine vinegar and 960 milliliters of olive oil. If you use 400 milliliters of olive oil to make the recipe, how much red wine vinegar should you use?

10. A recipe for Irish soda bread calls for 24 fluid ounces of milk and ¾ cup of butter. If you use 1 gallon of milk, how many pounds of butter should you use?

11. A recipe for banana bread calls for 3 cups of mashed bananas and 9 ounces of all-purpose flour. You have 5 pounds of peeled bananas that need to be used. If one cup of mashed banana weighs 4½ ounces, how many pounds of flour should you use with the 5 pounds of peeled bananas?

2.4 Standardizing Recipes

Recipe writers, like other writers, have individual styles and preferences. Whatever your preferences, the production needs of your business will be based on **standardized recipes.** When standardizing a recipe, a chef may prefer to measure some ingredients using nonstandard units of measure — measurements that are neither weight nor volume—because they are easy to use. (A good example of such a unit is "each." In the following recipe, the chicken breasts, the pineapple, the red onion, and the chipotle pepper are measured using this unit.) This is appropriate when an approximate measure is accurate enough for product consistency, or when planning, ordering, costing, or allocating labor usage is more efficient.

EXAMPLE 2.4.1 **STANDARDIZING A RECIPE**

Standardize the recipe below to yield the 32 servings needed daily for service.

Grilled Chicken with Mango, Red Onion, and Pineapple

Yields 4 servings

(Adapted from Techniques of Healthy Cooking *by The Culinary Institute of America, 2008)*

4 chicken breasts (8 oz each)

1 # mango, large dice

½ pineapple, large dice

1 large red onion, large dice

1 chipotle pepper in adobo, chopped

2½ fl oz orange juice

2 fl oz fresh lime juice

1 fl oz olive oil

Scaling factor = desired yield ÷ current recipe yield   Divide the desired yield by the current recipe yield.
                    = 32 servings ÷ 4 servings
                    = 8

Now multiply each recipe ingredient quantity by the scaling factor to calculate the scaled quantity of each ingredient.

Grilled Chicken with Mango, Red Onion, and Pineapple

(Adapted from Techniques of Healthy Cooking *by The Culinary Institute of America [2008])*

	Yields 4 servings		Yields 32 servings
INGREDIENT	**RECIPE QUANTITY**	**SCALING FACTOR**	**SCALED RECIPE QUANTITY**
Chicken breasts (8 oz each)	4 each	× 8	= 32 each
Mango, large dice	1 #	× 8	= 8 #
Pineapple, large dice	½ each	× 8	= 4 each
Red onion, large dice	1 each	× 8	= 8 each
Chipotle pepper, chopped	1 each	× 8	= 8 each
Orange juice	2½ fl oz	× 8	= 20 fl oz (or 1¼ pt)
Lime juice, fresh	2 fl oz	× 8	= 16 fl oz (or 1 pt)
Olive oil	1 fl oz	× 8	= 8 fl oz (or ½ pt)

EXAMPLE 2.4.2 STANDARDIZING A RECIPE

You want to standardize the following recipe for use in your bakery, which uses a digital scale accurate to $\frac{1}{100}$ of a pound. Calculate the recipe quantities needed for the standardized recipe.

Chocolate Chunk Cookies

Makes 12 dozen cookies

(Adapted from Baking at Home with the CIA *by The Culinary Institute of America)*

7½ C all-purpose flour

1 T baking soda

1 T salt (regular)

3 C unsalted butter

3 C granulated sugar

2¼ C packed brown sugar

6 eggs

1 T vanilla extract

1½ qt chocolate chips

Standardizing a recipe. Converting all ingredient quantities in a recipe so they are measured by weight means that a chef can weigh all ingredients in the same bowl, taring the scale after weighing each ingredient.

First, notice that almost all of the ingredient quantities need to be converted from volume to weight. Here are equivalents that can be used as part of the necessary unit conversions. These equivalents were found in *The Book of Yields*. (It is very likely your results will be more accurate if you weigh the items yourself.)

All-purpose flour: 1 C = 4.6 oz	Sugar, granulated: 1 C = 7.10 oz
Baking soda: 1 C = 8.4 oz	Brown sugar, packed: 1 C = 7.75 oz
Salt, regular: 1 T = 0.645 oz	Eggs: 1 ea (shelled) = 1.777 oz
Butter: 1 C = 8 oz	Chocolate chips: 1 C = 5.35 oz

Chocolate Chunk Cookies

Makes 12 dozen cookies

(Adapted from Baking at Home with the CIA *by The Culinary Institute of America)*

INGREDIENT	RECIPE QUANTITY		STANDARDIZED RECIPE QUANTITY
Flour, all-purpose	7½ C	$\dfrac{7.5\,C}{1} \times \dfrac{4.6\,oz}{1\,C} \times \dfrac{1\,\#}{16\,oz} = 2.1562\,\#$	2.16 #
Baking soda	1 T	$\dfrac{1\,T}{1} \times \dfrac{1\,C}{16\,T} \times \dfrac{8.4\,oz}{1\,C} \times \dfrac{1\,\#}{16\,oz} = 0.0328\,\#$	0.03 #
Salt, regular	1 T	$\dfrac{1\,T}{1} \times \dfrac{0.645\,oz}{1\,T} \times \dfrac{1\,\#}{16\,oz} = 0.0403\,\#$	0.04 #
Butter, unsalted	3 C	$\dfrac{3\,C}{1} \times \dfrac{8\,oz}{1\,C} \times \dfrac{1\,\#}{16\,oz} = 1.5\,\#$	1.5 #
Sugar, granulated	3 C	$\dfrac{3\,C}{1} \times \dfrac{7.1\,oz}{1\,C} \times \dfrac{1\,\#}{16\,oz} = 1.3312\,\#$	1.33 #
Brown sugar, packed	2¼ C	$\dfrac{2.25\,C}{1} \times \dfrac{7.75\,oz}{1\,C} \times \dfrac{1\,\#}{16\,oz} = 1.0898\,\#$	1.09 #
Eggs, large	6 ea	$\dfrac{6\,ea}{1} \times \dfrac{1.777\,oz}{1\,ea} \times \dfrac{1\,\#}{16\,oz} = 0.6663\,\#$	0.67 #
Vanilla extract	1 T	$\dfrac{1\,T}{1} \times \dfrac{1\,C}{16\,T} \times \dfrac{8\,oz}{1\,C} \times \dfrac{1\,\#}{16\,oz} = 0.0312\,\#$	0.03 #
Chocolate chips	1½ qt	$\dfrac{1.5\,qt}{1} \times \dfrac{4\,C}{1\,qt} \times \dfrac{5.35\,oz}{1\,C} \times \dfrac{1\,\#}{16\,oz} = 2.0062\,\#$	2.01 #

EXAMPLE 2.4.3 **STANDARDIZING A RECIPE**

Standardize the same chocolate chip cookie recipe for use on a metric scale that is accurate to 1 gram ($\frac{1}{1000}$ of a kilogram).

Chocolate Chunk Cookies

Makes 12 dozen cookies

(Adapted from Baking at Home with the CIA *by The Culinary Institute of America)*

INGREDIENT	RECIPE QUANTITY		STANDARDIZED RECIPE QUANTITY
Flour, all-purpose	7½ C	$\frac{7.5\,C}{1} \times \frac{4.6\,oz}{1\,C} \times \frac{28.35\,g}{1\,oz} \times \frac{1\,kg}{1000\,g} = 0.9780\,kg$	0.978 kg
Baking soda	1 T	$\frac{1\,T}{1} \times \frac{1\,C}{16\,T} \times \frac{8.4\,oz}{1\,C} \times \frac{28.35\,g}{1\,oz} = 14.8837\,g$	15 g
Salt, regular	1 T	$\frac{1\,T}{1} \times \frac{0.645\,oz}{1\,T} \times \frac{28.35\,g}{1\,oz} = 18.2857\,g$	18 g
Butter, unsalted	3 C	$\frac{3\,C}{1} \times \frac{8\,oz}{1\,C} \times \frac{28.35\,g}{1\,oz} \times \frac{1\,kg}{1000\,g} = 0.6804\,kg$	0.680 kg
Sugar, granulated	3 C	$\frac{3\,C}{1} \times \frac{7.1\,oz}{1\,C} \times \frac{28.35\,g}{1\,oz} \times \frac{1\,kg}{1000\,g} = 0.6038\,kg$	0.604 kg
Brown sugar, packed	2¼ C	$\frac{2.25\,C}{1} \times \frac{7.75\,oz}{1\,C} \times \frac{28.35\,g}{1\,oz} \times \frac{1\,kg}{1000\,g} = 0.4943\,kg$	0.494 kg
Eggs, large	6 ea	$\frac{6\,ea}{1} \times \frac{1.777\,oz}{1\,ea} \times \frac{28.35\,g}{1\,oz} \times \frac{1\,kg}{1000\,g} = 0.3022\,kg$	0.302 kg
Vanilla extract	1 T	$\frac{1\,T}{1} \times \frac{1\,C}{16\,T} \times \frac{8\,oz}{1\,C} \times \frac{28.35\,g}{1\,oz} = 14.175\,g$	14 g
Chocolate chips	1½ qt	$\frac{1.5\,qt}{1} \times \frac{4\,C}{1\,qt} \times \frac{1\,\#}{3\,C} \times \frac{1\,kg}{2.205\,\#} = 0.9070\,kg$	0.907 kg

EXAMPLE 2.4.4 **DETERMINING A STANDARDIZED RECIPE**

You have just standardized your recipe for Ancho Chile Crusted Salmon with Yellow Mole. Standardize the subrecipe for Yellow Mole so it yields 50 fluid ounces. Convert all quantities to weights that are rounded to the nearest hundredth.

Here is the standardized recipe for Ancho Chile Crusted Salmon with Yellow Mole, and your current recipe for Yellow Mole:

Ancho Chile Crusted Salmon with Yellow Mole
Yield: 25 servings

12½ oz ancho chiles

0.44 oz cumin seeds

½ oz fennel seeds

0.55 oz coriander seeds

0.52 oz black peppercorns

2¼ oz regular salt

9½ # salmon filets

3 oz clarified butter

50 fl oz Yellow Mole (recipe follows)

Yellow Mole
Makes 32 fluid ounces

1 fl oz olive oil

12 oz sliced onions

1 t sliced garlic

1½ # seeded and sliced yellow peppers

5 oz chopped fennel

½ t ground allspice

1½ t dried epazote

¾ oz granulated sugar

3 oz quartered tomatillos

1 fl oz fresh lime juice

As you can see, the Yellow Mole recipe is a subrecipe of the recipe for Ancho Chile Crusted Salmon, but it does not make 50 fluid ounces. Therefore, we need to standardize this recipe to make the necessary quantity.

Determine the scaling factor.

Scaling factor = desired yield ÷ current recipe yield
$$= 50 \text{ fl oz} \div 32 \text{ fl oz}$$
$$= 1.5625$$

Since we want exactly 50 fluid ounces of mole, we will use the exact scaling factor we just calculated. Here are equivalents that can be used as part of the necessary unit conversions. They were found in *The Book of Yields* (See Appendix V).

Garlic, sliced	1 C = 4.6 oz
Allspice, ground	1 T = 0.203 oz
Epazote, ground	1 T = 0.099 oz
Lime juice, fresh	1 C = 8.3 oz

Yellow Mole

Yields 32 fluid ounces   Standardized recipe yields 50 fl oz

INGREDIENT	RECIPE QUANTITY	SCALING FACTOR		STANDARDIZED RECIPE QUANTITY
Olive oil	1 fl oz	× 1.5625	$\dfrac{1.5625 \text{ fl oz}}{1} \times \dfrac{7.7 \text{ oz}}{8 \text{ fl oz}} = 1.5039 \text{ oz}$	1.5 oz
Onions, sliced	12 oz	× 1.5625	$\dfrac{18.75 \text{ oz}}{1} \times \dfrac{1\#}{16 \text{ oz}} = 1.1718 \#$	1.17 #
Garlic, sliced	1 t	× 1.5625	$\dfrac{1.5625 \text{ t}}{1} \times \dfrac{1 \text{ C}}{48 \text{ t}} \times \dfrac{4.6 \text{ oz}}{1 \text{ C}} = 0.1497 \text{ oz}$	0.15 oz
Yellow peppers, seeded and sliced	1½ #	× 1.5625	2.3437 #	2.34 #
Fennel, chopped	5 oz	× 1.5625	$\dfrac{7.8125 \text{ oz}}{1} \times \dfrac{1\#}{16 \text{ oz}} = 0.4882 \#$	0.49 #
Allspice, ground	½ t	× 1.5625	$\dfrac{0.7812 \text{ t}}{1} \times \dfrac{1 \text{ T}}{3 \text{ t}} \times \dfrac{0.203 \text{ oz}}{1 \text{ T}} = 0.0528 \text{ oz}$	0.05 oz
Epazote, dried	1½ t	× 1.5625	$\dfrac{2.3437 \text{ t}}{1} \times \dfrac{1 \text{ T}}{3 \text{ t}} \times \dfrac{0.099 \text{ oz}}{1 \text{ T}} = 0.0773 \text{ oz}$	0.08 oz
Sugar, granulated	¾ oz	× 1.5625	1.1718 oz	1.17 oz
Tomatillos, quartered	3 oz	× 1.5625	4.6875 oz	4.69 oz
Lime juice, fresh	1 fl oz	× 1.5625	$\dfrac{1.5625 \text{ fl oz}}{1} \times \dfrac{8.3 \text{ oz}}{8 \text{ fl oz}} = 1.6210 \text{ oz}$	1.62 oz

Testing a standardized recipe. After a recipe has been scaled, a chef should test it to see if the scaled quantities are acceptable. If not, adjustments should be made before the recipe is standardized.

If you want to measure the yield of the standardized Yellow Mole recipe by weight, add the weight of each ingredient in the revised recipe to calculate an approximate weight. In this case, the standardized weights of the ingredients add up to approximately 4.58 pounds. This recipe can now be tested (and finalized). Once that is accomplished, your Ancho Chile Crusted Salmon recipe is standardized using all weight measures.

2.4 PRACTICE PROBLEMS

Use the information from *The Book of Yields* in Appendix V as necessary to help you answer the following questions. Truncate answers at the ten-thousandths place (4 decimal places).

1. The following recipe makes enough filling for six pies that each yield 8 slices.

   a. What scaling factor should you apply to the given recipe to yield enough filling for 336 slices?

b. Standardize the following recipe by first applying the scaling factor from part (a), then converting the scaled ingredient quantities into the units given in the last column.

Coconut Cream Pie Filling

Original recipe makes enough filling for 6 pies (8 slices each)

INGREDIENT	RECIPE QUANTITY	SCALING FACTOR	STANDARDIZED RECIPE QUANTITY
Shredded coconut, packaged	9 C	×	#
Sugar, granulated	1½ C	×	#
Sweetened condensed milk (1 can = 14 fl oz)	¾ C	×	cans

2. The following recipe makes thirty 5½-ounce portions of glazed beets.

    a. What scaling factor will adjust the recipe to call for 20¼ pounds of cooked, peeled, and sliced beets?

b. Standardize the following recipe by first applying the scaling factor from part (a), then converting the scaled ingredient quantities into the units given in the last column.

Glazed Beets

Original recipe makes thirty 5½-ounce servings

(*Adapted from* The Professional Chef *[8th ed.] by The Culinary Institute of America*)

INGREDIENT	RECIPE QUANTITY	SCALING FACTOR	STANDARDIZED RECIPE QUANTITY
Beets, cooked, peeled, and sliced	7 # 8 oz	×	#
Sugar, granulated	10½ oz	×	#
Orange juice	4½ fl oz	×	qt
Chicken stock	1 qt	×	qt
Red wine vinegar	1½ fl oz	×	C
Butter	4½ oz	×	#

c. How many 4-ounce portions of glazed beets would the revised recipe yield?

3. The following recipe makes fifteen 9-inch pies.

a. If you only need to make six pies, what scaling factor will appropriately adjust the recipe?

b. Standardize the following recipe by first applying the scaling factor from part (a), then converting the scaled ingredient quantities into the units given in the last column.

Lemon Meringue Pie

Original recipe makes fifteen 9-inch pies

(Adapted from The Professional Chef *[8th ed.] by The Culinary Institute of America)*

INGREDIENT	RECIPE QUANTITY	SCALING FACTOR	STANDARDIZED RECIPE QUANTITY
Water	5¾ L	×	#
Sugar, granulated	2¾ kg	×	#
Salt, regular	42 g	×	#
Lemon juice	900 mL	×	pt
Lemon zest	84 g	×	#
Cornstarch	510 g	×	#
Egg yolks	24 ea	×	#
Butter	340 g	×	#

Yield Percent

KEY TERMS

as-purchased (AP) quantity

fabrication

edible portion (EP) quantity

yield percent

trim loss percent

yield test

by the count

KEY QUESTIONS

What does yield percent represent?

How do you calculate a product's yield percent?

What are some factors that affect product yield percent?

What does it mean to say an ingredient is measured by the count?

What are some words used to signify that an ingredient is measured by the count?

A successful business is efficient in its methods, effective in meeting its goals, and (most of all) profitable. In the hospitality industry, cost-saving measures can involve each of the facets of a business. One area that often comprises a significant portion of many businesses' budgets is the cost of food, and food preparation methods and purchasing practices can affect profitability in a very significant way. In this chapter, we discuss yield percent, factors that affect yield percent, and the importance of maximizing product utilization.

3.1   What Is Yield Percent?

When a vendor delivers a product to a business, the amount of product the business receives is called an **as-purchased** (abbreviated **AP**) **quantity**. Preparation, or **fabrication**, of this product before it is used in a recipe turns that AP quantity into an **edible portion** (abbreviated **EP**) **quantity**. For example, if a business purchases heads of cauliflower and the staff cuts them into florets, the heads are the AP quantity and the florets are the EP quantity.

Yield percent is the percent of your AP quantity that is usable after you prepare it for use in a recipe. To calculate the yield percent of an ingredient, divide the EP quantity by the AP quantity, and change the decimal to a percent.

$$\text{Yield percent} = \text{EP quantity} \div \text{AP quantity}$$

When you calculate a yield percent, you are calculating the percent of an AP quantity that is usable for a specific purpose. If you can fabricate 6 pounds of florets from 10 pounds of cauliflower heads, then the yield percent is 60%, because 6 pounds is 60% of 10 pounds. If you can strip 4 ounces of leaves from a bunch of rosemary that weighs 5 ounces, the yield percent is 80%.

EXAMPLE 3.1.1   CALCULATING A YIELD PERCENT

A restaurant purchased a 24-pound case of Granny Smith apples. After fabricating the apples, 17.2 pounds of usable apples remained. What was the yield percent of the case?

Yield percent = EP quantity ÷ AP quantity
$= 17.2 \# \div 24 \#$
$= 0.7166$
$= 71.66\%$

Since 24 pounds is the weight of the apples when they were purchased, 24 pounds is the AP quantity. Similarly, 17.2 pounds is the EP quantity because it is the weight of the apples after they were prepared.

EXAMPLE 3.1.2 CALCULATING A YIELD PERCENT

A member of a restaurant's kitchen staff fabricated a 35-pound box of squash. After fabrication, he had 415 ounces of prepared squash. What yield percent did this staff member achieve?

$$\frac{35\,\#}{1} \times \frac{16\,oz}{1\,\#} = 560\,oz$$

Convert either the AP weight (as shown here) or the EP weight so that both are expressed in the same unit.

Yield percent = EP quantity ÷ AP quantity
= 415 oz ÷ 560 oz
= 0.7410
= 74.1%

415 ounces is the EP weight, and 560 ounces is the AP weight.

Yield percent. Top: the original AP quantity. Bottom: 60% of the AP weight is usable florets (left scale) and 40% of the AP weight is trim loss (right scale).

TRIM LOSS

If fabricating cauliflower heads into florets gives a yield percent of 60%, then the other 40% is not florets. This 40% is an example of a **trim loss percent**. To calculate a trim loss percent, divide the amount of unused product by the AP quantity from which it came and change the decimal to a percent:

Trim loss percent = trim loss quantity ÷ AP quantity

As you may have deduced, the yield percent and the trim loss percent of an ingredient always add up to 100%. Therefore, there is another formula to calculate yield percent:

Yield percent = 100% − trim loss percent

Sometimes the waste generated while preparing a product for one recipe can be turned into usable product for another recipe. For example, the stems of the cauliflower heads may be used for soup or another application, but the yield percent for the cauliflower florets remains as originally calculated.

Effect of preparation method on yield percent. Making melon balls from a cantaloupe (left) gives a lower yield percent than dicing a cantaloupe (right).

YIELD TESTS

The most accurate method of determining the yield percent of a product is to perform a **yield test**: fabricate *your* product with *your* staff, using *your* equipment, under *your* normal working conditions, and determine the yield percent generated in your kitchen. A yield test is accurate, but also time consuming. This is one reason chefs may use resources such as *The Book of Yields.*

Many factors can affect the results of a yield test, but the most common ones are:

◼ **THE INTENDED USE OF THE PRODUCT:** As mentioned above, yield percent is the percent of an AP quantity that is usable *for a specific purpose.* Dicing cantaloupe yields about 58%, but making cantaloupe balls yields only about 37%.

◼ **THE QUALITY AND CONDITION OF THE PRODUCT:** No matter how skilled a chef is, technique cannot compensate for inferior product. Product that meets appropriate purchasing specifications will likely result in a higher yield.

◼ **THE SIZE OF THE PRODUCT BEING PREPARED:** Dicing medium-sized carrots gives about an 81% yield on average, but dicing jumbo carrots increases that yield to almost 84%. Along the same lines, a 24-pound case of romaine lettuce that contains twenty-four 1-pound heads will likely have a different yield percent than a case with twelve 2-pound heads.

◼ **THE SKILL LEVEL OF THE PERSON PREPARING THE PRODUCT:** Someone who is unfamiliar or inexperienced with a particular technique is likely to achieve a lower yield than someone who has taken time to practice that method.

◼ **ATTENTION TO DETAIL:** Conscientiousness in the kitchen can greatly improve yield. A sloppy job can negate any amount of experience.

◼ **THE EQUIPMENT USED:** Different designs for kitchen equipment may lead to a different product yield. A heavy, cumbersome peeler will dig deeper into a potato or a carrot than will one that weighs less; a dull knife blade may crush a tomato, while a finely honed edge will slice through almost effortlessly.

By affecting product yield, these factors also affect ingredient cost. Higher yields on products translate directly into smaller AP quantities. Thus, you spend less money on product because you are able to use more of what you purchase.

PRACTICE PROBLEMS

Answer the following questions. Truncate all percents at the hundredths place (2 decimal places), and all other quantities at the ten-thousandths place (4 decimal places).

1. A 24-pound case of Bosc pears yielded a total of 20 pounds 12 ounces of sliced pears. What percent of the case is usable after fabrication?

2. You purchase a 3-pound bunch of celery and are able to fabricate 31½ ounces of diced celery from the bunch. What yield percent did you achieve?

3. A 20-kilogram case of bananas yielded a total of 419 ounces of sliced bananas. What was the yield percent of the case?

4. Before it is drained, a number-10 can contains 107.3 ounces of sliced beets in water. If 75½ ounces of beets remain after draining the can, what percent of the original weight is beets?

5. A prep cook is given 50 pounds of potatoes to clean. After all the potatoes have been cleaned, the prep cook has 8 pounds of peels. What yield percent did the prep cook achieve?

6. Three large fryer chickens weigh 10.3 pounds. If you end up with 4 pounds 11 ounces of clean meat, what percent of the chicken is clean meat?

7. If 500 grams of whole Kalamata olives yield 14.7 ounces of pitted olives, what percent of the original weight do the pitted olives represent?

8. A case of bananas weighs 15 pounds and contains 60 bananas. After peeling the bananas, you are left with 6 pounds of waste. What is the yield percent for this case of bananas?

9. A 2½-pound whole bass will yield 18 ounces in filets. What percent of a whole bass is the filets?

10. Thirty pounds of Macintosh apples yielded 345 ounces of sliced apples. What percent yield was achieved?

11. Twelve kilograms of Roma tomatoes yielded 400 ounces of sliced tomatoes. What percent yield was achieved?

12. A case of kiwi fruits contained 12 fruits and weighed 4 pounds. If this case yielded 1500 grams of peeled and sliced kiwi, what percent of the original weight does the prepared fruit represent?

13. A case of mangoes contains 16 mangoes, and each mango weighs approximately 8 ounces. If this case yielded 5 pounds of diced mango, what percent of the case does the diced fruit represent?

14. While fabricating 3½ pounds of tangerines into sections, 1 pound of waste was generated. What percent of the tangerines do the sections represent?

15. Fabricating a kilogram of Mexican papaya generated 12 ounces of waste. What is the yield percent of this papaya?

3.2 Calculating EP Quantities and AP Quantities

In a professional kitchen, two calculations come up frequently: (1) calculating the expected EP quantity from a given AP quantity, and (2) calculating an AP quantity, given a necessary EP quantity. The formulas for each of those situations are:

$$\text{AP quantity} \times \text{yield \%} = \text{EP quantity}$$

$$\text{EP quantity} \div \text{yield \%} = \text{AP quantity}$$

(It is usually easier to convert yield percents to decimals when performing these calculations.)

When the yield of a product is less than 100%, EP quantities will always be less than their respective AP quantities. From the other perspective, the AP quantities will be larger than their respective EP quantities. For example, you will always end up with less than 3 pounds of florets after fabricating 3 pounds of broccoli. The underlying math supports this fact: changing a percent between 0% and 100% into a decimal will give you a value between 0 and 1. When you multiply a number by such a decimal, the answer is *less than* the original number. When you divide a number by such a decimal, the answer is *greater than* the original number.

Before we look at some examples involving yield percent, remember that the data presented in *The Book of Yields* are guidelines to help you make calculations. Measurements that you take in your kitchen may vary. For example, if *The Book of Yields* reports that a product has a 75% yield, you may not get a yield of exactly 75% each time you prepare that product because of the factors listed previously.

EXAMPLE 3.2.1 CALCULATING AN EP QUANTITY

If you purchase 15 pounds of pineapples, what EP weight of cubed pineapple can you expect?

AP weight × yield % = EP weight
15 # × 0.484 = 7.26 #

According to *The Book of Yields*, cubing pineapple gives a yield of 48.4%.

EXAMPLE 3.2.2 CALCULATING AN AP QUANTITY

You have a recipe that requires 700 grams of cubed honeydew melon. How many AP pounds of melon will yield this EP weight?

EP weight ÷ yield % = AP weight
700 g ÷ 0.575 = 1217.3913 g

$$\frac{1217.3913 \text{ g}}{1} \times \frac{1 \text{ \#}}{453.6 \text{ g}} = 2.6838 \text{ \#}$$

Calculate the AP weight, using the yield for cubed honeydew (57.5%, according to *The Book of Yields*).

Convert the AP weight into pounds.

You can, if you want, convert the EP weight of 700 grams into pounds, and then use the yield percent to calculate the AP weight.

EXAMPLE 3.2.3 CALCULATING AN EP QUANTITY AND AN AP QUANTITY

A recipe calls for 12 pounds of diced carrots, and you have 15 pounds (AP) of carrots on hand. Do you have enough carrots on hand for this recipe?

(a) AP weight × yield % = EP weight
15 # × 0.813 = 12.195 #

One option is to calculate the expected EP weight using the given AP weight. *The Book of Yields* reports that the yield percent of carrots is 81.3%.

(b) EP weight ÷ yield % = AP weight
12 # ÷ 0.813 = 14.7601 #

Alternatively, calculate the necessary AP weight using the given EP weight.

Calculation (a) shows an EP weight that is adequate to cover the amount needed for the recipe, but it is very close to the weight needed. Remember that the yield percent you achieve when fabricating carrots will determine the actual EP weight.

Calculation (b) shows, on average, how many pounds of carrots you would need to start with to get 12 pounds of diced carrots. This AP weight is very close to what you have on hand.

Both calculations are estimates, used for planning purposes. There is one more way that you could decide if having 15 pounds of carrots on hand is sufficient for your recipe. Since you know both the EP and AP weights, you can use them to calculate a yield percent:

12 # ÷ 15 # = 0.8
= 80%

Based on the yield percent in *The Book of Yields* (81.3%), an 80% yield seems to be a reasonable goal. You would have to decide if 1.3% is a comfortable margin of error.

EXAMPLE 3.2.4 CALCULATING AN AP QUANTITY

A high-end Japanese restaurant serves, on average, 100 pounds of sliced Asian pears per week. How many pounds of pears should this restaurant purchase?

To answer this question, the restaurant could look up the expected yield when slicing Asian pears. According to *The Book of Yields*, it's 74.5%. However, the staff may not always achieve a 74.5% yield when fabricating Asian pears. Below are the results of two yield tests performed by this restaurant:

	AP WEIGHT	EP WEIGHT	YIELD PERCENT
YIELD TEST 1	50 #	36 #	36 # ÷ 50 # = 0.72 = 72%
YIELD TEST 2	25 #	15.5 #	15.5 # ÷ 25 # = 0.62 = 62%

Depending on which yield percent is used, the calculated AP quantity will differ significantly:

EP weight ÷ yield % = AP weight
100 # ÷ 0.745 = 134.2281 #

Calculate an AP weight using the yield percent from *The Book of Yields*.

EP weight ÷ yield % = AP weight
100 # ÷ 0.72 = 138.8888 #

Use the yield percent from Yield Test 1.

EP weight ÷ yield % = AP weight
100 # ÷ 0.62 = 161.2903 #

Use the yield percent from Yield Test 2.

Because of the sizable discrepancy between the results of the two yield tests, this restaurant should not yet establish its standard yield for Asian pears; further testing is needed. To briefly illustrate the importance of both using a realistic yield and striving to achieve a high one, consider the impact of the 10% difference in product yield between the two tests:

161.2903 # − 138.8888 # = 22.4015 # difference (per week)
22.4015 #/week × 52 weeks/year = 1164.878 #/year

Calculate the yearly difference in AP quantity between the two tests.

1164.878 #/year × $2.09 = $2434.60/year

Research shows that Asian pears are currently selling for an average of $2.09 per pound.

While you may not always achieve a high yield each time you fabricate products, you can certainly see the benefits of striving to achieve as high a yield as possible. If you take care in your work, it will, quite literally, pay off in the long run.

3.2 PRACTICE PROBLEMS

Use the information from *The Book of Yields* in Appendix V as necessary to help you answer the following questions. Unless otherwise directed, truncate all percents at the hundredths place (2 decimal places), and all other quantities at the ten-thousandths place (4 decimal places).

1. You purchase 10 bunches of fresh tarragon and fabricate 7.8 ounces of tarragon leaves from the bunches. What percent yield did you achieve?

2. If a basket of oyster mushrooms yields 5.35 ounces of sliced mushrooms, what percent of the mushrooms is usable?

3. You need 12 pounds 8 ounces of chopped leeks for a soup recipe. On average, one bunch of leeks weighs 1½ pounds and has a 43.8% yield. How many bunches of leeks would you need to purchase in order to make this recipe?

4. If you were able to get 38½ ounces of diced carrots from a 3-pound bag, how many ounces should you be able to get from a 10-pound bag?

5. If you were able to get 6.8 ounces of sections from one grapefruit, how many ounces should you be able to get from 10 pounds of grapefruit?

6. How many bunches of fresh rosemary should you purchase if you need 1½ ounces of chopped rosemary leaves and a bunch of rosemary has an 80% yield?

7. For a party you are catering, you will need 45 pounds of shredded romaine lettuce. If a case of romaine weighs 24 pounds as purchased and has a 75% yield, how many cases of romaine should you purchase for this party?

8. How many ounces of chopped romaine lettuce should a case of romaine yield if the case has 12 heads?

9. You purchase 12 bunches of green onions. How many ounces of chopped green onions should you be able to fabricate?

10. How many cups of diced pears should you end up with after draining a number-10 can of diced pears in light syrup?

11. How many ounces of sweet basil leaves can you expect to fabricate from a bunch that weighs 60 grams?

12. If you need 18 ounces of chopped fresh garlic, how many heads of garlic should you purchase? (For this question, round your answer up to the next whole number.)

13. How many ounces of fresh Italian parsley should you purchase if you need 1 cup of chopped parsley?

14. How many daikon radishes should you purchase if you need 36 ounces of julienned radish? (For this question, round your answer up to the next whole number.)

15. You purchase one head each of Bibb lettuce, red leaf lettuce, and romaine lettuce. How many total ounces of chopped lettuce should you be able to fabricate?

16. You purchase 5 pounds of green bell peppers and 5 pounds of red bell peppers. Which color pepper should result in a higher fabricated weight? Why?

17. You need 1 trimmed pound each of butternut squash, spaghetti squash, and Hubbard squash. Which of these three varieties requires you to purchase the largest unfabricated weight? Which would require purchasing the smallest unfabricated weight?

18. You need 1½ pints of fresh orange juice. How many oranges would you need to purchase to make this recipe? (For this question, round your answer up to the next whole number.)

19. You need 2 cups of freshly squeezed lemon juice. How many pounds of lemons will yield the 2 cups of juice you need?

20. Is it reasonable to expect to fabricate 250 ounces of diced watermelon from a 25-pound watermelon?

21. Should 20 pounds of cauliflower heads be sufficient if you need 150 ounces of cauliflower florets?

22. After fabricating 15 pounds of apples, your extern reports to you that he has 213½ ounces of fabricated apples. If you asked him to fabricate the Macintosh apples in the pantry, is it likely that he fabricated the correct apples? If not, what variety did he most likely fabricate?

3.3 Quantities That Compensate for Waste

When a restaurant's staff determines how much of each ingredient it needs to purchase, it must consider many factors. Among the most important considerations is the way the restaurant's recipes are written. For example, in a recipe for apple pie, the amount of apples to use might be specified in one of the following ways:

VERSION A	VERSION B	VERSION C
2.88 kilograms peeled, cored, and sliced apples	1½ gallons peeled, cored, and sliced apples	20 medium apples, peeled, cored, and sliced

Recipe quantities. When a recipe calls for an EP weight (left) or for a volume (center), waste must be factored into a purchasing calculation, since volume and weight both decrease as a result of fabrication. When a recipe quantity is given by an AP count (right), the recipe writer has already compensated for the waste.

Both version A and version B specify an EP quantity to use in the recipe. (This will be our convention for this book: anytime a recipe quantity is measured by weight or by volume, it is an EP quantity.) Thus, you need to factor in the yield percent of the apples when making these purchasing calculations. This will help you determine how much more than 2.88 kilograms of apples you should purchase for version A and how much more than 1½ gallons (or an equivalent weight) of apples you should purchase for version B.

Version C, however, specifies an *AP* quantity. The recipe writer still wants you to peel and core the apples before putting them in the pie, but when you calculate how much to purchase for version C, you don't have to compensate for any waste you may generate, because the recipe writer has already done so.

Version C is an example of measuring an ingredient **by the count**. An ingredient is measured by the count if the measurement specifies a number of objects. In most cases, a count is an AP quantity. (See "Some Exceptions to the Rule" (below) for examples of counts that are EP quantities.) Words that indicate measuring by the count include *head* (used for lettuces, for example), *clove* (garlic), and *bunch* (herbs and some fruits and vegetables). Of course, you can use the name of the ingredient itself, and write a recipe that calls for 5 large onions or for 12 red peppers. A word frequently used to signify a count is the word *each*, often abbreviated *ea*. For example, a recipe might call for "24 ea Bosc pears."

Serving sizes also follow this convention. For example, consider the following three serving sizes:

SERVING SIZE A	SERVING SIZE B	SERVING SIZE C
3 ounces sliced strawberries	½ cup sliced strawberries	4 strawberries, sliced

Serving size A (which is measured by weight) and serving size B (measured by volume) are EP quantities, so you need to use the yield percent when making a calculation about purchasing or portioning. However, serving size C is measured by the count, so it is already an AP quantity. No yield is needed.

SOME EXCEPTIONS TO THE RULE

Occasionally a recipe will call for an ingredient by the count, but the objects that are counted out are an EP quantity. For example, if a fruit salad recipe calls for 120 melon balls, you will need to factor in the yield percent of the melon you are using to make the balls. If a recipe calls for a number of tournéed carrots, you must use the yield percent of your carrots when determining your AP quantity.

Also, some recipes are written such that a given weight or volume is an AP quantity. (As we mentioned before, weights and volumes in recipes in this book are EP quantities.) When a recipe writer wants you to treat a weight or a volume as an AP quantity, the recipe instructions should make it clear that this is the case. For example, a recipe may call for "10 pounds of russet potatoes" and the method will say, "First, peel the potatoes . . ." You will not end up with 10 pounds of peeled potatoes, but according to this recipe writer, that's fine. You should purchase the 10 pounds of unpeeled potatoes, as directed.

A word of caution: it is always a *recipe quantity's unit* (or a serving size's unit) that determines whether or not you should apply a yield percent, regardless of in what unit that ingredient will be purchased.

PRACTICE PROBLEMS

1. For each of the following recipe quantities, determine if you would need to use the ingredient's yield percent when calculating an AP quantity.

   a. 1½ # peeled diced potatoes
   b. 6 garlic cloves, minced
   c. 450 g sliced peaches
   d. 6 medium carrots, sliced
   e. ½ C fresh lemon juice

2. For each of the following serving sizes, determine if you would need to use the ingredient's yield percent when calculating an AP quantity.

   a. ¾ C shredded bok choy
   b. 60 g sliced oyster mushrooms
   c. 3 ounces drained canned tomatoes
   d. ½ tomato, peeled and seeded
   e. 5 baby carrots

3. For each ingredient in the chart, use the given recipe quantities, equivalents, and yield percents to determine the revised recipe quantity and the necessary AP quantity. For some ingredients, you do not need to use all of the given information. All given weights of objects are AP weights.

	INGREDIENT	RECIPE QUANTITY	REVISED RECIPE QUANTITY		YIELD	AP QUANTITY	
a.	Bananas, sliced (1 banana = 4 oz)	4 ea		#	66%		#
b.	Leeks, chopped (1 bu = 20 oz)	1½ #		bu	44%		bu
c.	Apples, peeled and cored (1 ea = 6 oz)	8 ea		#	74%		#
d.	Tarragon, leaves only (1 bu = 1½ oz)	2 bu		bu	78%		bu
e.	Grapefruit, sectioned (1 C = 7.4 oz, 1 ea = 13 oz)	5 C		ea	52%		ea

4. Calculate the number of servings of the specified size you can get from the given AP quantity.

	INGREDIENT	AP QUANTITY	YIELD	SERVING SIZE	NUMBER OF SERVINGS
a.	Watermelon (1 C = 5.36 oz)	12 #	49%	1 C	
b.	Green peppers (1 ea = 7 oz)	5 #	82%	3 oz	
c.	Grapefruit	12 ea	52%	¼ ea	
d.	Pears (1 ea = 6 oz)	6 ea	78%	4 oz	
e.	Limes (1 ea = 3.4 oz, 1 C = 8.3 oz)	24 ea	42.4%	⅓ C	

Purchasing and Portioning

KEY TERMS

portion (serving) size

par stock

KEY QUESTIONS

How do you calculate the number of portions you can get from an AP quantity?

How do you calculate the AP quantity that you need to produce a certain number of servings?

When and how is it appropriate to round calculated AP quantities?

When and how is it appropriate to round the number of servings?

When making decisions about purchasing and portioning (whether for a special event or for the day-to-day operations of a kitchen), a foodservice professional must understand yield percent and how to apply it in different situations. So far, we have discussed how to use yield percent to calculate the amounts you can expect to end up with after you fabricate AP quantities, and what quantities to purchase so you have adequate EP quantities for your recipes.

What if you needed to determine how many ounces of florets you could serve to each of 250 guests at a banquet? Or what if you needed to know the number of 3-ounce portions of sliced pears you could get from a 45-pound case? How do you apply your knowledge of EP quantities, AP quantities, and yield percent to make these types of purchasing decisions?

4.1 Calculating Portion Size or Number of Portions

To determine a **portion** (or **serving**) **size**—the prepared quantity of an ingredient or a recipe that is served to one person—or a number of portions, you first need to calculate the total EP quantity. Once you know that total EP quantity, you can use the appropriate formula below:

$$\text{Total EP quantity} \div \text{number of portions} = \text{portion size}$$

$$\text{Total EP quantity} \div \text{portion size} = \text{number of portions}$$

The formulas look very similar because, essentially, they do the same thing: take a total prepared quantity and divide it into smaller prepared quantities. Which of the two formulas you use depends on whether you know how many portions you want or how big you want those portions to be.

EXAMPLE 4.1.1 PORTIONING

You are planning on serving cauliflower florets as part of a banquet. Using 50 pounds of cauliflower heads, how many ounces of florets could you serve to each of 250 guests?

AP weight × yield % = EP weight
50 # × 0.6 = 30 #
　　　 = 480 oz

According to *The Book of Yields,* fabricating cauliflower into florets gives a 60% yield. Calculate the expected EP weight (in ounces) using this yield.

Total EP quantity ÷ number of portions = portion size
480 oz ÷ 250 guests = 1.92 oz per guest

Divide the total EP weight among the 250 guests.

A serving size like that may be hard to measure exactly—especially 250 times—even with an accurate digital scale. A serving size of 1.92 ounces per guest, remember, is an estimate based on a yield percent from *The Book of Yields.* When you actually fabricate the cauliflower, you may achieve a yield that is greater or less than 60%; your kitchen staff needs to be ready to make adjustments based on what actually happens in the kitchen.

Portioning. Accurate purchasing calculations will help ensure that a sufficient number of portions can be plated, and that those portions will be the correct size.

EXAMPLE 4.1.2 PORTIONING

How many 3-ounce portions of sliced pears should you be able to fabricate from a 45-pound case of Bosc pears?

AP weight × yield % = EP weight
45 # × 0.89 = 40.05 #
$\qquad$ = 640.8 oz

Calculate the expected EP weight of the case. *The Book of Yields* reports that slicing Bosc pears gives a yield of 89%.

Total EP quantity ÷ portion size = number of portions
640.8 oz ÷ 3 oz per portion = 213.6 portions

Divide the total EP weight into 3-ounce portions.

Should this answer be rounded up to 214 portions or down to 213 portions? Intuition should tell you that, since the calculated answer is less than 214, you do not have enough pears for 214 portions, and therefore you should round the answer down to 213 portions.

EXAMPLE 4.1.3 PORTIONING

For a banquet, each fruit plate will contain 3 sliced strawberries. How many servings can you make using 3½ pounds of medium strawberries?

$$\frac{3.5 \#}{1} \times \frac{24\,\text{ea}}{1 \#} = 84\,\text{ea}$$

According to *The Book of Yields*, there are (on average) 24 medium strawberries in a pound.

Total EP quantity ÷ portion size = number of portions
84 ea ÷ 3 ea per portion = 28 portions

Since the serving size is a count, do not use the yield percent of strawberries. Your EP quantity is the same as your AP quantity.

PRACTICE PROBLEMS

For questions 1–12, you do not need any additional information other than standard equivalents. Unless otherwise directed, truncate all percents at the hundredths place (2 decimal places), and all other quantities at the ten-thousandths place (4 decimal places).

1. You have a 24-pound case of Comice pears in your pantry. If dicing Comice pears gives a 78% yield, how many 4-ounce servings of peeled diced pears can you fabricate from this case?

2. You have purchased 48 kilograms of whole thin export asparagus to use to make 500 servings of sliced asparagus. If asparagus has a yield of 89%, how many full ounces would each guest get? (For this question, round your answer down to a whole number.)

3. You have 5 honeydew melons that weigh a total of 9 pounds. How many ounces of diced honeydew could you serve to 20 people if dicing honeydew gives a yield of 57%? (For this question, round your answer down to a whole number.)

4. You have purchased 4 watermelons that weigh 12 pounds each. How many 4-ounce portions will you get from these 4 melons, if the yield for watermelon is 49.4%? (For this question, round your answer down to a whole number.)

5. You are purchasing 22-pound turkeys for your carving station on the buffet line. If whole turkeys yield 36.3% of their original weight in cooked meat, how many 3-ounce portions of cooked meat will each turkey provide? (For this question, round your answer down to a whole number.)

6. A seafood entrée includes one-third of a head of braised sliced fennel. You have purchased 10 heads of fennel, which weigh an average of 10 ounces each. If braising and slicing fennel gives a yield of 55%, do you have enough for 25 entrées?

7. A salsa recipe includes 3 ounces of chopped fresh cilantro and serves 48 people. If chopping cilantro gives a 48% yield, how many servings of salsa can you make using the 1½ pounds of cilantro you have purchased? (For this question, round your answer down to a whole number.)

8. The results of a yield test in your kitchen show that each 20-pound case of cauliflower you purchase yields 12 pounds of florets. If you have 7 cases on hand, how many 5-ounce portions will you be able to prepare? (For this question, round your answer down to a whole number.)

9. Your recipe for jumbo blueberry muffins calls for 25 grams of fresh blueberries per muffin. If the yield of fresh blueberries is 89.4% , how many muffins will you be able to make with 4¼ pounds of berries? (For this question, round your answer down to a whole number.)

10. You need diced papaya for 58 tropical salad plates. If dicing papaya gives a 66.9% yield, how many ounces can each serving contain if you use a 5-kilogram case of papayas?

For questions 11–18, use the information from *The Book of Yields* in Appendix V as necessary. Unless otherwise directed, truncate all percents at the hundredths place (2 decimal places), and all other quantities at the ten-thousandths place (4 decimal places).

11. For a dinner event you need 1 tablespoon of chopped basil to garnish each of 125 bowls of winter vegetable soup. How many 1-tablespoon garnishes will you get from 8 bunches of basil? (For this question, round your answer to a whole number.)

12. You have a case of cantaloupe which you would like to use to make melon wrapped in prosciutto. If the case contains 12 melons, and one cantaloupe yields six servings, how many servings will you get from the case?

13. A lunch portion of Caesar salad contains 2 cups of chopped Romaine lettuce. How many Caesar salads will you be able to produce using 24 heads of Romaine lettuce?

14. A poached Bosc pear is a regular item on your dessert menu. Each plate contains one cored and peeled pear. Historically 20% of your customers have ordered this dessert. If you expect an average of 160 customers each day, how many full days of service should 1½ cases (100 pears per case) last?

15. Steamed bok choy with ponzu sauce is a favorite dish at your Japanese restaurant. If a serving contains one-third of a bunch of bok choy, how many servings can you expect to make using 24 pounds of bok choy?

16. You have 5 pints of grape tomatoes to divide evenly among 136 individual house salads. How many sliced tomatoes will each plate get? (For this question, round your answer down to a whole number.)

17. Each burrito made for your Tex-Mex drive-thru restaurant includes 3 slices of avocado. If each avocado is cut into 8 slices, how many servings can you make from 42 pounds of avocados?

18. You are serving freshly squeezed orange juice on your breakfast buffet. How many 5-fluid-ounce servings will you be able to get from 60 pounds of oranges?

4.2 Calculating AP Quantities Using Portion Sizes or Recipe Quantities

We have previously discussed how to calculate an AP quantity when you know the total EP quantity you need. In many cases, you must first calculate this total EP quantity by using information about the portions you want to produce.

$$\text{Number of portions} \times \text{portion size} = \text{total EP quantity}$$

EXAMPLE 4.2.1 CALCULATING AN AP QUANTITY

You plan to serve a 5-ounce portion of chopped romaine lettuce, as part of a Caesar salad, to each guest at a 250-person banquet. How many heads of romaine do you need to purchase?

Number of portions × portion size = total EP quantity
250 portions × 5 oz per portion = 1250 oz

Determine the total EP weight needed.

EP weight ÷ yield % = AP weight
1250 oz ÷ 0.75 = 1666.6666 oz

Determine the AP weight. *The Book of Yields* reports that chopping romaine lettuce gives a yield of 75%.

$$\frac{1666.6666 \text{ oz}}{1} \times \frac{1 \text{ head}}{24 \text{ oz}} = 69.4444 \text{ heads}$$

Convert the AP weight to heads. According to *The Book of Yields*, a head of romaine lettuce weighs, on average, 24 ounces, as purchased.

Since you cannot purchase exactly 69.4444 heads, you have to make a rounding decision. If this is the only use you have for lettuce, you would round the AP quantity up to 70 heads, even though 0.4444 is less than one-half. Do not automatically round decimal answers like this. There are times when you will keep numbers such as 69.4444 exact to increase the accuracy of calculations using those numbers.

Also, be careful about rounding AP quantities before it is appropriate to do so. Consider the following example:

RECIPE 1: 69.4444 heads (AP) needed → rounded up to 70 heads (AP)

RECIPE 2: 22.25 heads (AP) needed → rounded up to 23 heads (AP)

RECIPE 3: 13.5 heads (AP) needed → rounded up to 14 heads (AP)

Adding up the rounded AP quantities tells you that you should purchase 107 heads of romaine lettuce. However, you really need only 105.1944 heads (AP) of romaine for these three recipes, which only rounds up to 106 heads of romaine. One extra head of romaine may not seem like a large expense, but if that extra head is ordered every week, then you have a lot of unnecessary heads of romaine lettuce in your pantry and—perhaps more important—in your budget.

Portioning. When portions are measured by weight, the yield percent of the product must be taken into account when determining the number of portions that will come from that AP quantity.

EXAMPLE 4.2.2 CALCULATING AN AP QUANTITY

Instead of serving 5 ounces of romaine lettuce in each of the 250 salads, you will serve one-quarter of a trimmed head of lettuce per salad. How many heads of romaine do you need to purchase now?

Number of portions × portion size = total EP quantity   Determine the total EP quantity needed.

$$250 \text{ portions} \times \frac{1}{4} \text{ head per portion} = 62.5 \text{ heads}$$

This portion size (one-quarter of a head) is a count. No matter how much you remove from each quarter, you will still have the same number of quarters afterward. You do not need to use the yield percent of romaine lettuce this time. Therefore, 62.5 heads is also the AP quantity needed for this recipe. Alternatively, you could use the fact that each head of romaine will serve four people:

250 portions ÷ 4 portions per head = 62.5 heads

As before, you won't round this AP quantity until you have calculated the number of heads of romaine you need for all of your recipes.

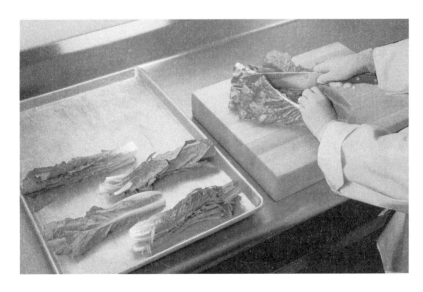

Portioning. When portions are measured by count, the yield percent of the product is not a factor in determining the number of portions that an AP quantity will yield.

EXAMPLE 4.2.3 CALCULATING AN AP QUANTITY

You need 2 cups of chopped thyme leaves for a recipe. How many bunches of thyme do you need to purchase for this recipe?

$$\text{cups} \rightarrow \overbrace{\underbrace{\text{ounces}}_{\text{weight of one cup}}}^{\text{weight of one bunch}} \rightarrow \text{bunches}$$

Convert the EP volume to bunches. Use ounces as a "connecting" unit between cups and bunches.

$$\frac{2\,C}{1} \times \frac{1.6\,oz}{1\,C} \times \frac{1\,bu}{1\,oz} = 3.2\,bu$$

According to *The Book of Yields,* 1 cup of thyme leaves weighs 1.6 ounces, and a bunch weighs 1 ounce, as purchased.

EP count ÷ yield % = AP count
3.2 bu ÷ 0.65 = 4.9230 bu

Convert the EP quantity to an AP quantity. A bunch of thyme is 65% leaves, according to *The Book of Yields.*

Because the recipe quantity is measured by volume, you need to use the yield percent as part of your calculations. Don't be misled by the purchasing unit, which is a count. Your recipe quantity (or the serving size) determines if you should apply the yield percent.

If this was the only recipe for which you needed to buy thyme, then you would purchase 5 bunches of thyme. If you have other recipes that call for thyme, you would make similar calculations for those recipes and add up all the exact AP quantities *before* rounding up to an appropriate level of accuracy.

EXAMPLE 4.2.4 CALCULATING AP QUANTITIES

How many pounds of apples would you need to purchase for each of the following recipes for apple pie?

RECIPE A: 2.88 kilograms of peeled, cored, and sliced apples

RECIPE B: 1½ gallons of peeled, cored, and sliced apples

RECIPE C: 20 medium apples, peeled, cored, and sliced

(Assume that one apple weighs an average of 6 ounces, as purchased.)

For each recipe, first convert the given quantity of apples into a number of pounds. Then use the yield percent (as appropriate) to calculate the necessary AP quantity. (For this example, let's say that your staff averages an 84.5% yield on Red Delicious apples, which is what you use to make the pies.)

RECIPE A

$$\frac{2.88\,kg}{1} \times \frac{2.205\,\#}{1\,kg} = 6.3504\,\#$$

Convert kilograms into pounds.

6.3504 # (EP) ÷ 0.845 = 7.5152 # (AP)

Use the yield percent, since the recipe specifies an EP quantity.

RECIPE B

$$\frac{1.5\,G}{1} \times \frac{16\,C}{1\,G} \times \frac{4.2\,oz}{1\,C} \times \frac{1\,\#}{16\,oz} = 6.3\,\#$$

Convert gallons into pounds. According to *The Book of Yields,* 1 cup of sliced Red Delicious apples weighs 4.2 ounces.

Use the yield percent, since the recipe specifies an EP quantity.

6.3 # (AP) ÷ 0.845 = 7.4556 # (AP)

RECIPE C

$$\frac{20\,apples}{1} \times \frac{6\,oz}{1\,apple} \times \frac{1\,\#}{16\,oz} = 7.5\,\#$$

Calculate the weight of 20 apples. No yield percent is necessary, since "20 apples" is an AP quantity.

As you can see, these three versions of the recipe specify three different quantities of apples, but require you to purchase essentially the same amount of apples. (If you used the yield percent on recipe C's quantity, the calculated AP quantity would be almost 1½ pounds greater than necessary.)

INFORMATION THAT COMPENSATES FOR PRODUCT YIELD

For some ingredients (usually fresh herbs, fruits, and vegetables), a reference such as *The Book of Yields* will provide information that you can use to simultaneously convert units *and* factor in a yield percent. In general, this information tells you how much usable product you can expect from an AP quantity. Facts such as "1 pound of cantaloupe yields 9.3 ounces diced cantaloupe" or "1 bunch of celery yields 5½ cups diced celery" take the waste into account since they give an EP quantity that comes from an AP quantity.

For example, *The Book of Yields* reports that from 1 AP pound of carrots, you can expect, on average, 13 ounces of trimmed carrots. Also, that same AP pound of carrots should produce 2.6 cups of diced carrots. These pieces of information relate an EP quantity to an AP quantity; thus, they factor in a yield percent. Equivalents such as "1 cup = 5 ounces" or "1 head = 30 ounces" do not factor in a yield percent, since the quantities in the equivalent are either both EP quantities or both AP quantities. Both measurements were taken either before the product was prepared or after the product was prepared.

Be careful if you decide to use this type of information. Like other information in *The Book of Yields*, these facts are based on specific yields and measurements. In your kitchen, the measurements that you take and yields that you achieve may vary. Using information that incorporates a yield percent makes it more difficult to compare the actual yield of your product to the yield that was used in the equivalent.

In Example 4.2.3, we calculated the number of purchased bunches that would yield 2 cups of chopped thyme. *The Book of Yields* reports that you can expect 0.65 ounces of leaves from each AP bunch of thyme. Using this fact, you can calculate the same AP quantity as before. (In this version, we have labeled the quantities as EP and AP to make it easier to see the transition.)

$$\frac{2\,C\,(EP)}{1} \times \frac{1.6\,oz\,(EP)}{1\,C\,(EP)} \times \frac{1\,bu\,(AP)}{0.65\,oz\,(EP)} = 4.9230\,bu\,(AP)$$

A word of caution about this method: even though we did not write down thyme's yield of 65% anywhere in the above calculation, it is there in the transition from 0.65 ounces (EP) to 1 bunch (AP). If you choose to calculate EP or AP quantities using a fact like this, make sure you are applying the yield percent appropriately.

PRACTICE PROBLEMS

Use the information from *The Book of Yields* in Appendix V as necessary to answer the following questions. Some of these problems require using a yield percent; some do not. Unless otherwise directed, truncate all percents at the hundredths place (2 decimal places), and all other quantities at the ten-thousandths place (4 decimal places).

1. You need 125 servings of diced avocado. How many avocados will you use if each serving is half an avocado?

2. A composed salad will include ½ ounce sliced red onion. How many large onions should you purchase for 48 salads?

3. You need 175 portions of sugar snap peas, each weighing 4 ounces. How many 10-pound cases of peas should you purchase?

4. A recipe for pesto calls for 5 bunches of fresh basil with the stems removed. How many bunches of basil would you need to purchase in order to make this recipe?

5. A popular side dish at your restaurant is a stuffed yellow bell pepper (which is actually one-third of a pepper). How many peppers should you purchase to serve 300 of these side dishes?

6. A serving of parsnip-celery purée contains 50 grams of diced celery. How many bunches of celery should you purchase to make 60 servings of purée?

7. Your version of Bananas Foster uses 6 ounces of peeled, sliced bananas per serving. How many pounds of bananas should you purchase to plate 76 servings of Bananas Foster?

8. How many pints of grape tomatoes will you use if you serve four grape tomatoes to each of 50 guests?

9. Each of 184 guests at a Sunday brunch will be served ⅓ pound of peeled, diced cantaloupe. The average cantaloupe weighs 2 pounds. If cantaloupes come 12 to a case, how many cases of cantaloupe should you purchase? (For this question, round your answer up to a whole number.)

10. A case of bok choy weighs 15 pounds. How many cases should you purchase to make 150 servings of sliced bok choy, each weighing 3 ounces? (For this question, round your answer up to a whole number.)

11. Each of 350 guests will be served two chocolate-dipped strawberries. How many pounds of strawberries should you purchase?

12. How many pounds of Brussels sprouts should you purchase if you want to serve five trimmed sprouts to each of 200 guests?

13. You are making individual pear tarts for 214 guests at a luncheon. Each tart uses 180 grams of peeled, cored, and sliced Bosc pear. If a case weighs 16 pounds and contains 45 pears, how many cases of pears would you need to purchase in order to make the tarts? (For this question, round your answer up to a whole number.)

14. In your recipe for stuffed zucchini, one zucchini can make six portions. How many zucchinis should you purchase to make 48 servings of stuffed zucchini?

4.3 Calculating AP Quantities for a Recipe

To calculate AP quantities for recipe ingredients, you combine two calculations: unit conversions that revise standardized recipe quantities so they are expressed in the appropriate purchasing units and the application of yield percents.

EXAMPLE 4.3.1 CALCULATING AP QUANTITIES

How much of each ingredient would you need to purchase to serve 32 portions of Grilled Chicken with Mango, Red Onion, and Pineapple?

Here is the recipe, which we standardized in Example 2.4.1:

Grilled Chicken with Mango, Red Onion, and Pineapple

Makes 32 portions

(Adapted from Techniques of Healthy Cooking *by The Culinary Institute of America)*

32 chicken breasts (8 oz each)

8 # mango, large dice

4 pineapples, large dice

8 large red onions, large dice

8 chipotle peppers in adobo, chopped

1¼ pt orange juice

1 pt fresh lime juice

½ pt olive oil

Chicken breasts: $\dfrac{32\,ea}{1}\times\dfrac{8\,oz}{1\,ea}\times\dfrac{1\,\#}{16\,oz}=16\,\#$

Mango: $\dfrac{8\,\#}{1}\times\dfrac{16\,oz}{1\,\#}\times\dfrac{1\,ea}{9\,oz}=14.2222\,ea$

Pineapple: [no unit conversion necessary]

Red onions: $\dfrac{8\,ea}{1}\times\dfrac{13.7\,oz}{1\,ea}\times\dfrac{1\,\#}{16\,oz}=6.85\,\#$

Chipotle peppers: $\dfrac{8\,ea}{1}\times\dfrac{1\,can}{4\,ea}=2\,cans$

Orange juice: $\dfrac{1.25\,pt}{1}\times\dfrac{1\,qt}{2\,pt}=0.625\,qt$

Convert the standardized ingredient quantities into the appropriate purchasing units. Use the following equivalents:

Mango: 1 ea = 9 oz
Red onion (large): 1 ea = 13.7 oz
Chipotles in adobo: 1 can = 4 ea
Lime juice: 1 C = 8.3 oz, 1 ea = 3.4 oz

Lime juice: $\dfrac{1\,pt}{1} \times \dfrac{2\,C}{1\,pt} \times \dfrac{8.3\,oz}{1\,C} \times \dfrac{1\,ea}{3.4\,oz} = 4.8823\,ea$

Olive oil: $\dfrac{0.5\,pt}{1} \times \dfrac{2\,C}{1\,pt} \times \dfrac{8\,fl\,oz}{1\,C} \times \dfrac{1\,L}{33.8\,fl\,oz} = 0.2366\,L$

Chicken breasts, pineapple, red onion, and chipotle peppers: No yield percent used (recipe quantities are counts)

Calculate the AP quantities by using the yield percent appropriately.

Orange juice and olive oil (100% yield): EP and AP quantities are equal

Mango (68.8% yield):
EP count ÷ yield % = AP count
14.2222 ea ÷ 0.688 = 20.6718 ea

Lime juice (42.4% yield):
EP count ÷ yield % = AP count
4.8823 ea ÷ 0.424 = 11.5148 ea

Grilled Chicken with Mango, Red Onion, and Pineapple
Makes 32 portions

(Adapted from Techniques of Healthy Cooking *by The Culinary Institute of America)*

INGREDIENT	RECIPE QUANTITY	REVISED RECIPE QUANTITY	YIELD	AP QUANTITY
Chicken breasts (8 oz ea)	32 ea	16 #		16 #
Mango, diced	8 #	14.2222 ea	68.8%	20.6718 ea
Pineapple, diced	4 ea	4 ea		4 ea
Red onion, diced	8 ea	6.85 #		6.85#
Chipotle pepper in adobo	8 ea	2 cans		2 cans
Orange juice	1¼ pt	0.625 qt	100%	0.625 qt
Lime juice, fresh	1 pt	4.8823 ea	42.4%	11.5148 ea
Olive oil	½ pt	0.2366 L	100%	0.2366 L

PRACTICE PROBLEMS

For problems 1–3, convert the given recipe quantities into amounts expressed in the appropriate purchasing units. Then use the appropriate yield percents to calculate the necessary AP quantities. You should not need any additional information other than standard equivalents. For some ingredients, you do not need all of the given information. Truncate all quantities at the ten-thousandths place (4 decimal places).

1. ## Tropical Salsa

Makes 20 servings

INGREDIENT	RECIPE QUANTITY	REVISED RECIPE QUANTITY	YIELD	AP QUANTITY
Mangoes, diced (1 ea = 14 oz)	2 #	ea	68.8%	ea
Red peppers, diced (1 ea = 10 oz)	2 ea	#	84.4%	#
Lime juice, fresh (1 C = 8.3 oz, 1 ea = 3.4 oz)	½ C	ea	42.4%	ea
Chili powder	½ oz	#	100%	#
Cilantro, chopped (1 bu = 2.8 oz)	1 bu	bu	46.43%	bu

2. Squash Casserole

Makes 30 servings

(Adapted from The New Moosewood Cookbook *by Mollie Katzen)*

INGREDIENT	RECIPE QUANTITY	REVISED RECIPE QUANTITY	YIELD	AP QUANTITY
Acorn squash, cubed (1 C = 4.6 oz)	6 qt	#	75.6%	#
Olive oil (1 C = 7.7 oz)	6 T	qt	100%	qt
Onion, ¼" dice (1 C = 4.45 oz)	9 C	#	90.6%	#
Salt, kosher flake (1 C = 9.41 oz, 1 box = 26 oz)	2 T	box	100%	box
Red peppers, chopped (1 ea = 10 oz)	12 ea	#	84.4%	#
Garlic cloves (12 ea = 2.1 oz)	24 ea	#	88.1%	#
Yogurt (1 C = 8.6 oz)	3 C	qt	100%	qt
Cotija, crumbled (1 C = 4.2 oz)	6 C	#	100%	#

3. Poached Chicken Florentine

Makes 48 servings

(Adapted from Cooking at Home with the CIA *by The Culinary Institute of America)*

INGREDIENT	RECIPE QUANTITY	REVISED RECIPE QUANTITY	YIELD	AP QUANTITY
Butter (1 # = 2 C)	3 C	#	100%	#
Shallots (1 C = 5.2 oz)	1 C	#	90.6%	#
Scallions, chopped (1 C = 2 oz, 1 bu = 3.5 oz)	1 C	bu	82.9%	bu
Chicken breasts (1 ea = 6 oz, 1 box = 24 ea)	48 ea	#	100%	#
Chicken broth	6 pt	qt	100%	qt
White wine (1 bottle = 750 mL)	1½ qt	bottles	100%	bottles
Sour cream	3 C	pt	100%	pt
Spinach, stemmed (1 C = 1½ oz, 1 bag = 2½ #)	2 G	bags	65.6%	bags
Parmesan, grated, fresh (1 # = 5.333 C)	5 C	#	100%	#
Salt, kosher flake (1 C = 9.41 oz, 1 box = 26 oz)	1 T	box	100%	box
Black pepper, cracked (1 C = 4 oz, 1 jar = 12 oz)	⅓ C	jar	100%	jar

For problems 4 and 5, convert the given recipe quantities into amounts expressed in the appropriate purchasing units. Then use the appropriate yield percents to calculate the necessary AP quantities. Use the information from *The Book of Yields* in Appendix V as necessary. Truncate all quantities at the ten-thousandths place (4 decimal places).

4. Vegetable Salad

Makes 8 servings

INGREDIENT	RECIPE QUANTITY	REVISED RECIPE QUANTITY	YIELD	AP QUANTITY
Carrots, sliced	1½ #	#		#
Pickled ginger, minced (1 jar = 40 oz)	2 oz	#	100%	#
Black sesame seeds	2 T	#	100%	#
Scallions, thinly sliced	¾ bu	bu		bu
Sesame oil (1 bottle = 300 mL)	4 t	bottle	100%	bottle

5. Corn Chowder

Makes 5 gallons

(Adapted from The Professional Chef *[8th ed.] by The Culinary Institute of America)*

INGREDIENT	RECIPE QUANTITY	REVISED RECIPE QUANTITY	YIELD	AP QUANTITY
Salt pork	12 oz	#	100%	#
Butter	10 oz	#	100%	#
Onion, small dice	2 #	#		#
Celery, small dice	12 oz	bu		bu
Red pepper, small dice	2¼ #	#		#
Flour, all-purpose	4¾ C	#	100%	#
Chicken stock	2½ G	G	100%	G
Corn niblets, fresh (1 ear = 17 oz)	8 #	dozen		dozen
Potatoes, peeled and diced (1 bag = 50 #)	10 #	bag		bag
Bay leaves (1 jar = 6 oz)	4 ea	jar	100%	jar
Half-and-half	6 pt	½ G	100%	½ G
Tabasco sauce (1 bottle = 6 fl oz)	¼ C	bottle	100%	bottle
Worcestershire sauce (1 bottle = 8 fl oz)	2 T	bottle	100%	bottle
Salt, kosher flake (1 box = 26 oz)	3 T	box	100%	box
Black pepper, cracked (1 jar = 12 oz)	1 T	jar	100%	jar

4·4 Creating a Grocery List

Chefs and managers need to know how to work with a menu's worth of recipes simultaneously. This may involve compiling a list of the products they need to order. A list such as this could be useful when purchasing ingredients for a special event, or when determining **par stock** (the maximum quantity of goods on hand at any given time). Depending on the breadth of the items to be prepared, this product list can often be many pages long. This procedure has four steps:

1. Standardize all recipes.

2. Convert all standardized recipe quantities to the appropriate purchasing units.

3. Use the appropriate yield percents to determine the AP quantity of all ingredients in each recipe separately.

4. Add up the AP quantities of any repeated ingredients and consolidate all AP quantities into a grocery list.

By calculating each recipe's AP quantities separately, you are ensuring that you are correctly applying yield percents. If you add EP quantities together before applying a yield percent, you may apply yield to ingredient quantities that don't need it, and you may not apply yield to ingredient quantities that do need it.

In this section, we are going to calculate the total AP quantities of the ingredients needed for three recipes. Continue to truncate these AP quantities at four decimal places. This can help prevent the ordering of excess product.

EXAMPLE 4.4.1 CALCULATING AP QUANTITIES

Your restaurant is preparing dinner service for a corporate event, and the menu will include:

> Spinach Salad with Oranges and Mango
>
> Grilled Chicken with Mango, Red Onion, and Pineapple
>
> Broiled Pineapple with Coconut

Determine the total AP quantities necessary for 32 servings of all three recipes.

In Example 4.3.1, we have already determined the AP quantities needed for Grilled Chicken with Mango, Red Onion, and Pineapple. Here are the other two recipes:

Spinach Salad with Oranges and Mango

Makes 48 servings

(Adapted from Gourmet Meals in Minutes *by The Culinary Institute of America)*

7½ # baby spinach

6 small red onions, sliced

96 oz orange sections

6 # sliced mango

¾ pt orange juice

¾ C pineapple juice

1 pt olive oil

¾ T balsamic vinegar

¾ T Dijon mustard

Broiled Pineapple with Coconut

Makes 8 servings

(Adapted from Gourmet Meals in Minutes *by The Culinary Institute of America)*

2 # sliced pineapple

¼ C dark rum

1½ T packed dark brown sugar

1 C pineapple juice

1 oz shredded fresh coconut

First, scale these two recipes to also yield 32 servings:

SPINACH SALAD	Scaling factor = desired yield ÷ recipe yield
	= 32 servings ÷ 48 servings
	= 0.6666 (or ⅔)
BROILED PINEAPPLE	Scaling factor = desired yield ÷ recipe yield
	= 32 servings ÷ 8 servings
	= 4

Using these scaling factors, calculate the ingredient quantities needed for 32 servings. The scaled ingredient quantities appear in the shaded boxes:

SPINACH SALAD WITH ORANGES AND MANGO Makes 48 servings (Adapted from **Gourmet Meals in Minutes** by The Culinary Institute of America)	**SCALED RECIPE:** Makes 32 servings
7½ # baby spinach 6 small red onions, sliced 96 oz orange sections 6 # sliced mango ¾ pt orange juice ¾ C pineapple juice 1 pt olive oil ¾ T balsamic vinegar ¾ T Dijon mustard	5 # spinach 4 small red onions, sliced 64 oz orange sections 4 # sliced mango 1 C orange juice ½ C pineapple juice 1⅓ C olive oil ½ T balsamic vinegar ½ T Dijon mustard

BROILED PINEAPPLE WITH COCONUT Makes 8 servings (Adapted from **Gourmet Meals in Minutes** by The Culinary Institute of America)	**SCALED RECIPE:** Makes 32 servings
2 # sliced pineapple ¼ C dark rum 1½ T packed dark brown sugar 1 C pineapple juice 1 oz shredded fresh coconut	8 # sliced pineapple 1 C dark rum 3 oz dark brown sugar 1 qt pineapple juice 4 oz shredded fresh coconut

Next, convert the recipe quantities to their purchasing units, and then use the appropriate yield percents to determine the AP quantities for each recipe. Use the following equivalents:

Small onion: 1 ea = 7.8 oz

Mango: 1 ea = 9 oz

Pineapple juice: 1 can = 46 fl oz

Dijon mustard: 1 T = 0.53 oz

Pineapple: 1 ea = 3½ #

Spinach Salad with Oranges and Mango
Makes 32 servings

(Adapted from Gourmet Meals in Minutes *by The Culinary Institute of America)*

INGREDIENT	SCALED RECIPE QUANTITY	REVISED SCALED RECIPE QUANTITY	YIELD	AP QUANTITY
Baby spinach	5 #	5 #	100%	5 #
Onions, small red	4 ea	1.95 #		1.95 #
Orange sections	64 oz	4 #	34.4%	11.6279 #
Mango, sliced	4 #	7.1111 ea	68.8%	10.3359 ea
Orange juice	1 C	0.25 qt	100%	0.25 qt
Pineapple juice	½ C	0.0869 can	100%	0.0869 can
Olive oil	1⅓ C	0.3155 L	100%	0.5521 L
Balsamic vinegar	½ T	7.3964 mL	100%	7.3964 mL
Dijon mustard	½ T	0.265 oz	100%	0.265 oz

Broiled Pineapple with Coconut
Makes 32 servings

(Adapted from Gourmet Meals in Minutes *by The Culinary Institute of America)*

INGREDIENT	SCALED RECIPE QUANTITY	REVISED SCALED RECIPE QUANTITY	YIELD	AP QUANTITY
Pineapple	8 #	2.2857 ea	48.4%	4.7225 ea
Dark rum	1 C	236.6863 mL	100%	236.6863 mL
Brown sugar	3 oz	0.1875 #	100%	0.1875 #
Pineapple juice	1 qt	0.6956 can	100%	0.6956 can
Coconut, shredded fresh	4 oz	0.25 #	100%	0.25 #

Now consolidate the three lists of AP quantities into one grocery (or ingredient) list. For ease of use, the list of ingredients used in the three recipes is alphabetized. Here is the completed grocery list:

Grocery List for Corporate Event
Makes 32 servings

INGREDIENT	AP QUANTITY FOR SPINACH SALAD	AP QUANTITY FOR CHICKEN WITH MANGO	AP QUANTITY FOR BROILED PINEAPPLE	TOTAL AP QUANTITY
Baby spinach	5 #			5 #
Balsamic vinegar	7.3964 mL			7.3964 mL
Brown sugar			0.1875 #	0.1875 #
Chicken breasts		16 #		16 #
Chipotle peppers in adobo		2 cans		2 cans
Coconut, shredded fresh			0.25 #	0.25 #
Dark rum			236.6863 mL	236.6863 mL
Dijon mustard	0.265 oz			0.265 oz
Limes		11.5148 ea		11.5148 ea
Mango	10.3359 ea	20.6718 ea		31.0077 ea
Olive oil	0.2958 L	0.2366 L		0.5324 L
Onions, red	1.95 #	6.85 #		8.8 #
Oranges	11.6279 #			11.6279 #
Orange juice	0.25 qt	0.625 qt		0.875 qt
Pineapples		4 ea	4.7225 ea	8.7225 ea
Pineapple juice	0.0869 can		0.6956 can	0.7825 can

Remember, these are the specific quantities that you need for the event recipes. Typically, they would not necessarily be the exact quantities that you would purchase. Since this grocery list is for a special event, these quantities should be considered along with the restaurant's needs, making allowances for what is in stock, and orders should be placed accordingly. Purchasing units should be rounded up to the next whole purchasing unit just prior to placing product orders. For this example, however, assume ingredients are to be purchased separately from other orders.

PRACTICE PROBLEMS

1. You will be catering a luncheon for 48 guests at the annual meeting of the Orange Growers of America and you need to assemble a grocery list.

   Scale recipe A and recipe C so they each make 48 servings.

   Scale recipe B so it makes the appropriate number of fluid ounces of Orange Dressing.

   Scale recipe D so it makes the appropriate number of crêpes.

   Transfer all scaled quantities to the charts following the four recipes.

   Convert all scaled ingredient quantities into amounts expressed in the appropriate purchasing units.

   Use the appropriate yield percents to calculate the necessary AP quantities.

   Enter all AP quantities in the grocery list and calculate the total AP quantities needed.

   Use the information from **The Book of Yields** in Appendix V as necessary.

Recipe A

Lobster Salad with Beets, Mango, Avocado, and Orange Dressing

Makes 8 servings *(Adapted from* The Professional Chef *[8th ed.] by The Culinary Institute of America)*	SCALED RECIPE: Makes 48 servings
1 # 8 oz lobster meat, cooked and sliced	_____ # lobster meat
12 oz cooked, peeled, and sliced red beets	_____ oz red beets
3 ea mangoes, sliced	_____ ea mangoes
4 ea avocados, sliced	_____ ea avocados
5 oz peeled, seeded, and sliced tomatoes	_____ oz tomatoes
1 t salt (regular)	_____ t salt
10 fl oz Orange Dressing (recipe follows)	_____ fl oz Orange Dressing

Recipe B

Orange Dressing

Makes 18 fluid ounces	SCALED RECIPE: Makes _____ fl oz
12 fl oz olive oil	_____ fl oz olive oil
6 fl oz fresh orange juice	_____ fl oz orange juice
1 t vanilla extract	_____ t vanilla extract
½ t cracked black pepper	_____ t black pepper
2 t salt (regular)	_____ t salt

Recipe C

Crêpes Suzette

Makes 12 servings *(Adapted from* The Professional Chef *[8th ed.] by The Culinary Institute of America)*	SCALED RECIPE: Makes 48 servings
85 g granulated sugar	_____ g granulated sugar
340 g butter, cubed	_____ g butter, cubed
180 mL fresh orange juice	_____ mL orange juice
180 mL Grand Marnier	_____ mL Grand Marnier
180 mL brandy	_____ mL brandy
36 ea Dessert Crêpes (recipe follows)	_____ ea Dessert Crêpes

Recipe D

Dessert Crêpes

Makes 24 crêpes *(Adapted from The Professional Chef [8th ed.] by The Culinary Institute of America)*	**SCALED RECIPE:** Makes _____ crêpes
4 ea eggs	_____ ea eggs
480 mL heavy cream	_____ mL heavy cream
227 mL whole milk	_____ mL milk
14 g butter, melted	_____ g butter, melted
227 g all-purpose flour	_____ g flour
51 g confectioners' sugar	_____ g confectioners' sugar
5 g salt (regular)	_____ g salt
8 mL vanilla extract	_____ mL vanilla extract

A. Lobster Salad with Beets, Mango, Avocado, and Orange Dressing

(Adapted from The Professional Chef [8th ed.] by The Culinary Institute of America)

INGREDIENT	SCALED RECIPE QUANTITY	REVISED SCALED RECIPE QUANTITY	YIELD	AP QUANTITY
Lobster meat, cooked and sliced	#		100%	#
Red beets, cooked, peeled, and sliced	#			#
Mangoes, sliced	ea			ea
Avocados, sliced	ea			ea
Tomatoes, peeled, seeded, and sliced	#			#
Salt, regular	oz		100%	oz

B. Orange Dressing

INGREDIENT	SCALED RECIPE QUANTITY	REVISED SCALED RECIPE QUANTITY	YIELD	AP QUANTITY
Olive oil		L	100%	L
Orange juice, fresh		ea		ea
Vanilla extract (1 bottle = 1 pt)		btl	100%	btl
Black pepper, cracked		oz	100%	oz
Salt, regular		oz	100%	oz

c. Crêpes Suzette

(Adapted from The Professional Chef *[8th ed.] by The Culinary Institute of America)*

INGREDIENT	SCALED RECIPE QUANTITY	REVISED SCALED RECIPE QUANTITY	YIELD	AP QUANTITY
Sugar, granulated		#	100%	#
Butter, cubed		#	100%	#
Orange juice, fresh		ea		ea
Grand Marnier (1 bottle = 750 mL)		btl	100%	btl
Brandy (1 bottle = 1½ L)		btl	100%	btl

D. Dessert Crêpes

(Adapted from The Professional Chef [8th ed.] by The Culinary Institute of America)

INGREDIENT	SCALED RECIPE QUANTITY	REVISED SCALED RECIPE QUANTITY	YIELD	AP QUANTITY
Eggs	dozen			dozen
Heavy cream	pt		100%	pt
Milk, whole	G		100%	G
Butter, melted	#		100%	#
Flour, all-purpose	#		100%	#
Confectioners' sugar	#		100%	#
Salt, regular	oz		100%	oz
Vanilla extract (1 bottle = 1 pt)	btl		100%	btl

Grocery List for Orange Growers of America Luncheon

Makes 48 servings

INGREDIENT	AP QUANTITY FOR LOBSTER SALAD	AP QUANTITY FOR ORANGE DRESSING	AP QUANTITY FOR CRÊPES SUZETTE	AP QUANTITY FOR DESSERT CRÊPES	TOTAL AP QUANTITY
Avocados					
Beets, red					
Black pepper					
Brandy					
Butter					
Confectioners' sugar					
Eggs					
Flour, all-purpose					
Grand Marnier					
Heavy cream					
Lobster					
Mangoes					
Milk, whole					
Olive oil					
Orange juice, fresh					
Salt, regular					
Sugar, granulated					
Tomatoes					
Vanilla extract					

PURCHASING AND PORTIONING

Recipe Costing

KEY TERMS

standard cost

AP cost per unit

ingredient cost

cost per portion

food cost percent

selling price

gross profit

cost of sales percent

EP cost per unit

butcher's yield

KEY QUESTIONS

How do you calculate the AP cost per unit of an ingredient?

How do you calculate the cost of an ingredient in a recipe?

How do you calculate the cost of a recipe?

What does the food cost percent of a menu item represent?

How do you calculate a food cost percent?

What are some ways to adjust food cost percent?

How do you compare the costs of different purchasing options for an ingredient?

Once you have standardized a recipe, the next step is to calculate the **standard cost** for that recipe. The cost of producing a loaf of bread, a menu item, or a catered event must be calculated to establish an appropriate selling price, based on the other expenses of your business.

5.1 Calculating AP Cost per Unit

When calculating the cost of a recipe or when comparison shopping, you will use ingredient prices (for example, $8.99 per 500-milliliter bottle of olive oil, or $13.50 for a 25-pound bag of flour) that you obtain from current vendor price lists. Often, you will need to calculate the **AP cost per unit** for that ingredient:

$$\text{AP cost} \div \text{number of units purchased} = \text{AP cost per unit}$$

You may need to determine an AP cost per unit in a different unit than that used by your vendor. To express the AP cost per unit in a different unit of measure, you can use unit equivalents.

EXAMPLE 5.1.1 CALCULATING AP COST PER UNIT

A vendor sells a 5-quart bottle of olive oil for $32.99. Calculate the AP cost per quart, per fluid ounce, and per liter.

PRICE PER QUART

$\text{AP cost} \div \text{number of units purchased} = \text{AP cost per unit}$

$\$32.99 \div 5 \text{ qt} = \$6.598 / \text{qt}$

The bottle size is given in quarts, so no unit conversion is needed before calculating the AP cost per quart.

PRICE PER FLUID OUNCE

$$\frac{5 \text{ qt}}{1} \times \frac{32 \text{ fl oz}}{1 \text{ qt}} = 160 \text{ fl oz}$$

Convert the bottle size into fluid ounces, then calculate the AP cost per fluid ounce.

$\text{AP cost} \div \text{number of units purchased} = \text{AP cost per unit}$

$\$32.99 \div 160 \text{ fl oz} = \$0.2061 / \text{fl oz}$

PRICE PER LITER

$$\frac{5 \text{ qt}}{1} \times \frac{32 \text{ fl oz}}{1 \text{ qt}} \times \frac{1 \text{ L}}{33.8 \text{ fl oz}} = 4.7337 \text{ L}$$

Convert the bottle size into liters, then calculate the AP cost per liter.

$\text{AP cost} \div \text{number of units purchased} = \text{AP cost per unit}$

$\$32.99 \div 4.7337 \text{ L} = \$6.9691 / \text{L}$

PRACTICE PROBLEMS

Using the given purchasing information, determine the specified AP costs per unit. Use the information from *The Book of Yields* in Appendix V as necessary. Truncate all answers at the ten-thousandths place (4 decimal places).

1. Red wine vinegar; AP cost: $18.35 / G

   a. AP cost per cup

   b. AP cost per fluid ounce

2. Semolina flour; AP cost: $13.65 / 50 #

   a. AP cost per pound

b. AP cost per kilogram

3. Pistachios; AP cost: $6.59 / #
   a. AP cost per ounce

   b. AP cost per kilogram

4. Celery; AP cost: $41.28 / 24 bu
   a. AP cost per bunch

RECIPE COSTING

b. AP cost per pound

5. Honey; AP cost: $18.00 / 5 # can

a. AP cost per ounce

b. AP cost per cup

6. Pine nuts; AP cost: $48.30 / 3 bags (2 # each)

   a. AP cost per gram

   b. AP cost per cup

7. Basil; AP cost: $16.20 / 12 bu

   a. AP cost per bunch

   b. AP cost per ounce

8. Blue cheese; AP cost: $32.75 / 6 # wheel

    a. AP cost per ounce

    b. AP cost per cup

9. Extra virgin olive oil; AP cost: $21.42 / 3 L

    a. AP cost per milliliter

b. AP cost per fluid ounce

10. Sweetened condensed milk; AP cost: $46.56 / 24 cans (10 oz each)

a. AP cost per can

b. AP cost per ounce

c. AP cost per cup

5.2 Recipe Costing

To calculate the **cost of an ingredient** in a recipe you can use the following formula:

$$\text{AP quantity} \times \text{AP cost per unit} = \text{ingredient cost}$$

In the culinary field, things get complicated when a recipe uses a product in one unit of measure and the item is sold or packaged in another unit of measure. When calculating the costs of your recipe ingredients, make sure your AP quantity and your AP cost per unit are expressed in the same unit of measure.

CALCULATING COSTS FOR INGREDIENTS WHEN WASTE IS NOT A FACTOR

When calculating the cost of a recipe ingredient that has no waste, remember that the necessary AP quantity is the same as the specified EP quantity.

EXAMPLE 5.2.1 CALCULATING THE COST OF AN INGREDIENT WHEN WASTE IS NOT A FACTOR

You need to use 2½ cups of vegetable oil in a recipe. If your vendor sells a 5-quart bottle of vegetable oil for $9.30, how much will the oil used in this recipe cost?

$$\frac{2.5\,C}{1} \times \frac{1\,qt}{4\,C} = 0.625\,qt$$

Convert the recipe quantity to quarts so it is expressed in the purchasing unit.

AP cost ÷ number of units purchased = AP cost per unit
$9.30 ÷ 5 qt = $1.86/qt

Calculate the AP cost per quart.

AP quantity × AP cost per unit = ingredient cost
0.625 qt × $1.86/qt = $1.1625

Calculate the ingredient cost.

EXAMPLE 5.2.2 CALCULATING THE COST OF AN INGREDIENT WHEN WASTE IS NOT A FACTOR

You have a recipe that calls for 3 pounds of chocolate, but imported chocolate is packaged in 5-kilogram blocks for $38.25. How much will the chocolate used in this recipe cost?

$$\frac{3\,\#}{1} \times \frac{1\,kg}{2.205\,\#} = 1.3605\,kg$$

Convert the recipe quantity to kilograpms so it is expressed in the purchasing unit.

AP cost ÷ number of units purchased = AP cost per unit
$38.25 ÷ 5 kg = $7.65/kg

Calculate the AP cost per kilogram.

AP quantity × AP cost per unit = ingredient cost
1.3605 kg × $7.65/kg = $10.4078

Calculate the ingredient cost.

You can also calculate this ingredient cost by converting the AP quantity to a number of pounds and then calculating the cost per pound of the chocolate:

$$\frac{5\,kg}{1} \times \frac{2.205\,\#}{1\,kg} = 11.025\,\#$$

Convert the purchased amount to pounds so it is expressed in the ingredient quantity's unit.

AP cost ÷ number of units purchased = AP cost per unit
$38.25 ÷ 11.025 # = $3.4693/#

Calculate the AP cost per pound.

AP quantity × AP cost per unit = ingredient cost
3 # × $3.4693/# = $10.4079

Calculate the ingredient cost.

Notice that there is a slight difference between the two calculated ingredient costs, depending on which unit is used and whether some of the numbers are truncated. You may also calculate slightly different values depending on whether or not you clear your calculator screen between steps. For example, if you do not truncate the AP cost per unit of $3.4693877 per pound, you will calculate an ingredient cost of $10.4081.

As discussed in the previous chapter, you do not need to factor in the ingredient's yield percent when calculating AP quantities for recipe ingredients that are measured by the count. This also applies when determining the cost of these recipe ingredients.

EXAMPLE 5.2.3 CALCULATING THE COST OF AN INGREDIENT WHEN WASTE IS NOT A FACTOR

You will be serving stuffed avocado to 38 people at an upcoming event. Your recipe calls for half an avocado per person, and avocados have a yield of 78.6%. If a vendor sells avocados for $0.89 each, how much will the avocados purchased for this event cost?

38 portions × ½ avocado per person = 19 avocados

The recipe quantity is already an AP quantity, so do not use the given yield percent.

AP quantity × AP cost per unit = ingredient cost
19 ea × $0.89/ea = $16.91

Calculate the ingredient cost.

CALCULATING COSTS FOR INGREDIENTS WHEN WASTE IS A FACTOR

When a recipe specifies an EP quantity of an ingredient you need to fabricate, you must start with a greater quantity than the recipe calls for, to compensate for the waste. Thus, to accurately determine the cost of such an ingredient, you must include the cost of the waste. When finding the cost of ingredients that have waste, calculate the necessary AP quantity, then use the ingredient cost formula as above.

EXAMPLE 5.2.4 CALCULATING THE COST OF AN INGREDIENT WHEN WASTE IS A FACTOR

A recipe calls for 3½ pints of cleaned, halved apricots for a recipe. If a vendor sells a flat of apricots (which contains 12 pints) for $28.74, how much will the apricots purchased for this recipe cost?

EP quantity ÷ yield % = AP quantity
3.5 pt ÷ 0.919 = 3.8084 pt

Calculate the AP quantity that will yield the required 3½ pints for the recipe. According to *The Book of Yields*, apricots have a 91.9% yield.

AP cost ÷ number of units purchased = AP cost per unit
$28.74 ÷ 12 pt = $2.395/pt

Calculate the AP cost per pint.

AP quantity × AP cost per unit = ingredient cost
3.8084 pt × $2.395/pt = $9.1211

Calculate the ingredient cost.

You could also use flat as the common unit of measure:

$$\frac{3.8084\,pt}{1} \times \frac{1\,flat}{12\,pt} = 0.3173\,flat$$

Convert the AP quantity to the purchasing unit.

AP quantity × AP cost per unit = ingredient cost
0.3173 flat × $28.74/flat = $9.1192

Calculate the ingredient cost.

EXAMPLE 5.2.5 CALCULATING THE COST OF AN INGREDIENT WHEN WASTE IS A FACTOR

You have a recipe that calls for 3 pounds of diced carrots. If a vendor sells a 10-pound case of carrots for $4.99, how much will the carrots purchased for this recipe cost?

EP quantity ÷ yield % = AP quantity
3 # ÷ 0.813 = 3.6900 #

Calculate the AP quantity that will yield the required 3 pounds for the recipe. *The Book of Yields* reports the yield percent of carrots is 81.3%.

AP cost ÷ number of units purchased = AP cost per unit
$4.99 ÷ 10 # = $0.499/#

Calculate the AP cost per pound.

AP quantity × AP cost per unit = ingredient cost
3.6900 # × $0.499/# = $1.8413

Calculate the ingredient cost.

EXAMPLE 5.2.6 CALCULATING THE COST OF AN INGREDIENT WHEN WASTE IS A FACTOR

A recipe calls for 50 grams of papaya per salad. On average, you sell 25 of these salads every evening. Papaya has a yield percent of 66.9%, and one papaya weighs 185 grams. If a vendor sells papaya for $2.29 per pound, how much will the papaya for one evening's worth of salads cost?

25 servings × 50 g/serving = 1250 g	Calculate the total necessary EP quantity.
$\dfrac{1,250\,g}{1} \times \dfrac{1\#}{435.6} = 2.7557\,\#$	Convert the EP quantity to the purchasing unit. The weight of a papaya is irrelevant in this case.
EP quantity ÷ yield % = AP quantity 2.7557 # ÷ 0.669 = 4.1191 #	Calculate the necessary AP quantity.
AP quantity × AP cost per unit = ingredient cost 4.1191 # × $2.29/# = $9.4327	Calculate the ingredient cost.

CALCULATING THE TOTAL COST OF A RECIPE

To calculate the total cost of a recipe, add the costs of all ingredients in the recipe. (In an upcoming section, we will introduce a form that can help you with costing a recipe.)

EXAMPLE 5.2.7 CALCULATING THE TOTAL COST OF A RECIPE

Calculate the cost of the following recipe:

Caramelized Apples

Makes 20 servings

(Adapted from The Professional Chef *[8th ed.] by The Culinary Institute of America)*

96 oz peeled and cored Granny Smith apples

2 C granulated sugar

Juice of 2 lemons

Here are the AP costs for the ingredients:

Apples, Granny Smith	$0.79 / #
Granulated sugar	$1.84 / 5 # (or $0.368 / #)
Lemons	$0.24 / ea

APPLES

$$\frac{96\ oz}{1} \times \frac{1\ \#}{16\ oz} = 6\ \#$$

$$6\ \# \div 0.7388 = 8.1212\ \#$$

SUGAR

$$\frac{2\ C}{1} \times \frac{7.1\ oz}{1\ C} \times \frac{1\ \#}{16\ oz} = 0.8875\ \#$$

LEMONS 2 ea
(no unit conversion is needed)

AP quantity × AP cost per unit = ingredient cost

APPLES
8.1212 # × $0.79/# = $6.4157

SUGAR
0.8875 # × $0.368/# = $0.3266

LEMONS
2 ea × $0.24/ea = $0.48

Total recipe cost = $6.4157 + $0.3266 + $0.48
= $7.2223 ≈ $7.23

Calculate the AP quantity of each ingredient needed for the recipe. *The Book of Yields* reports that Granny Smith apples give a 73.88% yield and 1 cup of granulated sugar weighs 7.1 ounces.

Calculate the cost of each ingredient.

Add the ingredient costs to calculate the total cost of the recipe.

In this book, we will round total recipe costs up to the next whole cent, even if the partial cent is less than half a cent.

Leave individual AP quantities exact, since recipe costs should reflect what is used *for a particular recipe*, which is most likely not the entire amount of the ingredients that were purchased. For example, if you have a recipe that requires 8 pounds (AP) of onions, the fact that you purchased a 25-pound bag of onions should not be reflected in the cost of that recipe. The assumption is that the person making the recipe takes only what is required for that application and leaves the remainder in storage to be used at another time. Calculating recipe costs as precisely as possible helps you to plan for profitability and control costs.

COST PER PORTION

A restaurant will often prepare multiple portions of a dish simultaneously but sell them individually. Thus, a restaurant owner would need to know the ingredient cost for an individual portion of a menu item. To determine the **cost per portion** for a recipe, divide the total recipe cost by the number of portions the recipe yields:

Total recipe cost ÷ number of portions = cost per portion

EXAMPLE 5.2.8 CALCULATING A COST PER PORTION

Using the total recipe cost calculated in Example 5.2.7, determine the cost per portion of Caramelized Apples.

Total recipe cost ÷ number of portions = cost per portion
$7.23 ÷ 20 portions = $0.3615 per portion

According to the recipe card, you can make 20 portions.

If the recipe yielded fewer portions (say, 17) or more portions (say, 23), the cost per portion would be affected accordingly:

Total recipe cost ÷ number of portions = cost per portion
$7.23 ÷ 17 portions = $0.4252 per portion

Calculate the cost per portion using 17 portions.

Total recipe cost ÷ number of portions = cost per portion
$7.23 ÷ 23 portions = $0.3143 per portion

Calculate the cost per portion using 23 portions.

Note that for a given recipe yield, there is an inverse relationship between the number of portions and the cost per portion: the more portions, the lower the cost per portion, and vice versa. You should carefully monitor portion sizes to keep the expected cost per portion as consistent as possible.

EXAMPLE 5.2.9 CALCULATING A COST PER PORTION

A recipe for Manhattan clam chowder makes 3 gallons. If this recipe has a total cost of $37.65, calculate the cost of a 1½-cup portion.

$$\frac{3\,G}{1} \times \frac{16\,C}{1\,G} \times \frac{1\,portion}{1.5\,C} = 32\,portions$$

Calculate the number of 1½-cup portions in 3 gallons.

Total recipe cost ÷ number of portions = cost per portion
$37.65 ÷ 32 portions = $1.1765 per portion

Calculate the cost per portion.

PRACTICE PROBLEMS

Calculate the cost of the specified recipe ingredient amount, using the given purchasing information. Use the information from *The Book of Yields* in Appendix V as necessary. Round all ingredient costs up to the next cent.

1.   1½ # light brown sugar; AP cost: $0.92 / #

2.   3½ # shredded coconut; AP cost: $3.98 / 2 #

3.   5 oz curry paste; AP cost: $0.70 / 4-oz can

4. 4 # frozen lima beans; AP cost: $2.43 / 2½ #

5. 2½ qt sour cream; AP cost: $1.79 / pt

6. 500 g brown rice; AP cost: $0.85 / #

7. 3 T baking soda (1 C = 8.4 oz); AP cost: $0.63 / #

8.   12 oz molasses; AP cost: $3.45 / 1½ # jar

9.   1½ C maple syrup; AP cost: $19.86 / ½ G

10. 3 T ground dried tarragon (1 T = 0.169 oz); AP cost: $6.89 / 4 oz

11.   5 t baking powder (1 C = 6.9 oz); AP cost: $3.61 / 10 oz

_____

_____

_____

_____

12.   4¾ # diced carrots (81.3% yield); AP cost: $0.35 / #

_____

_____

_____

_____

13.   10 heads Bibb lettuce (80% yield); AP cost: $0.38 / head

_____

_____

_____

_____

14.   150 g chopped fresh Sicilian oregano (78% yield); AP cost: $4.11 / 25 g

_____

_____

15. ½ oz diced habanero peppers (87.75% yield); AP cost: $2.21 / 4-oz bag

16. 12 diced avocados; AP cost: $34.08 / 48 ea

17. 3 kg sliced green beans; AP cost: $0.86 / #

18.   3 C sliced strawberries; AP cost: $1.78 / pt

19.   4 # halved grape tomatoes; AP cost: $1.15 / pt (use 1 pt = 11.2 oz)

20.   9 oz diced celery; AP cost: $41.28 / 48 #

21.   6 oz fresh lemon juice; AP cost: $16.80 / 35 # case

22.   18 oz sliced kiwifruit; AP cost: $10.00 / 27 ea (3 oz ea)

Use the following recipe and the given information to answer problem 23. You do not need any additional information from *The Book of Yields*.

23.   # Gingered Fruit Coulis

Yields 1 quart

2 oranges, juiced

1 C honey

2 oz peeled and chopped ginger

3 # sliced fresh strawberries

INGREDIENT	YIELD/PERCENT	AP COST	NOTES
Oranges	37.6%	$0.50 / ea	
Honey	100%	$9.25 / 5 #	1 C = 12 oz
Ginger	70%	$2.50 / #	
Strawberries	91.9%	$5.00 / qt	1 C = 5.85 oz

a. What is the total recipe cost?

b. What is the cost of a ½-cup portion?

c. What is the cost of a 1-fluid-ounce portion?

Use the following recipe and the given information to answer problem 24. Use information from *The Book of Yields* in Appendix V, as necessary.

24. Italian Spaghetti Squash

Yields 15 portions

3 T olive oil

6 garlic cloves, chopped

1 pint canned diced tomatoes, drained

3 # peeled spaghetti squash

2 t regular salt

INGREDIENT	AP COST
Olive oil	$10.11 / L
Garlic	$1.89 / #
Canned diced tomatoes	$6.32 / number-10 can
Spaghetti squash	$0.89 / #
Salt, regular	$0.40 / 26-oz box

a. What is the total recipe cost?

b. What is the cost per portion?

c. If you divided the recipe yield into 20 portions, what would the resulting cost per portion be?

5·3 Food Cost Percent

A restaurant sells its dishes for significantly more than the cost of the ingredients in order to cover that expense and others (payroll, mortgage, utilities, etc.) and, hopefully, make a profit. Many restaurants use a number called **food cost percent** to help them plan for profitability. Food cost percent tells you what percent of a menu item's **selling price** (the amount the customer pays for the item) is covering the cost of the ingredients. For example, consider a menu item that sells for $10.00 and whose ingredients cost $3.00:

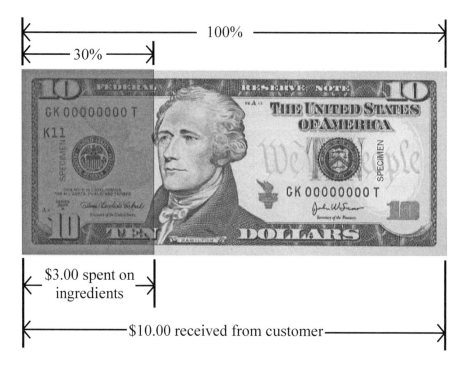

This item has a food cost percent of 30%, because $3.00 (the cost per portion) is 30% of $10.00 (the selling price). The relationship between cost per portion, selling price, and food cost percent is a part-whole-percent relationship. We will always know the standard cost per portion (from our recipe costing procedure), so the unknown quantity will either be the food cost percent or the selling price.

CALCULATING FOOD COST PERCENT

The introduction to this section and the example of the $10.00 menu item may have already given you an idea of how to calculate a food cost percent. Once you know the cost per portion, calculate the food cost percent by dividing the cost per portion by the selling price:

Cost per portion ÷ selling price = food cost percent

(This division will result in an answer expressed as a decimal, which you will need to rewrite as a percent.)

EXAMPLE 5.3.1 **CALCULATING FOOD COST PERCENT**

Below are the selling prices of three entrées on a menu. Based on the information provided, which entrée has the highest food cost percent? Which entrée has the lowest food cost percent?

PORK CHOPS WITH SAUTÉED APPLES	$13.95 (cost per portion: $3.92)
T-BONE STEAK WITH MASHED POTATOES	$18.95 (cost per portion: $7.74)
PASTA PUTTANESCA	$11.95 (cost per portion: $2.67)

Cost per portion ÷ selling price = food cost percent

PORK CHOPS
$3.92 ÷ $13.95 = 0.2810
= 28.10%

STEAK
$7.74 ÷ $18.95 = 0.4084
= 40.84%

PASTA
$2.67 ÷ $11.95 = 0.2234
= 22.34%

Divide the given cost per portion by the listed selling price, then rewrite the answer as a percent.

As you may have predicted, the steak has the highest food cost percent. This is often the case with high-priced items such as steak or lobster: they are expensive for a restaurant to purchase, so a large percent of the selling price covers that cost. The pasta, on the other hand, has the lowest food cost percent. The tendency is for a recipe with predominantly low-cost ingredients to have a low food cost percent and one with higher-cost ingredients to have a higher food cost percent. However, it is possible for a high-cost item to have a low food cost percent, but a restaurant would need to set a rather high selling price—and have a customer base willing to pay such a price.

CALCULATING GROSS PROFIT

In the opening discussion of the $10.00 menu item, the other $7.00—the remaining 70% of the selling price—helps cover other expenses and is called the **gross profit** of the dish (the 70% is called the gross profit percent). Gross profit is another key indicator of profitability, along with food cost percent. If your gross profit is not sufficient to cover your expenses, you will need to find a way to remedy the situation.

Does a low food cost percent for a menu item always result in a high profit? To answer this question, you need to know how to calculate the gross profit of the dish. Gross profit is calculated by subtracting the ingredient cost from the selling price:

Selling price − ingredient cost = gross profit

EXAMPLE 5.3.2 CALCULATING GROSS PROFIT

Which of these three menu items has the highest gross profit? Which has the lowest gross profit?

PORK CHOPS WITH SAUTÉED APPLES $13.95
(cost per portion: $3.92)

T-BONE STEAK WITH MASHED POTATOES $18.95
(cost per portion: $7.74)

PASTA PUTTANESCA $11.95
(cost per portion: $2.67)

Selling price − ingredient cost = gross profit   *Subtract the given cost per portion from the listed selling price.*

PORK CHOPS
$13.95 − $3.92 = $10.03
STEAK
$18.95 − $7.74 = $11.21
PASTA
$11.95 − $2.67 = $9.28

In the preceding examples, the steak has the highest food cost percent, but also the highest gross profit. The pasta—which has the lowest food cost percent—also has the lowest gross profit. (This will not always be the case: menu items with high food cost percents can have low gross profits, and vice versa.) Items with high food cost percents should not be removed from a menu based solely on their food cost percent, since they often make significant contributions to the bottom line. The best way to analyze menu profitability is to look at both food cost percent and gross profit.

If you calculate the total ingredient cost of all of the food items sold during a particular time period and divide it by the total sales generated by those items during the same period, you will calculate the **cost of sales percent** for food. This percent represents an *overall average* food cost for that time period.

For example, consider an establishment that generated $10,000 in sales during a one-month period, and used $3,200 worth of ingredients to make those dishes. The cost of sales percent for food for that one-month period was 32%, since $3,200 is 32% of $10,000. It does not mean that every single dish on the menu had a food cost percent of 32%, nor does it mean that 32% was necessarily used to establish the selling price of any of the individual dishes. It is the goal of the chef, manager, or business owner to keep the cost of sales percent as consistently low as possible from one budget period to the next, which will help maximize gross profit.

ADJUSTING FOOD COST PERCENT

If a restaurant needs to adjust the food cost percent of a menu item (usually this means lowering it), what are some possible ways to do this? The following graph illustrates the effect that selling price has on food cost percent.

Effect of selling price on food cost percent. If the cost per portion remains constant, a lower selling price results in a higher food cost percent.

Even though the cost per portion of $2.50 (represented by the darker shading in each bar) is the same for all three restaurants in the graph, it represents a different percent of each bar. When cost per portion remains constant, there is an inverse relationship between selling price and food cost percent: as the selling price decreases, food cost percent will increase and vice versa. Restaurant A's food cost percent for this dish is the lowest of the three, because restaurant A's selling price of $15 is the highest.

If the selling price of a dish remains the same, a change in the cost per portion will affect food cost percent. In the graph below, three restaurants sell a particular dish for the same amount, but each restaurant's cost per portion (again, depicted by the darker portion of each bar) is different.

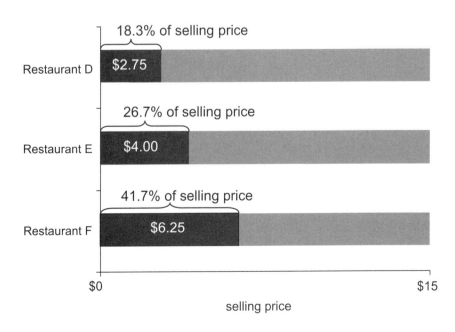

Effect of cost per portion on food cost percent. If the selling price remains constant, a higher cost per portion results in a higher food cost percent.

Restaurant D's dish has the lowest food cost percent, since its cost per portion (of $2.75) is the lowest. When the selling price remains constant, there is a direct relationship between cost per portion and food cost percent: if one increases, the other will also increase. If one decreases, the other will also decrease.

You can adjust a food cost percent by:

◼ **ADJUSTING THE SELLING PRICE. If the cost per portion remains the same, changing how much money you get from a customer for a dish changes the percentage you take out to cover the ingredient costs.**

◼ **ADJUSTING THE COST PER PORTION. If the selling price remains the same, this can be accomplished in two ways:**

   ◼ **ADJUSTING THE PORTION SIZE. This will change the number of portions the recipe makes, which will in turn change the cost per portion. Changing the cost per portion means a different amount of money (and therefore a different percentage) is taken from the selling price to cover ingredient costs.**

   ◼ **ADJUSTING INGREDIENT COSTS. This will change the total recipe cost, which will in turn change the cost per portion. As explained above, this will change the food cost percent.**

If you are not able to reduce the food cost percent to a desirable level, the item may need to be removed from the menu, since it may not generate sufficient profit.

CALCULATING AN ESTIMATED SELLING PRICE

Often a foodservice establishment has an acceptable range for the food cost percent for each category of menu item (e.g., appetizers, main dishes, desserts, breads, cookies). A desired food cost percent can be used to estimate a selling price that will help the restaurant achieve its necessary gross profit. To calculate an estimated minimum selling price, divide the menu item's cost per portion by the desired food cost percent:

cost per portion ÷ food cost percent = estimated selling price

EXAMPLE 5.3.3 CALCULATING AN ESTIMATED SELLING PRICE

Below are three items on a menu. Based on the information provided, calculate an estimated selling price for each dessert.

FRESH FRUIT TART	(cost per portion: $0.56, 15% food cost)
SEAFOOD CHOWDER	(cost per portion: $0.92, 22% food cost)
CHIPOTLE CHICKEN WRAP	(cost per portion: $1.97, 28% food cost)

Cost per portion ÷ food cost percent = estimated selling price

Divide the given cost per portion by the listed food cost percent.

FRESH FRUIT TART
$0.56 ÷ 0.15 = $3.7333
≈ $3.74

SEAFOOD CHOWDER
$0.92 ÷ 0.22 = $4.1818
≈ $4.19

CHIPOTLE CHICKEN WRAP
$1.97 ÷ 0.28 = $7.0357
≈ $7.04

Using a desired food cost percent to calculate an estimated minimum selling price helps ensure that you will generate a sufficient gross profit. You do not want to charge less than this price, but if your customers are willing to pay more, you should charge a price based on what your market will bear.

5.3 PRACTICE PROBLEMS

For the following problems, round dollar amounts up to the next penny, and truncate percents at the hundredths place (2 decimal places).

1. Calculate the missing quantities.

	COST PER PORTION	ESTIMATED MINIMUM SELLING PRICE	FOOD COST PERCENT
a.	$1.25	$5.00	
b.	$6.28	$18.50	
c.	$3.73	$13.95	
d.	$2.18		23%
e.	$1.85		19%
f.	$5.07		33%

2. Your recipe for mango chutney yields 48 servings, at a recipe cost of $18.50. If a serving sells for $1.79, what is your approximate food cost percent for mango chutney?

3. Your recipe for corned beef hash yields 50 portions, at a recipe cost of $25.50. If a portion sells for $3.29, what is your approximate food cost percent for corned beef hash?

4. Your recipe for spinach and goat cheese turnovers yields 72 servings, at a recipe cost of $37.20. Calculate a selling price for this dish using a food cost percent of 19%.

5. Your recipe for Thai coconut soup yields 64 servings, at a recipe cost of $51.35. Calculate a selling price for this dish using a food cost percent of 22%.

6. Over the course of the week, your guests ordered 389 servings of Manhattan clam chowder. Each serving sold for $3.29. If your food cost percent on Manhattan clam chowder is 23%, how much money will be left after you pay for the chowder ingredients?

7. Over the course of the week, your guests ordered 391 portions of leek and potato soup. Each portion sold for $4.59. If your food cost percent on leek and potato soup is 27%, how much money will be left after you pay for the ingredients for those 391 portions?

8. A recipe for 10 portions of roast pork loin has a total cost of $40.00. If your target food cost percent for roast pork loin is 25%, in what range should the selling price fall?

   (A) less than $10   (B) between $10 and $15
   (C) between $15 and $20   (D) more than $20

9. Which of the following actions would definitely help you lower the food cost percent of a menu item?

   (A) use more expensive ingredients   (B) divide the recipe into larger portions
   (C) increase the selling price   (D) none of these will help

10. Which of the following actions would definitely help you lower the food cost percent of a menu item?

    (A) double the recipe   (B) divide the recipe into fewer portions

    (C) decrease the selling price   (D) none of these will help

11. Which of the following actions would definitely help you lower the food cost percent of a menu item?

    (A) divide the recipe into more portions   (B) reduce your labor costs for this item

    (C) use pre-fabricated products   (D) none of these will help

For questions 12–21, assume any quantities that change as a result of your adjustment will do so, but all others will remain constant.

12. A menu item that sells for $11.95 has a food cost percent of 26%. What should the minimum selling price be if you want to lower the food cost percent of this item to 23%?

13. A menu item that sells for $7.50 has a food cost percent of 38%. What should the minimum selling price be if you want to lower the food cost percent of this item to 34%?

14. A menu item that sells for $14.00 has a food cost percent of 18%. What would the food cost percent be if the selling price was increased to $15.00?

15. A menu item that sells for $16.95 has a food cost percent of 20%. What would the food cost percent be if the selling price were decreased by $0.45?

16. A menu item that sells for $8.50 has a food cost percent of 21%. By how much would the food cost percent change if the selling price was increased to $9.25?

17. A menu item that sells for $23.00 has a food cost percent of 40%. By how much would the food cost percent change if the selling price was decreased by $1.00?

18. Your recipe for taco salad yields 50 portions at a recipe cost of $103.25. You sell one portion for $7.95. If the total recipe cost increased to $108.00, by how much would the food cost percent change?

19. Your recipe for peanut brittle yields 24 portions at a recipe cost of $17.65. You sell one portion for $5.00. If the total recipe cost increased by $2.80, by how much would the food cost percent change?

20. Your recipe for shrimp scampi yields 18 portions at a recipe cost of $98.30. You sell one portion for $17.00. If the total recipe cost decreased to $94.85, by how much would the food cost percent change?

21. Your recipe for chocolate chunk cookies yields 36 cookies at a recipe cost of $13.70. You sell one cookie for $2.75. If the total recipe cost decreased by $2.50, by how much would the food cost percent change?

22. Next week you expect your restaurant to record the following appetizer sales:

86 portions of Coconut Shrimp at $8.95 each (cost per portion: $2.63)

121 portions of Spinach and Artichoke Dip at $7.95 each (cost per portion: $1.16)

92 portions of Mucho Nachos at $9.95 each (cost per portion: $2.12)

102 portions of Spicy Calamari at $10.95 each (cost per portion: $3.63)

What is your projected cost of sales percent for these four appetizers?

The 2-in-1 Recipe Costing Form

This form combines three concepts we have discussed previously: unit conversions, product yield, and ingredient cost. We call this recipe costing form a "2-in-1" form because it allows you to calculate both the list of AP quantities needed for the recipe and the total recipe cost.

RECIPE COSTING FORM

Menu item _____   Date _____

Number of portions _____   Size _____

Cost per portion _____   Selling price _____   Food cost % _____

RECIPE QUANTITY		REVISED RECIPE QUANTITY (IN PURCHASING UNIT)	QUANTITY TO PURCHASE		TOTAL COST	
Ingredient	Quantity	Revised Quantity	Yield %	AP Quantity	AP Cost	Ingredient Cost
					TOTAL RECIPE COST	

How to Use the 2-in-1 Recipe Costing Form

1. Write in the Menu Item name, the date, the number of portions, and the portion size, if desired.
2. Write the recipe quantities in the Recipe Quantity column.
3. Write in the appropriate yield percent for each ingredient, if necessary.
4. Write in the AP cost for each ingredient. Convert from a nonstandard unit such as "bottle," "case," or "pack" to a standard unit of measure, if desired.

5. Determine the unit into which each recipe ingredient will be revised. Revise each recipe quantity so it is expressed in your chosen unit and enter it into the Revised Quantity column.

6. Calculate each AP quantity by appropriately applying each ingredient's yield percent.

7. Use the ingredient cost formula to calculate the cost of each ingredient.

8. Calculate the total recipe cost by adding the ingredient costs.

9. Calculate the cost per portion.

10. a) Calculate the food cost percent, using a given selling price.

    or

    b) Calculate an estimated selling price, using a given food cost percent.

EXAMPLE 5.4.1 DETERMINING THE COST OF A RECIPE

Determine the cost of the standardized recipe for Grilled Chicken with Mango, Red Onion, and Pineapple.

We have already completed steps 1,2, 3, 5, and 6 (in Sections 2.4 and 4.3).

RECIPE COSTING FORM

Menu item Grilled Chicken with Mango, Red Onion, and Pineapple   Date _____

Number of portions 32 _____   Size 8 oz breast _____

Cost per portion _____   Selling price _____   Food cost % _____

RECIPE QUANTITY		REVISED RECIPE QUANTITY (IN PURCHASING UNIT)	QUANTITY TO PURCHASE		TOTAL COST	
Ingredient	Quantity	Revised Quantity	Yield %	AP Quantity	AP Cost	Ingredient Cost
Chicken breasts (8 oz ea)	32 ea	16 #		16 #		
Mango, diced	8 #	14.2222 ea	68.8%	20.6728 ea		
Pineapple, diced	4 ea	4 ea		4 ea		
Red onion, diced	8 ea	6.85 #		6.85 #		
Chipotle pepper in adobo	8 ea	2 cans		2 cans		
Orange juice	1¼ pt	0.625 qt	100%	0.625 qt		
Lime juice, fresh	1 pt	4.8823 ea	42.4%	11.5148 ea		
Olive oil	½ pt	0.2366 L	100%	0.2366 L		
				TOTAL RECIPE COST		

For step 4, refer to the as-purchased costs for the ingredients:

Chicken breasts	$2.65 / #
Mango	$1.99 / each
Pineapple	$3.16 / each
Red onion	$0.48 / #
Chipotle pepper in adobo	$2.57 / can
Orange juice	$3.68 / quart
Lime juice	$0.42 / each
Olive oil	$11.50 / 1½ L bottle

Since sizes of bottles, cans, and cases are not consistent, we recommend that you record prices using weights or volumes, when possible. This way, you can easily update recipe costing forms if you purchase a different size package of an ingredient.

RECIPE COSTING FORM

Menu item Grilled Chicken with Mango, Red Onion, and Pineapple   Date _____

Number of portions 32 _____   Size 8 oz breast _____

Cost per portion _____   Selling price _____   Food cost % _____

RECIPE QUANTITY		REVISED RECIPE QUANTITY (IN PURCHASING UNIT)	QUANTITY TO PURCHASE		TOTAL COST	
Ingredient	Quantity	Revised Quantity	Yield %	AP Quantity	AP Cost	Ingredient Cost
Chicken breasts (8 oz ea)	32 ea	16 #		16 #	$2.65 / #	
Mango, diced	8 #	14.2222 ea	68.8%	20.6728 ea	$1.99 / ea	
Pineapple, diced	4 ea	4 ea		4 ea	$3.16 / ea	
Red onion, diced	8 ea	6.85 #		6.85 #	$0.48 / #	
Chipotle pepper in adobo	8 ea	2 cans		2 cans	$2.57 / can	
Orange juice	1¼ pt	0.625 qt	100%	0.625 qt	$3.68 / qt	
Lime juice, fresh	1 pt	4.8823 ea	42.4%	11.5148 ea	$0.42 / ea	
Olive oil	½ pt	0.2366 L	100%	0.2366 L	$7.6666 / L	
					TOTAL RECIPE COST	

You can now complete step 7 in the costing procedure: apply the ingredient cost formula to each ingredient. The results of the calculations are shown below. We have also added the ingredient costs to find the total recipe cost (step 8).

RECIPE COSTING FORM

Menu item Grilled Chicken with Mango, Red Onion, and Pineapple   Date _____

Number of portions 32 _____   Size 8 oz breast _____

Cost per portion _____   Selling price _____   Food cost % _____

RECIPE QUANTITY		REVISED RECIPE QUANTITY (IN PURCHASING UNIT)	QUANTITY TO PURCHASE		TOTAL COST	
Ingredient	Quantity	Revised Quantity	Yield %	AP Quantity	AP Cost	Ingredient Cost
Chicken breasts (8 oz ea)	32 ea	16 #		16 #	$2.65 / #	$42.40
Mango, diced	8 #	14.2222 ea	68.8%	20.6728 ea	$1.99 / ea	$41.1388
Pineapple, diced	4 ea	4 ea		4 ea	$3.16 / ea	$12.64
Red onion, diced	8 ea	6.85 #		6.85 #	$0.48 / #	$3.288
Chipotle pepper in adobo	8 ea	2 cans		2 cans	$2.57 / can	$5.14
Orange juice	1¼ pt	0.625 qt	100%	0.625 qt	$3.68 / qt	$2.30
Lime juice, fresh	1 pt	4.8823 ea	42.4%	11.5148 ea	$0.42 / ea	$4.8362
Olive oil	½ pt	0.2366 L	100%	0.2366 L	$7.6666 / L	$1.8139
					TOTAL RECIPE COST	$113.56

According to these calculations, $113.56 worth of ingredients from inventory are used to make 32 portions of Grilled Chicken with Mango, Red Onion, and Pineapple. With this information, it is possible to calculate the cost per portion (step 9).

Total recipe cost ÷ number of portions = cost per portion
$113.56 ÷ 32 portions = $3.5487 per portion

Divide the total recipe cost by 32, the number of portions the recipe makes.

RECIPE COSTING FORM

Menu item Grilled Chicken with Mango, Red Onion, and Pineapple   Date _____

Number of portions 32 _____   Size 8 oz breast _____

Cost per portion $3.5487 _____   Selling price _____   Food cost % _____

The next two examples will demonstrate steps 10a and 10b in the procedure.

EXAMPLE 5.4.2 CALCULATING A FOOD COST PERCENT

You are currently selling one portion of Grilled Chicken with Mango, Red Onion, and Pineapple for $12.95. Based on the calculated cost per portion, what is the food cost percent for this dish?

Cost per portion ÷ selling price = food cost percent

$3.5487 ÷ $12.95 = 0.2740

= 27.40%

Calculate the food cost percent using the calculated cost per portion of $3.5487.

RECIPE COSTING FORM

Menu item <u>Grilled Chicken with Mango, Red Onion, and Pineapple</u>   Date _____

Number of portions <u>32</u>   Size <u>8 oz breast</u>

Cost per portion <u>**$3.5487**</u>   Selling price <u>**$12.95**</u>   Food cost % <u>**27.40%**</u>

EXAMPLE 5.4.3 CALCULATING AN ESTIMATED SELLING PRICE

You want to lower the food cost percent for Grilled Chicken with Mango, Red Onion, and Pineapple to 25%. Estimate a selling price that will allow you to achieve this food cost percent.

Cost per portion ÷ food cost percent = estimated selling price

$3.5487 ÷ 0.25 = $14.1948

≈ $14.20

Calculate the minimum selling price using the calculated cost per portion of $3.5487.

RECIPE COSTING FORM

Menu item <u>Grilled Chicken with Mango, Red Onion, and Pineapple</u>   Date _____

Number of portions <u>32</u>   Size <u>8 oz breast</u>

Cost per portion <u>**$3.5487**</u>   Selling price <u>**$14.20**</u>   Food cost % <u>**25%**</u>

As you may have noticed, there is a place to record the date that you make these costing calculations. Why is it important to make note of this? Since many of the ingredients used in the kitchen are commodities, prices are constantly changing. One portion of a recipe could cost $3.55 today, $3.49 next week, and $3.75 six months from now. It is good business practice to periodically recalculate the cost per portion for your recipes to make sure you are charging an appropriate selling price.

Also, remember that when you use a recipe costing form, you are *forecasting* what you expect to happen. In practice, many things can happen that may cause the restaurant to not achieve expected food costs, including overportioning, underportioning, vendor price fluctuations, and inconsistent yields.

PRACTICE PROBLEMS

For each of the following recipes, determine the cost of each ingredient, the total recipe cost, the cost per portion, and an estimated selling price. You should not need any additional information, other than standard unit equivalents.

1. RECIPE COSTING FORM

Menu item   Big Jim's Chili   Date _____

Number of portions   15   Size _____

Cost per portion _____ Selling price _____   Food cost %   25%

RECIPE QUANTITY		REVISED RECIPE QUANTITY (IN PURCHASING UNIT)	QUANTITY TO PURCHASE		TOTAL COST	
Ingredient	Quantity	Revised Quantity	Yield %	AP Quantity	AP Cost	Ingredient Cost
Lean beef, cubed	5 #		95%		$2.29 / #	
Onions, diced	1½ #		90.6%		$0.28 / #	
Garlic cloves, minced (1 bulb = 12 cloves = 2.1 oz)	6 ea		88.1%		$1.73 / #	
Vegetable oil (1 bottle = 5 qt)	4 fl oz		100%		$6.40 / bottle	
Beef stock	3 pt		100%		$2.50 / G	
Tomato purée (1 can = 1 # 13 oz)	20 oz		100%		$3.50 / can	
Fresh jalapeños, diced	1 oz		93.5%		$1.99 / #	
Chili powder, hot	2 oz		100%		$5.15 / #	
Cumin, ground (1 C = 3.33 oz)	6 T		100%		$8.46 / #	
Kidney beans, dried	½ #		100%		$0.59 / #	
Salt (1 C = 8.55 oz, 1 bag = 25 #)	1½ T		100%		$2.99 / bag	
					TOTAL RECIPE COST	

2. RECIPE COSTING FORM

Menu item   <u>Stir-Fried Chicken with Gin</u>   Date _____

Number of portions   <u>12</u>   Size _____

Cost per portion _____   Selling price _____   Food cost %   <u>20%</u>

RECIPE QUANTITY		REVISED RECIPE QUANTITY (IN PURCHASING UNIT)	QUANTITY TO PURCHASE		TOTAL COST	
Ingredient	Quantity	Revised Quantity	Yield %	AP Quantity	AP Cost	Ingredient Cost
Boneless chicken breasts (1 breast = 6 oz)	12 ea		100%		$2.25 / #	
Yogurt	4 C		100%		$2.76 / qt	
Cayenne pepper (1 C = 3 oz)	½ t		100%		$5.00 / #	
Iceberg lettuce, shredded (1 head = 26 oz)	1 head		73.1%		$1.62 / head	
Shallots, chopped (1 C = 5.2 oz)	¾ C		90.6%		$0.59 / #	
Olive oil	6 T		100%		$15.75 / 3 L	
Gin (1 bottle = 1 L)	⅔ C		100%		$17.32 / bottle	
Grapes, green seedless (1 C = 3.24 oz)	3 C		93.8%		$1.87 / #	
Chicken stock	2 C		100%		$2.50 / G	
Dark corn syrup (1 jar = 16 oz, 1 C = 11½ oz)	4 T		100%		$1.89 / jar	
Thyme leaves, fresh (1 bu = 1 oz, 1 T = 0.1 oz)	4 t		65%		$0.67 / bu	
Cornstarch (1 C = 4.7 oz)	2 T		100%		$0.03 / oz	
					TOTAL RECIPE COST	

For each of the following recipes, determine the cost of each ingredient, the total recipe cost, the cost per portion, and either an estimated selling price or a food cost percent. Use the information from *The Book of Yields* in Appendix V as necessary.

3. **RECIPE COSTING FORM**

Menu item   Pizza with Tomatoes and Cheese   Date _____

Number of portions   10   Size _____

Cost per portion _____   Selling price _____   Food cost %   25%

RECIPE QUANTITY		REVISED RECIPE QUANTITY (IN PURCHASING UNIT)	QUANTITY TO PURCHASE		TOTAL COST	
Ingredient	Quantity	Revised Quantity	Yield %	AP Quantity	AP Cost	Ingredient Cost
Basic pizza dough	1 ea		100%		$1.00 / ea	
Olive oil, extra-virgin	30 mL		100%		$8.99 / L	
Basil leaves, fresh, chiffonade	3 g				$5.67 / #	
Oregano, fresh, chopped	2 g				$1.89 / bu	
Tomatoes, Roma, sliced	375 g				$0.99 / #	
Mozzarella, shredded	300 g		100%		$5.63 / #	
Parmesan, grated fresh	25 g		100%		$8.99 / #	
Black pepper, freshly cracked	3 g		100%		$5.65 / 12 oz	
Garlic cloves, minced	3 ea		100%		$1.12 / #	
					TOTAL RECIPE COST	

4. RECIPE COSTING FORM

Menu item   Sour Cream Shortcake Biscuits _____   Date _____

Number of portions   72 _____   Size _____

Cost per portion _____   Selling price _____   Food cost %   12%

RECIPE QUANTITY		REVISED RECIPE QUANTITY (IN PURCHASING UNIT)	QUANTITY TO PURCHASE		TOTAL COST	
Ingredient	Quantity	Revised Quantity	Yield %	AP Quantity	AP Cost	Ingredient Cost
Flour, all-purpose (1 bag = 25 #)	6 qt				$7.75 / bag	
Baking powder	¼ C				$1.70 / #	
Baking soda	2 T				$0.61 / #	
Salt, regular (1 box = 3 #)	1 T				$1.50 / box	
Sugar, granulated (1 bag = 5 #)	4½ C				$3.06 / bag	
Butter, unsalted	3 C				$2.05 / #	
Sour cream	3 qt				$1.59 / pt	
Milk, whole	3 C				$4.19 / G	
				TOTAL RECIPE COST		

5. RECIPE COSTING FORM

Menu item   Stir-Fried Vegetables _____   Date _____

Number of portions   10 _____   Size _____

Cost per portion _____   Selling price _____ $8.95 _____   Food cost % _____

RECIPE QUANTITY		REVISED RECIPE QUANTITY (IN PURCHASING UNIT)	QUANTITY TO PURCHASE		TOTAL COST	
Ingredient	Quantity	Revised Quantity	Yield %	AP Quantity	AP Cost	Ingredient Cost
Onion, sliced	350 g				$0.40 / #	
Red pepper, julienne	500 g				$3.99 / #	
Green pepper, sliced	600 g				$0.90 / #	
Carrots, chopped	450 g				$0.39 / #	
Celery, diced	⅔ bu				$1.69 / bu	
Garlic cloves, chopped	3 ea				$1.73 / #	
Sesame oil (1 bottle = 64 fl oz)	15 mL				$9.18 / bottle	
Soy sauce (1 bottle = 750 mL)	250 mL				$5.25 / bottle	
Five-spice powder (1 jar = 12 oz)	2 g				$8.95 / jar	
Sesame seeds	15 g				$1.17 / #	
Green onions, chopped	125 g				$0.59 / bu	
					TOTAL RECIPE COST	

6. For the following recipe, determine the cost of each ingredient, the total recipe cost, and the cost per portion.

RECIPE COSTING FORM

Menu item   Pie Dough _____   Date _____

Number of portions   96 _____   Size   10 oz _____

Cost per portion _____ selling price _____   Food cost % _____

RECIPE QUANTITY		REVISED RECIPE QUANTITY (IN PURCHASING UNIT)	QUANTITY TO PURCHASE		TOTAL COST	
Ingredient	Quantity	Revised Quantity	Yield %	AP Quantity	AP Cost	Ingredient Cost
Flour, pastry	30 #				$11.75 / 50 #	
Butter	10 #				$2.05 / #	
Shortening	10 #				$4.24 / 3 #	
Water	10 #					$0.00
Salt, kosher	5 oz				$1.33 / 26 oz	
					TOTAL RECIPE COST	

7. For the following recipe, determine the cost of each ingredient, the total recipe cost, the cost per portion, and the food cost percent. Use the information from *The Book of Yields* in Appendix V as necessary. Use the cost per portion from the recipe in practice problem 6 as the AP cost for the pie dough in this recipe.

RECIPE COSTING FORM

Menu item   Apple Crumb Pie   Date _____

Number of portions   8   Size _____

Cost per portion _____   Selling price ____ $3.25 ____   Food cost % _____

RECIPE QUANTITY		REVISED RECIPE QUANTITY (IN PURCHASING UNIT)	QUANTITY TO PURCHASE		TOTAL COST	
Ingredient	Quantity	Revised Quantity	Yield %	AP Quantity	AP Cost	Ingredient Cost
Apples, Macintosh (1 ea = 6 oz)	2 ea				$1.10 / #	
Apples, Granny Smith (1 ea = 6 oz)	2 ea				$1.08 / #	
Sugar, granulated (1 bag = 5 #)	6 oz				$3.06 / bag	
Lemon juice	1 T				$0.40 / ea	
Flour, all-purpose (1 bag = 25 #)	1 oz				$7.75 / bag	
Cinnamon, ground (1 jar = 16 oz)	2 t				$5.28 / jar	
Crumb topping	2 C				$0.75 / cup	
Pie dough	10 oz					
					TOTAL RECIPE COST	

Use the following recipe costing form to answer questions 8–22. It is not necessary to complete the entire form to answer the questions.

RECIPE COSTING FORM

Menu item   Oat Bran and Fruit Muffins _____   Date _____

Number of portions   1 dozen _____   Size _____

Cost per portion _____ Selling price _____   Food cost %   12%

RECIPE QUANTITY		REVISED RECIPE QUANTITY (IN PURCHASING UNIT)	QUANTITY TO PURCHASE		TOTAL COST	
Ingredient	Quantity	Revised Quantity	Yield %	AP Quantity	AP Cost	Ingredient Cost
Oat bran (1 C = 5.3 oz)	2 C		100%		$11.70 / 50 #	
Rolled oats (1 C = 3 oz)	1½ C		100%		$0.98 / #	
Flour, all-purpose	5 oz		100%		$15.00 / 50 #	
Brown sugar, light	3 oz		100%		$0.93 / #	
Baking powder (1 C = 6.9 oz)	2 t		100%		$10.72 / 10 #	
Egg whites (1 C = 8.75 oz, 1 egg = 2 oz)	½ C		66.6%		$1.29 / dozen	
Bananas, mashed (1 ea = 7 oz)	2 ea		66.3%		$0.49 / #	
Apples, peeled and shredded (1 ea = 6 oz)	½ #		85%		$0.89 / #	
Orange juice, fresh (1 C = 8.3 oz, 1 ea = 8 ½ oz)	⅔ C		37.6%		$0.45 / ea	
Vegetable oil	2 fl oz		100%		$6.40 / 5 qt	
Skim milk	1 pt		100%		$0.96 / qt	
				TOTAL RECIPE COST		

8.   How many pounds of flour are used in this recipe?

9. How many pounds of oat bran are used in this recipe?

10. How many ounces of baking powder are used in this recipe?

11. For which ingredient in this recipe can you ignore the given yield percent?

12. How many pounds of apples do you need to purchase for this recipe?

13.   How many eggs do you need to purchase for this recipe?

14.   If you tripled this recipe, how many oranges would you need to purchase?

15.   What is the AP cost per ounce of the all-purpose flour?

16.   What is the AP cost per fluid ounce of the vegetable oil?

17. What is the cost of the skim milk purchased for this recipe?

18. What is the cost of the rolled oats purchased for this recipe?

19. What is the cost of the apples purchased for this recipe?

20. If the total recipe cost is $3.37, how much do the ingredients for each muffin cost?

21. Based on customer demand, you have increased the size of the muffin, which now has a cost per portion of $0.329. If you want to maintain a food cost of 12%, what should the minimum selling price of each muffin be?

22. A small coffee and muffin combo sells for $2.50. If the ingredient cost for the items in the combo is $0.3808, what is the food cost percent for the combo?

Use the following recipe costing form to answer questions 23–35. It is not necessary to complete the entire form to answer the questions.

RECIPE COSTING FORM

Menu item   Pork Roast with Jus Lié   Date _____

Number of portions   6   Size _____

Cost per portion _____   Selling price ____$13.00____   Food cost % _____

RECIPE QUANTITY		REVISED RECIPE QUANTITY (IN PURCHASING UNIT)	QUANTITY TO PURCHASE		TOTAL COST	
Ingredient	Quantity	Revised Quantity	Yield %	AP Quantity	AP Cost	Ingredient Cost
Pork roast, bone-in	2 kg		100%		$1.64 / #	
Garlic, minced (1 bulb = 2.1 oz)	15 g		88.1%		$1.10 / #	
Rosemary, minced (1 bu = 1 oz)	2 g		80%		$0.47 / bu	
Salt, kosher (1 box = 3 #)	6 g		100%		$1.33 / box	
Pepper, ground (1 jar = 20 oz)	4 g		100%		$5.89 / jar	
Onions, small dice (1 onion = 4 oz)	113 g		90.6%		$0.26 / #	
Carrots, small dice (1 bag = 500 g)	57 g		81.3%		$0.35 / bag	
Celery, small dice (1 bu = 32 oz, 1 case = 24 bu)	57 g		68.8%		$39.52 / case	
White wine, dry (1 btl = 750 mL)	120 mL		100%		$7.35 / bottle	
Tomato paste (1 can = 12 oz)	33 g		100%		$1.12 / can	
Brown veal stock (1 cup = 8 oz)	1 L		100%		$7.35 / G	
Thyme sprigs, fresh (1 bu = 23 sprigs)	2 ea		65%		$0.30 / bu	
Bay leaves (1 oz = 130 ea, 1 jar = 2 oz)	1 ea		100%		$4.79 / jar	
Arrowroot (1 T = .281 oz, 1 box = 1.25 #)	15 g		100 %		$5.55 / box	
					TOTAL RECIPE COST	

23. How many ounces of celery are used in this recipe?

_____

_____

_____

24. How many ounces of arrowroot are used in this recipe?

25. What percent of a can of tomato paste is used in this recipe?

26. How many pounds of garlic do you need to purchase for this recipe?

27. How many pounds of onions do you need to purchase to make this recipe ten times?

RECIPE COSTING

28. What is the AP cost per fluid ounce of the brown veal stock?

29. What is the AP cost per milliliter of the white wine?

30. What is the cost of the white wine purchased for this recipe?

31. What is the cost of the onion purchased for this recipe?

32. What is the cost of the thyme purchased for this recipe?

33. If the total recipe cost is $11.05, how much do the ingredients for each portion cost?

34. If the selling price for this dish is $13.00, what is the food cost percent?

35. If you wanted to lower the food cost percent of this dish to 12%, what should the minimum selling price of each portion be?

For each of the following recipes, fill in a recipe costing form. Use the information from *The Book of Yields* in Appendix V to complete the forms in questions 38 and 39 as necessary.

36.   Halibut Steaks Provençal

Makes 4 servings

24 oz halibut steaks

¾ C minced onion

4 garlic cloves, minced

1¼ # peeled and seeded plum tomatoes

2 T olive oil

INGREDIENTS	YIELD	AP COST	NOTES
Halibut steaks	100%	$10.85/#	
Onions	90.6%	$0.05/oz	1 C = 4 oz
Garlic	88.1%	$1.28/#	1 bulb = 2.1 oz = 12 cloves
Plum tomatoes	78.4%	$1.09/#	
Olive oil	100%	$6.50/L	

Food cost percent = 39%

RECIPE COSTING FORM

Menu item _____   Date _____

Number of portions _____   Size _____

Cost per portion _____ Selling price _____   Food cost % _____

RECIPE QUANTITY		REVISED RECIPE QUANTITY (IN PURCHASING UNIT)	QUANTITY TO PURCHASE		TOTAL COST	
Ingredient	Quantity	Revised Quantity	Yield %	AP Quantity	AP Cost	Ingredient Cost
					TOTAL RECIPE COST	

37. Asian Noodle Soup

Makes 8 servings

175 g buckwheat noodles

2 L chicken broth

100 g trimmed and crushed lemongrass

½ bu cilantro, chopped

5 g chile flakes

INGREDIENTS	YIELD	AP COST	NOTES
Buckwheat noodles	100%	$2.00/box	1 box = 500 g
Chicken broth	100%	$2.19/G	
Lemongrass	65%	$3.58/#	1 bu = 170 g
Cilantro	46%	$1.50/bu	1 bu = 2.8 oz
Chile flakes	100%	$3.95/jar	1 jar = 6 oz, 1 T = 0.238 oz

Selling price = $6.95

RECIPE COSTING FORM

Menu item _____   Date _____

Number of portions _____   Size _____

Cost per portion _____ Selling price _____   Food cost % _____

RECIPE QUANTITY		REVISED RECIPE QUANTITY (IN PURCHASING UNIT)	QUANTITY TO PURCHASE		TOTAL COST	
Ingredient	Quantity	Revised Quantity	Yield %	AP Quantity	AP Cost	Ingredient Cost
					TOTAL RECIPE COST	

38. Berry Coulis

Makes 24 servings

1 qt cleaned raspberries

½ # hulled and sliced strawberries

12 oz granulated sugar

Juice of 2 lemons

1 t vanilla

INGREDIENT	AP COST
Raspberries	$1.95/pt
Strawberries	$3.00/qt
Granulated sugar	$2.04/5 #
Lemons	$0.25/ea
Vanilla	$6.00/300 mL

Food cost percent = 22%

RECIPE COSTING FORM

Menu item _____   Date _____

Number of portions _____   Size _____

Cost per portion _____ Selling price _____   Food cost % _____

RECIPE QUANTITY		REVISED RECIPE QUANTITY (IN PURCHASING UNIT)	QUANTITY TO PURCHASE		TOTAL COST	
Ingredient	Quantity	Revised Quantity	Yield %	AP Quantity	AP Cost	Ingredient Cost
					TOTAL RECIPE COST	

39. Butternut Squash Soup

Makes 6 servings

1 large onion, diced

3½ C peeled and cubed butternut squash

1 qt chicken stock

2 t kosher salt

1 C heavy (whipping) cream

INGREDIENT	AP COST
Onion	$0.69/#
Butternut squash	$0.46/#
Chicken stock	$2.00/G
Salt, kosher flake	$1.00/26 oz
Heavy cream	$3.00/qt

Food cost percent = 12%

RECIPE COSTING FORM

Menu item _____   Date _____

Number of portions _____   Size _____

Cost per portion _____ Selling price _____   Food cost % _____

RECIPE QUANTITY		REVISED RECIPE QUANTITY (IN PURCHASING UNIT)	QUANTITY TO PURCHASE		TOTAL COST	
Ingredient	Quantity	Revised Quantity	Yield %	AP Quantity	AP Cost	Ingredient Cost
					TOTAL RECIPE COST	

5.5 The 2-in-1 Recipe Costing Form: The Excel Version

Ingredient costs can fluctuate based on a number of factors: seasonality, market demand, and weather conditions, among others. Manually recalculating recipe costs based on new ingredient prices could be very time-consuming, so most businesses (foodservice-related or otherwise) employ some form of technology to help them organize information about their products.

To this end, we have developed a version of our recipe costing form using a Microsoft Excel spreadsheet. The interactive Excel spreadsheet is available at www.wiley.com/college/cia.com. A blank version appears below:

To illustrate how to use the Excel recipe costing form, we will calculate the cost of the same recipe for Caramelized Apples used in Example 5.2.7.

RECIPE COSTING FORM

Menu item _____   Date _____

Number of portions _____   Portion size _____

Cost per portion   **#DIV/0!**   Selling price _____   Food cost percent _____

RECIPE QUANTITY			REVISED RECIPE QUANTITY		QUANTITY TO PURCHASE			AP COST			INGREDIENT COST
Ingredient	Quantity	Unit	Quantity	Unit	Yield %	APQ	Unit	APC	No.	Unit	
				0		0.0000	0				$0.0000
				0		0.0000	0				$0.0000
				0		0.0000	0				$0.0000
				0		0.0000	0				$0.0000
				0		0.0000	0				$0.0000
				0		0.0000	0				$0.0000
				0		0.0000	0				$0.0000
				0		0.0000	0				$0.0000
				0		0.0000	0				$0.0000
				0		0.0000	0				$0.0000
				0		0.0000	0				$0.0000
				0		0.0000	0				$0.0000
				0		0.0000	0				$0.0000
				0		0.0000	0				$0.0000
									TOTAL RECIPE COST		$0.00

Caramelized Apples

Makes 20 servings

(Adapted from The Professional Chef [8th ed.] by The Culinary Institute of America)

96 oz Granny Smith apples, peeled and cored

2 C granulated sugar

Juice of 2 lemons

Here again is the relevant purchasing information:

Apples, Granny Smith $0.79/#

Sugar, granulated $1.84/5 #

Lemons $0.24/each

For purposes of this example, after we calculate the cost to make this recipe, we will calculate an estimated selling price using a food cost percent of 14%.

HOW TO USE THE EXCEL 2-IN-1 RECIPE COSTING FORM

Before entering information, remember the following:

- Formulas are locked to assist you in completing the form properly and to prevent you from deleting key formulas. You cannot type data into a locked cell.

- On this form, recipe quantities need to be converted into the same unit as the AP cost.

- Convert all fractions to their decimal equivalents. (Even if Excel displays a rounded version of a number you have entered, it will perform calculations with the exact number that you entered.)

1.   Enter the given information.

    a. **The menu item as listed on your recipe card and the date.**

RECIPE COSTING FORM

Menu item	Caramelized Apples	Date	7/16/20XX
Number of portions		Portion size	
Cost per portion	#DIV/0! Selling price	Food cost percent	

    b. **The number of portions and , if desired, the portion size.** Do not include a word such as "portions" or "servings" with the number of portions, as Excel will not calculate the cost per portion if you put text in this cell.

       Before the number of portions is entered, the "Cost per portion" cell will contain "#DIV/0!."

RECIPE COSTING FORM

Menu item	Caramelized Apples	Date	7/16/20XX
Number of portions	20	Portion size	
Cost per portion	$0.0000 Selling price	Food cost percent	

After the number of portions is entered, the form will calculate the cost per portion. (The cell contains $0 at this point because $0—the total recipe cost at this point—divided by 20 is $0.)

c. **The recipe ingredients and the quantities.** Enter numbers in the "Quantity" column and the units of measure (or other text) in the "Unit" column. (Remember that Excel will not calculate certain formulas if numbers are mixed with letters or symbols.)

RECIPE QUANTITY		
Ingredient	**Quantity**	**Unit**
Apples, Granny Smith	96.00	oz
Sugar, granulated	2.00	C
Lemons, juiced	2.00	ea

d. **The AP cost for each item, the number of units purchased for that cost, and the purchasing unit.** (Once again, do not mix numbers and letters or symbols in the same cell.) This form is set up to handle costs that are AP costs per single unit and AP costs per multiple units. In the second row below, Excel will calculate the AP cost per pound as part of the ingredient cost calculation for that ingredient.

Also, the units you enter in this section will be copied to the two other indicated "Unit" columns to remind you of the unit in which your original recipe quantity needs to be expressed.

REVISED RECIPE QUANTITY		QUANTITY TO PURCHASE			AP COST		
Quantity	**Unit**	**Yield %**	**APQ**	**Unit**	**APC**	**No.**	**Unit**
	#		0.0000	#	$0.79	1	#
	#		0.0000	#	$1.84	5	#
	ea		0.0000	ea	$0.24	1	ea

e. **The yield percent.** Enter 100% for ingredients that have no waste, and when the recipe quantity is given as an AP quantity. (Ordinarily in that instance, you would simply not use the yield percent. However, Excel will not calculate an ingredient's cost without a yield percent, so do the next best thing and enter 100%.)

Ingredient	Quantity	Unit	Quantity	Unit	Yield %
Apples, Granny Smith	96.00	oz		#	73.88%
Sugar, granulated	2.00	C		#	100.00%
Lemons, juiced	2.00	ea		ea	100.00%

2. Revise each recipe quantity so it is expressed in the purchasing unit and enter the revised quantity in the "Revised Recipe Quantity" column.

RECIPE QUANTITY			REVISED RECIPE QUANTITY	
Ingredient	Quantity	Unit	Quantity	Unit
Apples, Granny Smith	96.00	oz	6.0000	#
Sugar, granulated	2.00	C	0.8875	#
Lemons, juiced	2.00	ea	2.0000	ea

3. The values in the "APQ" and "Ingredient Cost" columns will calculate automatically, as will "Total Recipe Cost." You cannot calculate these values on your own and enter them. Remember, you will get an error message if you try to type data into a protected cell.

QUANTITY TO PURCHASE			AP COST			INGREDIENT COST
Yield %	APQ	Unit	APC	No.	Unit	
73.88%	8.1213	#	$0.79	1	#	$6.4158
100.00%	0.8875	#	$1.84	5	#	$0.3266
100.00%	2.0000	ea	$0.24	1	ea	$0.4800

TOTAL RECIPE COST	$7.23

4. Enter either the food cost percent or the selling price, as given. Calculate the unknown quantity, based on the cost per portion (which, remember, will be calculated automatically). You can type the answer into the appropriate cell, or you can type in a formula so Excel calculates it for you. For this form, the formulas to use are:

selling price: = B5/K5   food cost percent: =B5/F5

RECIPE COSTING FORM

Menu item	**Caramelized Apples**		Date	**7/16/20XX**
Number of portions	**20**		Portion size	
Cost per portion	**$0.3615**	Selling price **$2.58**	Food cost percent	**14.00%**

PRACTICE PROBLEMS

For each of the following recipes, fill in the Excel recipe costing form. Use the information from *The Book of Yields* in Appendix V to complete the forms in questions 3 and 4 as necessary. (Note: These are the same recipes from questions 36 through 39 in Section 5.4.)

1. ## Halibut Steaks Provençal

Makes 4 servings

24 oz halibut steaks

¾ C minced onion

4 garlic cloves, minced

1¼ # peeled and seeded plum tomatoes

2 T olive oil

INGREDIENT	YIELD	AP COST	NOTES
Halibut steaks	100%	$10.85/#	
Onion	90.6%	$0.05/oz	1 C = 4 oz
Garlic	88.1%	$1.28/#	1 bulb = 2.1 oz = 12 cloves
Plum tomatoes	78.4%	$1.09/#	
Olive oil	100%	$6.50/L	

Food cost percent = 39%

2. # Asian Noodle Soup

Makes 8 servings

175 g buckwheat noodles

2 L chicken broth

100 g trimmed and crushed lemongrass

½ bu cilantro, chopped

5 g chile flakes

INGREDIENTS	YIELD	AP COST	NOTES
Buckwheat noodles	100%	$2.00/box	1 box = 500 g
Chicken broth	100%	$2.19/G	
Lemongrass	65%	$3.58/#	1 bu = 170 g
Cilantro	46%	$1.50/bu	1 bu = 2.8 oz
Chile flakes	100%	$3.95/jar	1 jar = 6 oz, 1 T = 0.238 oz

Selling price = $6.95

3. # Berry Coulis

Makes 24 servings

1 qt cleaned raspberries

½ # hulled and sliced strawberries

12 oz granulated sugar

Juice of 2 lemons

1 t vanilla

INGREDIENTS	AP COST
Raspberries	$1.95/pt
Strawberries	$3.00/qt
Granulated sugar	$2.04/5 #
Lemons	$0.25/ea
Vanilla	$6.00/300 mL

Food cost percent = 22%

4. Butternut Squash Soup

Makes 6 servings

1 large onion, diced

3½ C peeled and cubed butternut squash

1 qt chicken stock

2 t kosher salt

1 C heavy (whipping) cream

INGREDIENTS	AP COST
Onion	$0.69/#
Butternut squash	$0.46/#
Chicken stock	$2.00/G
Salt, kosher flake	$1.00/26 oz
Heavy cream	$3.00/qt

Food cost percent = 12%

5.6 Comparative Costing

In a foodservice establishment, two of the primary concerns of the person responsible for purchasing food are the quality of the products and the cost of those products. The purchaser must take care to select the products that provide the best value for their level of quality. A business may be run very efficiently in terms of cost control measures, but if too much is spent on raw ingredients, the bottom line will suffer. Some wholesalers provide comparative costing information; others do not. If your vendors do not provide unit prices for you, you can calculate them using the AP cost per unit formula (Section 5.1). These calculations can help you make prudent purchasing decisions.

COMPARING AP COSTS PER UNIT FOR PRODUCTS WHEN WASTE IS NOT A FACTOR

When waste is not an issue, comparing the unit prices of multiple purchasing options is most often a matter of calculating an AP cost per unit expressed in the same unit for all options.

EXAMPLE 5.6.1 COMPARING AP COSTS PER UNIT

Below are three options for purchasing all-purpose flour from your supplier. Which bag has the lowest cost per pound?

  A.   a 10-pound bag for $5.00

  B.   a 25-pound bag for $11.50

  C.   a 50-pound bag for $22.00

AP cost ÷ number of units purchased = AP cost per unit

A. $5.00 ÷ 10 # = $0.50 / #
B. $11.50 ÷ 25 # = $0.46 / #
C. $22.00 ÷ 50 # = $0.44 / #

Divide each price by the number of pounds in the corresponding bag.

The 50-pound bag is the cheapest per pound. This is often the case: the more product purchased, the lower the cost per unit.

EXAMPLE 5.6.2 COMPARING AP COSTS PER UNIT

Which of the following three options for purchasing olive oil is the least expensive per AP unit?

A. a 3-liter bottle for $21.42

B. a 1-gallon bottle for $23.42

C. a 5-quart can for $27.76

A. $\dfrac{3\,L}{1}\times\dfrac{33.8\,\text{fl oz}}{1\,L} = 101.4\,\text{fl oz}$

Express all three bottles' quantities in the same unit of measure.

B. $\dfrac{1\,G}{1}\times\dfrac{128\,\text{fl oz}}{1\,G} = 128\,\text{fl oz}$

C. $\dfrac{5\,qt}{1}\times\dfrac{32\,\text{fl oz}}{1\,qt} = 160\,\text{fl oz}$

AP cost ÷ number of units purchased = AP cost per unit

A. $21.42 ÷ 101.4 fl oz = $0.2112 / fl oz
B. $23.42 ÷ 128 fl oz = $0.1829 / fl oz
C. $27.76 ÷ 160 fl oz = $0.1735 / fl oz

Divide each bottle's price by the number of fluid ounces in the bottle.

The largest bottle is the least expensive per fluid ounce. We chose to compare the prices of the three options by converting the bottle sizes to fluid ounces, but you could choose another unit if the conversions would be more efficient for you.

In the foodservice industry, investigating a range of purchasing options and selecting those with the lowest unit prices is frequently a primary concern. There are, however, other factors that should also be considered when buying products: the amount of available storage space and how quickly you will use the product, for example. There may not be room in your establishment to properly store 50 pounds of flour or 5 quarts of olive oil, particularly if only small quantities of those ingredients are used on a daily basis. Since some items deteriorate over time, buying larger pack sizes to save money may actually cost you money in the long run. Additionally, funds that could be used elsewhere are now tied up in excessive inventory. Both mathematical calculations and practicality should be considered when making purchasing decisions.

COMPARING UNIT PRICES FOR PRODUCTS WHEN WASTE IS A FACTOR

Product yield can be used to help make appropriate purchasing decisions: calculating accurate AP quantities helps ensure you do not underestimate food costs. It can also be used to help make decisions when comparing ingredient prices. Consider, for example, the option of purchasing 24-ounce heads of romaine lettuce at $1.69 each versus purchasing 30-ounce bags of romaine hearts for $2.28 each.

Purchasing options. When deciding between two purchasing options, the AP cost of each option is only one aspect of making a prudent decision. Yield percent, quality and labor costs (among other considerations) must also factor into your decision. An option with a lower AP cost could end up costing much more after all dimensions are considered.

HEADS OF ROMAINE	BAGS OF ROMAINE HEARTS
AP cost: $1.69 / 24 oz 75% yield	AP cost: $2.28 / 30 oz 90% yield

At first, it appears that the heads of romaine are cheaper, since the price per AP ounce is slightly lower ($0.0704 per ounce versus $0.076 per ounce for the hearts). However, there is a 15% difference in yield between the two options. What effect will this difference in yield have on the total cost of each option? (We will investigate this scenario in more detail in Example 5.6.6.)

Also, there would most likely be labor costs associated with each of these options—which would add to the overall cost of each option—but those costs would not be included in what we are calling ingredient cost. Example 5.6.7 will show how labor costs can affect the overall cost of a particular purchasing option.

EDIBLE PORTION COST PER UNIT

Calculating the **EP cost per unit**—also called the cost per usable unit—can help a chef decide which of multiple options for purchasing a specific product is the most cost effective, if each option has a different yield. We will discuss two methods of calculating EP cost per unit. The first method applies product yields to unit prices to calculate the EP cost per unit:

METHOD 1:   AP cost per unit ÷ yield percent = EP cost per unit

Alternatively, you can calculate the amount of usable product you can expect from a purchased quantity, then divide the total cost of that purchased quantity by the usable amount:

METHOD 2:   AP cost ÷ EP quantity = EP cost per unit

In each of the following examples, we will calculate the EP cost per unit for each option using both methods. When you calculate EP costs per unit, use whichever method you prefer. Each method uses the same information in different ways, but produces the same result.

EXAMPLE 5.6.3 CALCULATING EP COST PER UNIT

Your kitchen is using broccoli florets for a new menu item. A vendor has bunches of broccoli available for $21.12 per 16-pound case. What is the EP cost per unit for this broccoli?

USING METHOD 1:

AP cost ÷ number of units purchased = AP cost per unit
$21.12 ÷ 16 # = $1.32 / #

Calculate the AP cost per pound.

AP cost per unit ÷ yield percent = EP cost per unit
$1.32 / # ÷ 0.628 = $2.1019 / #

Calculate the EP cost per pound using the yield percent of broccoli (62.8%, according to *The Book of Yields*).

Why is the EP cost per unit of the broccoli higher than the AP cost per unit? The calculated price of $2.1019 per pound is the cost of 100% usable florets. Remember, you had to purchase more than one pound of broccoli for each pound of usable product you needed.

USING METHOD 2:

AP weight × yield % = EP weight
16 # × 0.628 = 10.048 #

Calculate the weight of florets you can expect from the case.

AP cost ÷ EP weight = EP cost per unit
$21.12 ÷ 10.048 # = $2.1019 / #

Divide the amount spent on the case by the usable weight.

Regardless of how much usable product you get from the case, you paid $21.12 for it. Many chefs use method 2 when doing a cost per portion calculation for proteins such as meats, seafood, and poultry, since a chef can quickly divide the total price paid for, say, a fish or a cut of beef by the number of trimmed portions that the chef expects from that quantity.

Edible portion cost. Prefabricated products (left) will not incur any additional costs for waste, but products that must be fabricated (right) will. Calculating edible portion cost helps a chef factor in the cost of the waste that must be purchased to obtain a certain EP quantity.

As we mentioned in Section 3.1, the trim loss of a product doesn't always go in the garbage. Generally, even if fruit and vegetable scraps can be used for another purpose, such as stock, no value is assigned to them. It is customary in the foodservice industry to assign a trim value only to higher-cost ingredients such as meat, poultry, and fish products. (A formula called the **butcher's yield** can be used to calculate the costs of usable trim. See Appendix IV for more information on the butcher's yield.)

EXAMPLE 5.6.4 **CALCULATING EP COST PER UNIT**

You are making fresh apple pies for a holiday party. Prior to giving your client a price quote for the pies, you want to know the EP cost per pound for peeled, cored, and sliced apples. If the wholesale price for apples is currently $71.60 per 40-pound case, what is the EP cost per pound?

For the purposes of this example, let's say that you achieved a 61.8% yield the last time you fabricated apples for pies. (You could look up the yield in *The Book of Yields*, of course, but using your own calculated yields will provide a much more accurate result.)

USING METHOD 1:

AP cost ÷ number of units purchased = AP cost per unit
$71.60 ÷ 40 # = $1.79 / #

Calculate the AP cost per pound.

AP cost per unit ÷ yield percent = EP cost per unit
$1.79 / # ÷ 0.618 = $2.8964 / #

Calculate the EP cost per pound using your yield percent.

USING METHOD 2:

AP weight × yield % = EP weight
40 # × 0.618 = 24.72 #

Calculate the weight of prepared apples you can expect from the case.

AP cost ÷ EP weight = EP cost per unit
$71.60 ÷ 24.72 # = $2.8964 / #

Divide the amount spent on the case by the usable weight.

If you had used $1.79 per pound as part of your price quote, you would have underestimated the actual cost of the prepared apples by over $1.00 per pound.

COMPARING COSTS OF INGREDIENTS

Foodservice establishments often have several purchasing options for products. Generally, having more than one supplier will give you more options if you are shopping around for the best prices on the products used in your establishment.

EXAMPLE 5.6.5 COMPARING COSTS OF INGREDIENTS

Your vendor has noticed that you are purchasing quite of bit of bunch broccoli (at $1.95 per bunch) lately, and offers you another option: 5-pound bags of prefabricated broccoli florets for $12.45 each. Which item has the lower EP cost per pound?

FOR THE PREFABRICATED FLORETS:

AP cost ÷ number of units purchased = AP cost per unit
$12.45 ÷ 5 # = $2.49 / #

Since the prefabricated florets have a 100% yield, EP quantity = AP quantity.

FOR THE BUNCHES:

USING METHOD 1:

AP cost ÷ number of units purchased = AP cost per unit
$1.95 ÷ 1.3437 # = $1.4512 / #

Calculate the AP cost per pound. *The Book of Yields* reports that a bunch of broccoli weighs 21.5 ounces, which is equivalent to 1.3437 pounds.

AP cost per unit ÷ yield percent = EP cost per unit
$1.4512 / # ÷ 0.628 = $2.3108 / #

Calculate the EP cost per pound using the yield percent of broccoli (62.8%, according to *The Book of Yields.*).

USING METHOD 2:

AP weight × yield % = EP weight
1.3437 # × 0.628 = 0.8438 #

Calculate the weight of a prepared bunch of broccoli.

AP cost ÷ EP weight = EP cost per unit
$1.95 ÷ 0.8438 # = $2.3109 / #

Divide the amount spent on the bunch by the usable weight.

By calculating the EP cost per unit, you can see that bunch broccoli has a lower EP cost per pound than the prefabricated florets. Information like this can help a chef make a well-informed decision on which form of broccoli (or other products) to buy.

EXAMPLE 5.6.6 COMPARING COSTS OF INGREDIENTS

A restaurant has two options for buying romaine lettuce: 24-ounce heads at $1.69 each or 30-ounce bags of romaine hearts for $2.28 each. Which option has the lower EP cost per ounce?

FOR THE HEADS:

USING METHOD 1:

AP cost ÷ number of units purchased = AP cost per unit
$1.69 ÷ 24 oz = $0.0704 / oz

Calculate the AP cost per pound.

AP cost per unit ÷ yield percent = EP cost per unit
$0.0704 / oz ÷ 0.75 = $0.0938 / oz

Calculate the EP cost per pound using the yield percent of romaine (75%, according to *The Book of Yields.*)

USING METHOD 2:

AP weight × yield % = EP weight
24 oz × 0.75 = 18 oz

Calculate the weight of a prepared head of romaine.

AP cost ÷ EP quantity = EP cost per unit
$1.69 ÷ 18 oz = $0.0938 / oz

Divide the amount spent on the head by the usable weight.

FOR THE HEARTS:

USING METHOD 1:

AP cost ÷ number of units purchased = AP cost per unit
$2.28 ÷ 30 oz = $0.076 / oz

Calculate the AP cost per pound.

AP cost per unit ÷ yield percent = EP cost per unit
$0.076 / oz ÷ 0.90 = $0.0844 / oz

Calculate the EP cost per pound using the yield percent for romaine hearts (90%, according to *The Book of Yields.*)

USING METHOD 2:

AP weight × yield % = EP weight
30 oz × 0.90 = 27 oz

Calculate the weight of a prepared bag of romaine hearts.

AP cost ÷ EP weight = EP cost per unit
$2.28 ÷ 27 oz = $0.0844 / oz

Divide the amount spent on the bag by the usable weight.

Would you automatically buy whole produce (like bunches of broccoli or heads of romaine) over prefabricated products (like broccoli florets or shredded lettuce) because they have a lower EP cost per unit? Among other factors (including quality, delivery issues, and availability), labor costs should also be considered when purchasing products which require fabrication. When buying broccoli, for example, the bunches themselves may be cheaper, but the amount of money spent to pay an employee to fabricate those bunches into florets may make it more expensive than buying prefabricated florets. In most foodservice operations, labor costs are substantial and can heavily impact the purchasing decisions made by a business.

EXAMPLE 5.6.7 IMPACT OF LABOR ON INGREDIENT COST

Your prep cook is paid $13.00 per hour, which includes the cost of mandatory benefits. If it takes 5 minutes for this cook to fabricate 1 pound of florets from bunches of broccoli, how much does this add to the EP cost per pound?

While five minutes of labor per bunch might not seem like much, it would certainly add up if you were using 50 pounds of florets a week. Here is one way to calculate how much you would pay your prep cook to fabricate each pound of broccoli:

Labor cost per hour ÷ 60 minutes / hour = labor cost per minute
$13.00 / hr ÷ 60 min / hr = $0.2166 / min

Calculate the cost of each minute of labor.

Labor cost per minute × fabrication time = total labor cost
$0.2166 / min × 5 minutes = $1.083

Multiply by the length of time it takes to complete the job.

If you add this $1.083 labor cost per pound to the $2.3109 EP cost per pound (calculated in Example 5.6.5), it is no longer cheaper to fabricate your own florets. The net cost of $3.3939 per EP pound is substantially higher than the $2.49 per EP pound for the prefabricated florets.

PRACTICE PROBLEMS

For questions 1–4, determine which purchasing option has the lowest AP cost per given unit. Do not consider any potential labor costs, and assume that each option is of equal quality.

1. AP cost per fluid ounce of olive oil

   Option A: $6.06 / 5 quarts
   Option B: $1.59 / liter

2. AP cost per pound of chocolate

   Option A: $38.70 / 5 kilograms
   Option B: $59.99 / 20-pound case

3. AP cost per gallon of yogurt

   Option A: pre-made: $1.25 / pint
   Option B: house-made: $2.25 / ½ gallon

4. AP cost per fluid ounce of maple syrup

Option A: $57.00 / gallon
Option B: $29.82 / ½ gallon
Option C: $7.69 / pint

For questions 5–9, use the given information to calculate the EP cost per given unit. Do not consider any potential labor costs.

5. EP cost per pound of leeks

AP cost: $24.20 / 24 # case; 43.8% yield

6. EP cost per pound of shiitake mushrooms

AP cost: $31.44 / 5 # box; 80.38% yield

7. EP cost per pound of grapefruit

AP cost: $25.91 / 40-count case (13.3 oz ea); 52.6% yield

8. EP cost per ounce of basil leaves

AP cost: $12.24 / 12 bunches (2.5 oz ea); 56% yield

9. EP cost per ounce of cooked long-grain white rice

AP cost: $43.16 / 50 # bag; 334% yield

For questions 10–15, determine which purchasing option has the lowest EP cost per unit. Do not consider any potential labor costs, and assume that each option is of equal quality. Yields not listed can be assumed to be 100%.

10. Option A: whole tomatoes (78.1% yield): $2.75 / #
    Option B: prefabricated tomato concassée: $3.99 / #

11. Option A: prefabricated broccoli florets: $2.09 / #
    Option B: bunch broccoli (1½ pounds per bunch, 62% yield): $1.82 / bunch

12. Option A: fresh chopped clams: $3.34 / 1-# container
    Option B: canned chopped clams: $7.85 / 51-ounce can

13.　Option A:　tomato sauce: $1.06 / 12-fluid-ounce jar
　　Option B:　tomato sauce: $7.00 / number-10 can (104.9 fluid ounces)

14.　Option A:　whole artichokes (8 ounces each, 45% yield): $1.48 / ea
　　Option B:　number-10 cans (drained weight: 64 ounces): $17.78 / can
　　Option C:　artichoke hearts: $65.05 / 10-kilogram case

15.　Option A:　large eggs (2 ounces each, 89% yield): $1.28 / dozen
　　Option B:　medium eggs (1.75 ounces each, 89% yield): $1.19 / dozen
　　Option C:　shelled and pooled eggs: $13.00 / 20 #

16. Using the given pricing information, calculate the lowest possible total cost for the following recipe by selecting the cheaper purchasing option for each ingredient. Enter the appropriate yields and AP costs in the form after you make your selections. (Yields not listed below or already entered on the recipe costing form can be assumed to be 100%.) Use the information from *The Book of Yields* in Appendix V as necessary.

White wine	Option A: $4.95 / 750 mL	Option B: $8.50 / 1½ L
Crème de cassis	Option A: $4.45 / 375 mL	Option B: $7.90 / 750 mL
Orange juice	Option A: $1.90 / 3-qt can	Option B: $0.35 / orange (37.6%)
Strawberry jam	Option A: $1.80 / 12-oz jar	Option B: $6.52 / 112-oz can
Red plums	Option A: $1.29 / #	Option B: $20.50 / 18 #
Basil	Option A: $1.99 / bu	Option B: $21.00 / 12 bu
Red grapes	Option A: $1.62 / #	Option B: $28.35 / 18 # flat
Sweet cherries	Option A: $2.39 / # (87.5%)	Option B: $11.32 / #10 can (60%)
Strawberries	Option A: $1.75 / pt (91.9%)	Option B: $19.50 / 10 # box (IQF)
Crème fraiche	Option A: $5.38 / pt	Option B: $6.20 / 500 g

RECIPE COSTING FORM

Menu item   <u>Red Fruit Compote</u>   Date _____

Number of portions   <u>10</u>   Size _____

Cost per portion _____   Selling price _____   Food cost % _____

RECIPE QUANTITY		REVISED RECIPE QUANTITY (IN PURCHASING UNIT)	QUANTITY TO PURCHASE		TOTAL COST	
Ingredient	Quantity	Revised Quantity	Yield %	AP Quantity	AP Cost	Ingredient Cost
White wine	1 C		100%			
Crème de cassis	1 C		100%			
Orange juice	⅓ C					
Strawberry jam (1 C = 11.3 oz)	¼ C		100%			
Red plums, diced	1 # 3 oz		90%			
Fresh basil sprigs	½ oz		56%			
Red grapes, halved	1 # 5 oz		93.8%			
Sweet cherries, pitted	1 #					
Strawberries, halved (1 pt = 15 oz)	13½ oz					
Crème fraiche	1 C		100%			
					TOTAL RECIPE COST	

6 Kitchen Ratios

KEY TERMS

ratio

kitchen ratio

part size

baker's percent

KEY QUESTIONS

What is the difference between a ratio and a recipe?

How do you determine the size of one part in a ratio?

How do you change a ratio's part values into percents?

What ingredient's percent forms the basis for the baker's percent?

6.1 What Is a Ratio?

A **ratio** is a relationship between two quantities that are expressed in the same unit. (The ratio itself, however, is not written with any units.) You may have used a ratio in your daily life without even knowing it: anytime you have said something like "It's twice as far from my house to the restaurant as it is from yours" or "This saucepan is three times as expensive as this other one," you are using a ratio. Knowing one quantity (the price of the cheaper saucepan, for example) means you can figure out any other quantities involved in the ratio (the price of the expensive saucepan, in this case).

The game of roulette uses ratios to tell the players how much money they will win if the number they choose comes up. For example, a bet on a single number has 35-to-1 odds, which means a player will win $35 for each dollar bet on that number. A common way to express a ratio is to separate each number in the ratio with a colon (:), so you could write those odds as "35 : 1." This 35-to-1 ratio does not mean that you can only bet $1 on any particular number, or that you will always win exactly $35. Rather, it says that for *every* dollar you bet, you will win $35: if you bet $2, you will win $70, and a winning bet of $100 pays $3,500.

Ratios are used in the kitchen as well. Professional chefs and bakers prepare many things that are based on a ratio: mirepoix, custard, and stocks, among numerous others. (It should be noted that the mathematical definition of ratio involves only two related quantities, but in the culinary field a **kitchen ratio**—also called a kitchen formula—can be a relationship between as many ingredients as are necessary.)

Ratios give a chef tremendous flexibility when it comes to preparing certain dishes. You can use the same ratio to create two different dishes (say, by using a different kind of melon in two fruit salads). Also, adjusting the relative amounts of ingredients is made significantly easier using a ratio. Ratios allow chefs to adapt a basic relationship between a set of ingredients to many different situations.

A common ratio used in a kitchen is the weight ratio for mirepoix:

MIREPOIX				
2 parts diced onion 1 part diced carrot 1 part diced celery	diced onion	diced onion	diced carrot	diced celery
	← 2 parts →		← 1 part →	← 1 part →

This ratio says that the weight of carrot will be the same as the weight of celery. It also says that the weight of diced onion will be twice the weight of celery or carrot. For example, if you use 9 ounces of diced carrot, you must use 9 ounces of diced celery and 18 ounces of diced onion.

Mirepoix. The standard weight ratio for mirepoix is 2 parts diced onion to 1 part diced celery to 1 part diced carrot.

Even though ratios are not written with specific units, some ratios are only accurate when the ingredients are measured in a certain way. For example, the ratio for roux is 1 part flour to 1 part fat when measured by *volume*. If you measure the ingredients for roux by *weight*, the ratio is 3 parts fat to 2 parts flour. When working with a kitchen ratio, be mindful of the way the quantities are being measured (by weight or by volume).

Volume ratios versus weight ratios. The volume ratio for roux is 1 part fat to 1 part flour (equal volumes), but when the ingredients are measured by weight, the ratio is 3 parts fat to 2 parts flour.

Before we begin some calculations involving ratios, keep in mind some key differences between a ratio and a recipe:

▨ **A ratio is a general formula; a recipe is a specific set of ingredient quantities.**

▨ **A ratio sets a fixed relationship between ingredient quantities; a recipe may not have ingredient quantities that are in any particular relationship.**

▨ **A ratio will generate ingredient quantities that are all (initially) measured in the same unit; a recipe can measure ingredients by whatever units are appropriate.**

▨ **A ratio does not produce a specific quantity; a recipe will yield a specific amount of product.**

In this chapter, we will investigate two scenarios involving ratios that you are likely to encounter in a kitchen. In one case, we will start with a specific amount of one ingredient (e.g., 3 pounds of diced apples to use in a fruit salad). In the other, we will have a total yield as the goal (e.g., produce 24 ounces of roux). We will end this chapter by showing how you can work with both of these types of ratio scenarios using percents.

PART SIZE

In ratios, the word "part" represents some unknown quantity. (It's sort of like using a variable in algebra to stand for an unknown number.) The key idea behind a ratio is that no matter how many parts each ingredient represents in a ratio, *each part must represent the same quantity*, which we call the **part size**. Depending on the situation, the part size could be 5 ounces, 14 cups, or 7½ liters. The size of one part can be determined by using a known quantity in the situation:

Known quantity ÷ corresponding number of parts = part size

Even though each part in a ratio represents the same quantity, the amounts of each ingredient you will use may differ, based on the number of parts each ingredient represents in the ratio.

In the upcoming sections, we are going to demonstrate how to use the part size formula to calculate ingredient quantities. This formula will work for any ratio. However, when it is relatively simple to compare part values in a ratio (mirepoix is a good example of this), you may be able to calculate ingredient quantities or total yields without using the part size formula.

PRACTICE PROBLEMS

1. What are three differences between a recipe and a ratio?

2. What are three advantages of working with a ratio versus working with a recipe?

3. Why is it important to know if the part values in a ratio are based on weight or volume?

4. Can you modify a basic recipe to change it into a ratio? If so, how?

5. Joe was given a weight ratio of 3 parts flour to 2 parts fat to 1 part water for pie dough. He didn't have a scale, so he grabbed a pint container and measured his ingredients by volume. Will Joe's ingredient quantities work out correctly? Why or why not?

6. The standard weight ratio for pâte à choux consists of 2 parts water, 2 parts egg, 1 part butter, and 1 part flour.

    a. A chef is using a recipe that calls for 1½ pounds of water, 1 pound 4 ounces of egg, 10 ounces of butter, and 10 ounces of flour. What is the quickest way to rewrite this recipe so the ingredient amounts are in the correct ratio?

b. If you wanted to use 1½ pounds of water in this ratio, what amounts of the other ingredients should you use?

7. The standard weight ratio for pasta dough is 3 parts flour to 2 parts egg. After reviewing a recipe that calls for ½ pound all-purpose flour, ½ pound buckwheat flour, ½ pound semolina flour, and 18 eggs, a chef says, "That won't work."

a. If 1 pound of pooled eggs is equivalent to 9 eggs, explain how the chef knew this recipe was not following the standard weight ratio for pasta dough.

b. What are two ways to rewrite the recipe so it would follow the standard weight ratio?

8. Convert the following recipe into a volume ratio.

Sherry Vinegar Marinade
Makes ten 30-milliliter servings

125 mL vegetable oil

50 mL sherry vinegar

50 mL white wine

50 mL chopped parsley

25 mL salt

9. Convert the following recipe into a volume ratio.

Popover Batter
Makes 3½ quarts

1½ qt whole milk

4½ C all-purpose flour

1 qt large eggs

1½ C butter

10. Convert the following recipe into a volume ratio. Use the information from *The Book of Yields* in Appendix V as necessary. (You will need to adjust the part values slightly after converting the ingredient quantities into a ratio.)

Tomato Chutney
Makes 4 pounds

1¾ # diced Roma tomatoes

2½ C vinegar

5 oz raisins, unpacked

1 C granulated sugar

1 C diced onions

11. Convert the following recipe into a three-ingredient weight ratio (flour : fat : liquid).

Biscuit Dough
Makes 8 pounds

2 # cake flour

2 # all-purpose flour

1 # butter

⅓ # shortening

2⅔ # buttermilk

6.2 Using a Ratio When One Ingredient Quantity Is Known

Knowing the quantity of one ingredient in a ratio can help you calculate the rest of the ingredient quantities and the total yield. The ratio gives you a general relationship between the ingredients; you are looking for specific amounts that satisfy that relationship. Use the part size formula to calculate the quantity per part, then use the part values to calculate the ingredient quantities:

$$\text{part size} \times \text{ingredient's number of parts} = \text{ingredient quantity}$$

You can also multiply the part size by the total parts in the ratio to calculate the total quantity of product you will produce.

EXAMPLE 6.2.1 USING A RATIO WHEN ONE INGREDIENT QUANTITY IS KNOWN

The chef has asked you to prepare mirepoix using the 6 pounds of diced onion that is on hand. How much of the other ingredients will you need? How much total mirepoix can you make?

In this example, the ratio does not need to be explicitly stated, since a standard mirepoix is always 2 parts diced onion to 1 part diced carrot to 1 part diced celery (and, therefore, 4 parts total).

	DICED ONION	DICED CARROT	DICED CELERY	TOTAL
QUANTITY	6 #			
PARTS	2	1	1	4

Enter the given information.

Known quantity ÷ corresponding number of parts = part size
6 # ÷ 2 parts = 3 # per part

Calculate the part size using the given information.

Part size × ingredient's number of parts = ingredient quantity
DICED CARROT: 3 # per part × 1 part = 3 #
DICED CELERY: 3 # per part × 1 part = 3 #

Calculate the remaining ingredient quantities using the part size.

TOTAL: 6 # + 3 # + 3 # = 12 #
(also, 3 # per part × 4 parts = 12 #)

Add up the ingredient quantities to get the total yield.

	DICED ONION	DICED CARROT	DICED CELERY	TOTAL
QUANTITY	6 #	3 #	3 #	12 #
PARTS	2	1	1	4

We have used the ratio for mirepoix to create a specific recipe that yields 12 pounds:

RATIO	RECIPE
MIREPOIX	MIREPOIX makes 12 pounds
2 parts diced onion	6 pounds diced onion
1 part diced carrot	3 pounds diced carrot
1 part diced celery	3 pounds diced celery

When using a ratio, changing the quantity of any ingredient will change all of the other ingredient amounts—and the total amount produced—accordingly. It would be extremely inefficient for a chef to start with a ratio and create recipes for every possible total yield. This is what makes a ratio so useful in the kitchen: a chef can adapt it to any specific situation that might come up. One ratio can be used to create an unlimited number of recipes. Remember, though, that a ratio is a formula. By itself, *it does not tell you the exact quantity of any ingredient to use, nor the exact total yield you will produce.*

EXAMPLE 6.2.2 USING A RATIO WHEN ONE INGREDIENT QUANTITY IS KNOWN

A local gourmet food store sells its own brand of trail mix. It uses a weight ratio of 2½ parts peanuts, 2 parts raisins, 1 part chocolate chips, and ½ part dried cranberries. If the manager asks you to make trail mix using the 4-pound bag of shelled peanuts in the pantry, how much of the other ingredients will you need?

	PEANUTS	RAISINS	CHOCOLATE CHIPS	CRANBERRIES	TOTAL
QUANTITY	4 #				
PARTS	2½	2	1	½	6

Enter the given information.

Known quantity ÷ corresponding number of parts = part size
4 # ÷ 2.5 parts = 1.6 # per part

Calculate the part size using the given information.

Part size × ingredient's number of parts = ingredient quantity

RAISINS: 1.6 # per part × 2 parts = 3.2 #
CHOCOLATE CHIPS: 1.6 # per part × 1 part = 1.6 #
CRANBERRIES: 1.6 # per part × 0.5 parts = 0.8 #

Calculate the remaining ingredient quantities using the part size.

TOTAL: 4 # + 3.2 # + 1.6 # + 0.8 # = 9.6 #
(also, 1.6 # per part × 6 parts = 9.6 #)

Add up the ingredient quantities to get the total yield.

	PEANUTS	RAISINS	CHOCOLATE CHIPS	CRANBERRIES	TOTAL
QUANTITY	4 #	3.2 #	1.6 #	0.8 #	9.6 #
PARTS	2½	2	1	½	6

You could also organize this information in another format:

	PARTS	PART SIZE	QUANTITY
PEANUTS	2½		4 #
RAISINS	2		3.2 #
CHOCOLATE CHIPS	1	× 1.6 # =	1.6 #
CRANBERRIES	½		0.8 #
TOTAL	6		9.6 #

PRACTICE PROBLEMS

Use your knowledge of ratios to answer the following questions. Truncate answers after 4 decimal places, if necessary. Use the information from *The Book of Yields* in Appendix V as necessary.

1.   The weight ratio for mirepoix is 2 parts diced onion to 1 part diced carrot to 1 part diced celery.

   a.   If you have 15 pounds of diced onion, how much mirepoix can you make?

   b.   If you have 6 pounds of diced carrot to use, how many pounds of onions would you need to purchase?

2.   The weight ratio for cookie dough is 3 parts flour to 2 parts fat to 1 part sugar.

   a.   How many 2-ounce cookies will you be able to make if you use 1½ pounds of butter to make the dough?

b. If you use 2 kilograms of flour to make the dough, how many kilograms of the other two ingredients do you need to use?

3. The volume ratio for a Cosmopolitan is 3 parts vodka to 2 parts triple sec to 1 part cranberry juice.

   a. What volume of Cosmopolitans can you make with a quart bottle of cranberry juice?

   b. How many 5-fluid-ounce Cosmopolitans will you be able to make with one 750-milliliter bottle of vodka?

4. A volume ratio for fruit punch consists of 3 parts cranberry juice, 2 parts club soda, 1 part ginger ale, 1 part orange juice, and ½ part orange slices.

   a. You have 3 liters of club soda that you would like to use for your punch. How many liters of cranberry juice should you use?

b. How much fruit punch can you make with a 2-liter bottle of ginger ale?

5. The weight ratio for Rib Rub consists of 4 parts brown sugar, 3 parts kosher salt, 2 parts chili powder, ¾ part granulated garlic, and ½ part black pepper.

a. Your jar of granulated garlic has 3 ounces of garlic left in it. How much Rib Rub can you make using this garlic?

b. The chef asks you to make Rib Rub with a 1-kilogram box of kosher salt. How many pounds of rub will you be able to make if you use all of the salt?

6. A weight ratio for fruit salad consists of 5 parts cubed seedless watermelon, 3 parts blueberries, 2 parts sliced peaches, 2 parts halved strawberries, and ½ part shredded coconut.

   a. How much of the other ingredients should you use with a 24-ounce bag of shredded coconut?

   b. You have purchased a 6-pound seedless watermelon that you would like to use for the fruit salad. Assuming you have enough of the other ingredients, how many pounds of fruit salad will you be able to make using this watermelon?

7. A weight ratio for trail mix is 5 parts rolled oats to 2 parts almonds to 2 parts raisins to 1½ parts banana chips.

   a. How many kilograms of trail mix can you make with 400 grams of banana chips?

b. How many kilograms of trail mix can you make with 1½ pounds of almonds?

8. The volume ratio for South of the Border Marinade consists of 6 parts olive oil, 2 parts pureéd mango, 1 part tequila, 1 part fresh lime juice, and ½ part chopped fresh cilantro.

   a. If you have 1 pint of olive oil to use, how many cups of marinade can be made?

   b. If a mango yields a cup of pureéd fruit, how many mangoes do you need to use with a 500-milliliter bottle of tequila?

9. A weight ratio for a bagel topping consists of 3 parts poppy seeds, 2 parts sesame seeds, 1 part dried garlic, 1 part onion flakes, and ½ part kosher salt.

   a. If you use 9 ounces of sesame seeds, how much kosher salt should you use?

b. If each bagel uses ¼ ounce of topping, how many bagels would you be able to top if you made this topping using 5 ounces of poppy seeds?

10. The volume ratio for a fresh fruit smoothie is 2 parts sliced bananas to 1 part orange juice to 1 part crushed ice to ½ part plain yogurt.

a. If you have 1 quart of yogurt to use, how many 12-fluid-ounce servings of fruit smoothie will you be able to make?

b. How many pounds of bananas should you purchase to make smoothies with your 1 quart of yogurt?

6.3 Using a Ratio When the Desired Yield Is Known

When your goal is to prepare a specific yield using a ratio, you cannot use any ingredient amounts you want, even if they do add up to the desired total. You have to preserve the relationships between the ingredient amounts indicated by the ratio. You can use the part size formula with a desired yield in the same way you used it with ingredient quantities in the previous section. As before, we will multiply the part size by each ingredient's parts to determine the ingredient quantities.

Adaptability of ratios. The specific quantities of oil and vinegar in each container are different, but the ratio of oil to vinegar in both containers is 3 : 1.

EXAMPLE 6.3.1 USING A RATIO WHEN THE TOTAL YIELD IS KNOWN

The weight ratio for 3-2-1 Pie Dough is 3 parts flour to 2 parts fat to 1 part water. How much of each ingredient is needed to make 15 pounds of pie dough?

	FLOUR	FAT	WATER	TOTAL
QUANTITY				15 #
PARTS	3	2	1	6

Enter the given information.

Known quantity ÷ corresponding number of parts = part size
15 # ÷ 6 parts = 2.5 # per part

Calculate the part size using the given information.

Part size × ingredient's number of parts = ingredient quantity
FLOUR: 2.5 # per part × 3 parts = 7.5 #
FAT: 2.5 # per part × 2 parts = 5 #
WATER: 2.5 # per part × 1 part = 2.5 #

Calculate the remaining ingredient quantities using the part size.

	FLOUR	FAT	WATER	TOTAL
QUANTITY	7.5 #	5 #	2.5 #	15 #
PARTS	3	2	1	6

The ingredient amounts add up to the required 15 pounds.

A note about the water: weighing ingredients is often the most accurate way to measure them. If, in the end, you decide not to weigh certain ingredients, use an accurate weight-to-volume conversion to determine the correct volume. Depending on the equivalents you use, you may or may not preserve the part values in the ratio.

The part size formula will work with *any* ratio. However, working with a simple ratio such as 3 : 2 : 1 is a good example of when you may be able to use some shortcuts. For example, flour represents three out of the six total parts in the pie dough ratio above. Since three-sixths is equivalent to one-half, flour represents one-half of the total weight of the pie dough. Therefore, if you know the total weight of 3-2-1 Pie Dough you want to produce, you know that you need half that amount in flour. You can use similar reasoning with the butter (two out of the six total parts in the ratio, or one-third of the total amount) and the water (one out of the six total parts, or one-sixth of the total amount).

EXAMPLE 6.3.2 USING A RATIO WHEN THE TOTAL YIELD IS KNOWN

You have been assigned the task of preparing a citrus vinaigrette using a volume ratio consisting of 8 parts blood orange juice, 2 parts canola oil, 1 part lemon juice, 1 part honey, and ⅓ part white wine vinegar. If you need 1 quart of vinaigrette, how much of each ingredient should you use?

This ratio has 12⅓ total parts. Dividing 1 quart into 12⅓ parts means each of the ingredient amounts will be expressed as a decimal part of a quart. It will likely make the calculations (and probably the measuring) more manageable if you convert one quart to some smaller unit. Using fluid ounces seems like it would be useful in this situation.

	ORANGE JUICE	OIL	LEMON JUICE	HONEY	VINEGAR	TOTAL
QUANTITY						32 fl oz
PARTS	8	2	1	1	⅓	12⅓

Enter the given information.

Known quantity ÷ corresponding number of parts = part size
32 fl oz ÷ 12⅓ parts = 2.5945 fl oz per part

Convert 1 quart to 32 fluid ounces, then calculate the part size using the given information.

This part size is likely to give ingredient amounts that are not easy to measure, so you may need to adjust some of them slightly to make them practical to measure. Before you do any adjusting, however, calculate all of the ingredient amounts using the exact part size you just figured out.

Part size × ingredient's number of parts = ingredient quantity
ORANGE JUICE: 2.5945 fl oz per part × 8 parts = 20.756 fl oz
OIL: 2.5945 fl oz per part × 2 parts = 5.189 fl oz
LEMON JUICE: 2.5945 fl oz per part × 1 part = 2.5945 fl oz
HONEY: 2.5945 fl oz per part × 1 part = 2.5945 fl oz
VINEGAR: 2.5945 fl oz per part × ⅓ part = 0.8648 fl oz

Calculate the remaining ingredient quantities using the part size.

	ORANGE JUICE	OIL	LEMON JUICE	HONEY	VINEGAR	TOTAL
QUANTITY	20.756 fl oz	5.189 fl oz	2.5945 fl oz	2.5945 fl oz	0.8648 fl oz	32 fl oz
PARTS	8	2	1	1	⅓	12⅓

Or you could use the other chart format:

	PARTS	PART SIZE	QUANTITY
ORANGE JUICE	8		20.756 fl oz
OIL	2		5.189 fl oz
LEMON JUICE	1	× 2.5945 fl oz =	2.5945 fl oz
HONEY	1		2.5945 fl oz
VINEGAR	⅓		0.8648 fl oz
TOTAL	12⅓		32 fl oz

Adding up the exact ingredient amounts just calculated gives a total of 31.9988 fluid ounces, so the calculations seem to check. However, those ingredient quantities would most likely not be easy for someone on your staff to measure, so what should you do?

There isn't a single right answer to that question; different situations might call for different solutions. One possibility could be to round each ingredient amount to a reasonably measured quantity (e.g., 20 fluid ounces of orange juice, 5 fluid ounces of oil, etc.) and adjust the taste accordingly. Use your culinary expertise to advise your staff on how to work with ingredient quantities that are difficult or impractical to measure.

PRACTICE PROBLEMS

Use your knowledge of ratios to answer the following questions. Truncate answers after 4 decimal places if necessary. Use the information from *The Book of Yields* in Appendix V as necessary.

1. The volume ratio for a Cosmopolitan is 3 parts vodka to 2 parts triple sec to 1 part cranberry juice.

    a. How many fluid ounces of each ingredient would you need to make a 1-cup Cosmopolitan?

    b. If you need to make 3 gallons of Cosmopolitans, how many 375-milliliter bottles of triple sec would you need to use?

2. A volume ratio for fruit punch consists of 3 parts cranberry juice, 2 parts club soda, 1 part ginger ale, 1 part orange juice, and ½ part orange slices.

    a. If you need to make 12 gallons of fruit punch for a party, how many gallons of each ingredient would you need?

b. How many fluid ounces of cranberry juice would be in a 1-pint serving of fruit punch?

3. The weight ratio for Rib Rub consists of 4 parts brown sugar, 3 parts kosher salt, 2 parts chili powder, ¾ part granulated garlic, and ½ part black pepper.

   a. How much kosher salt will you use in making 2 pounds of Rib Rub?

   b. You will need 115 portions (10 ounces each) of Rib Rub for your retail sales division. How many pounds of each ingredient will you need? (For this question, round your quantities to the hundredths place, or 2 decimal places.)

4. A weight ratio for fruit salad consists of 5 parts cubed seedless watermelon, 3 parts blueberries, 2 parts sliced peaches, 2 parts halved strawberries, and ½ part shredded coconut.

    a. You need an 8-ounce serving of fruit salad for each of 68 guests. How many pounds of halved strawberries will you use in the fruit salad for this party?

    b. If you need to make 16 pounds of fruit salad, how many pounds of peaches would you need to purchase?

5. A weight ratio for trail mix is 5 parts rolled oats to 2 parts almonds to 2 parts raisins to 1½ parts banana chips.

    a. For your company picnic you would like to make to-go bags of trail mix for the guests. How many pounds of each ingredient would you need to make in order to give a 5-ounce portion to each of your 55 guests?

b. Is a 12-pound bag of rolled oats sufficient to make 30 pounds of trail mix?

6. The volume ratio for South of the Border Marinade consists of 6 parts olive oil, 2 parts pureéd mango, 1 part tequila, 1 part fresh lime juice, and ½ part chopped fresh cilantro.

   a. You need to make 5 pints of marinade. How many bunches of cilantro do you need to purchase to make this amount?

   b. How many limes would you need to purchase for the 5 pints of marinade?

7. A weight ratio for a bagel topping consists of 3 parts poppy seeds, 2 parts sesame seeds, 1 part dried garlic, 1 part onion flakes, and ½ part kosher salt.

    a. For a wholesale order, you need to produce enough topping for 18 dozen jumbo bagels. If each bagel uses ½ ounce of topping, how many pounds of each ingredient would you need for the topping?

    b. To get the nutritional information for your bagel topping, you need to convert all the ingredient quantities to grams. How many grams of each ingredient would be required for each ½-ounce portion of topping?

The following problems represent a mixture of both types of ratio scenarios discussed in this section and the previous section. You should not need any additional information, other than standard equivalents.

8. The volume ratio for Kahlúa Coconut Mudslide consists of 1 part vodka, 1 part cream of coconut, ¾ part heavy cream, ½ part Kahlúa, and ½ part Irish cream liqueur.

    a. If you need to make forty-eight 6-fluid-ounce servings of Kahlúa Coconut Mudslide, how many quarts of each ingredient would you need to use?

b. If you only have one 750-milliliter bottle of Kahlúa available, how many 6-fluid-ounce Mudslides can you make?

9. The standard weight ratio for pâte à choux is 2 parts water to 2 parts eggs to 1 part butter to 1 part flour.

   a. How many kilograms of each ingredient would you need to make 15 kilograms of pâte à choux?

   b. If you used 2 pounds of butter to make pâte à choux, how many dozen large eggs (shelled weight: 1.7 ounces per egg) would you need to use?

10. The standard weight ratio for consommé is 12 parts stock to 3 parts ground meat to 1 part mirepoix to 1 part egg whites.

   a. If you have 3 gallons of stock to use for consommé, how many pounds of mirepoix would you need? (Assume 1 cup of stock weighs 8 ounces.)

   b. The standard weight ratio for mirepoix is 2 parts diced onion, 1 part diced carrot, and 1 part diced celery. How many pounds of each vegetable would you need to purchase to make the amount of mirepoix you calculated in part (a)?

6.4 Working with Ratios Using Percents

When you work with ratios using part values, the part size is an important quantity to know. When you work with ratios using percents, the amount that corresponds with 100% can be used in a similar way to the part size. For most ratios, the total yield corresponds with 100%. (In an application of ratios called the **baker's percent,** the quantity of flour corresponds with 100%. We will discuss the baker's percent in Section 6.5.)

To calculate ingredient quantities using percents when the total yield corresponds to 100%:

1. Calculate a percent for each ingredient.

    ingredient's parts ÷ total parts in ratio = ingredient's percent

    (This formula gives an answer in decimal form.)

2. Calculate the total yield.

    known quantity ÷ corresponding percent = total yield

3. Calculate ingredient quantities.

    total yield × ingredient's percent = ingredient quantity

EXAMPLE 6.4.1 WORKING WITH RATIOS USING PERCENTS

The chef has given you the task of preparing 9 pounds of mirepoix. How much of each ingredient do you need to use?

Ingredient's parts ÷ total parts in ratio = ingredient's percent

ONION:	2 parts ÷ 4 parts (total) = 0.5 = 50%
CARROT:	1 part ÷ 4 parts (total) = 0.25 = 25%
CELERY:	1 part ÷ 4 parts (total) = 0.25 = 25%

Divide each ingredient's part value by 4 (the total number of parts in mirepoix) to calculate the percent.

	DICED ONION	DICED CARROT	DICED CELERY	TOTAL
QUANTITY				9 #
PERCENT	50%	25%	25%	100%

Enter the known information.

Total yield × ingredient's percent = ingredient quantity

ONION:	9 # × 0.50 = 4½ #
CARROT:	9 # × 0.25 = 2¼ #
CELERY:	9 # × 0.25 = 2¼ #

You already know the total yield (9 pounds). Calculate the remaining ingredient quantities by multiplying 9 pounds by each ingredient's percent.

	DICED ONION	DICED CARROT	DICED CELERY	TOTAL
QUANTITY	4.5 #	2.25 #	2.25 #	9 #
PERCENT	50%	25%	25%	100%

The ingredient quantities add up to the required 9 pounds.

EXAMPLE 6.4.2 **WORKING WITH RATIOS USING PERCENTS**

A local gourmet food store sells its own brand of trail mix, which uses a weight ratio of 2½ parts peanuts, 2 parts raisins, 1 part chocolate chips, and ½ part dried cranberries. If the manager asks you to make trail mix using the 4-pound bag of shelled peanuts in the pantry, how much of the other ingredients will you need?

Ingredient's parts ÷ total parts in ratio = ingredient's percent

PEANUTS:	2½ ÷ 6 = 0.4166 = 41.66%
RAISINS:	2 ÷ 6 = 0.3333 = 33.33%
CHOCOLATE CHIPS:	1 ÷ 6 = 0.1666 = 16.66%
CRANBERRIES:	½ ÷ 6 = 0.0833 = 8.33%

Divide each ingredient's part value by 6 (the total number of parts in the ratio) to calculate the percents.

	PEANUTS	RAISINS	CHOCOLATE CHIPS	CRANBERRIES	TOTAL
QUANTITY	4 #				
PERCENT	41.66%	33.33%	16.66%	8.33%	100%

Enter the known information.

Known quantity ÷ corresponding percent = total yield
4 # ÷ 0.4166 = 9.6015 #

Use the known ingredient amount (for peanuts, in this case) and its percent to calculate the total yield.

Total yield × ingredient's percent = ingredient quantity

RAISINS:	9.6015 # × 0.3333 = 3.2001 #
CHOCOLATE CHIPS:	9.6015 # × 0.1666 = 1.5996 #
CRANBERRIES:	9.6015 # × 0.0833 = 0.7998 #

Calculate the remaining ingredient quantities by multiplying 9.6015 pounds by each ingredient's percent.

	PEANUTS	RAISINS	CHOCOLATE CHIPS	CRANBERRIES	TOTAL
QUANTITY	4 #	3.2001 #	1.5996 #	0.7998 #	9.6015 #
PERCENT	41.66%	33.33%	16.66%	8.33%	100%

The calculated quantities are not exactly the same as those calculated the first time through this trail mix example in Section 6.2 because we rounded the percents this time. (Rounding numbers such as 3.2004 pounds to 3.2 pounds is almost always fine in this type of situation.)

PRACTICE PROBLEMS

For questions 1–6, express the given ratios using percents. Round percents to the nearest tenth, if necessary.

1. Pasta dough

   3 parts flour : 2 parts egg

2. Custard

   2 parts liquid : 1 part egg

3. Crêpe batter

   1 part liquid : 1 part egg : ½ part flour

4. Stock

    8 parts water : 8 parts bones : 1 part mirepoix

5. Crème anglaise

    4 parts milk or cream : 1 part egg yolks : 1 part sugar

6. Popover batter

    6 parts milk : 4½ parts flour : 4 parts egg : 1½ parts butter

Use your knowledge of ratios to answer the following questions. You should not need any additional information, other than standard equivalents. Round to the nearest hundredth, if necessary.

7. The standard weight ratio for roux is 60% flour to 40% fat.

   a. How many grams of flour are in a 50-gram portion of roux?

   b. To make 1 pound of roux, how many ounces of fat would you need to add?

8. The volume ratio for a Cosmopolitan is 50% vodka to 33⅓% triple sec to 16⅔% cranberry juice.

   a. If you use 300 milliliters of vodka, how many milliliters of triple sec and cranberry juice would you need to use?

b. How many fluid ounces of each ingredient would you need to make a 5-fluid-ounce Cosmopolitan?

9. The standard weight ratio for pâte à choux is 33⅓% water to 33⅓% eggs to 16⅔% butter to 16⅔% flour.

a. How many grams of each ingredient would you need to make ½ kilogram of pâte à choux?

b. If you make pâte à choux using 1 dozen large eggs (shelled weight: 1.7 ounces each), how many ounces of flour do you need?

10. The standard volume ratio for vinaigrette is 75% oil to 25% acid.

a. For a banquet you are catering you will need twenty-four 1-fluid-ounce portions of vinaigrette. How many cups of each ingredient would you need to use?

b. You are making a vinaigrette that calls for equal parts vegetable oil and sesame oil. If you use 6 fluid ounces of rice wine vinegar, how many fluid ounces of each oil would you need to add?

11. The volume ratio for a quiche custard is 66⅔% liquid to 33⅓% eggs.

a. If your liquid is 1 quart of heavy cream plus 1 pint of whole milk, how many pints of eggs do you need to add?

b. One cup of pooled eggs weighs 8.57 ounces. If you use 1 pound of pooled eggs, how many pints of custard will you be able to make?

6.5 The Baker's Percent

Much of baking relies on formulas, and ratios are a type of formula that is precise and adaptable. One frequently used ingredient in baking recipes is flour, and because of this, it is used as the basis for another application of ratios: the baker's percent.

In this process, the necessary amounts of the rest of the ingredients are calculated based on the amount of flour. The amount of flour (*not* the total yield) is designated as 100%. Then, an appropriate percent is assigned to the other ingredients—and to the total yield—based on how those amounts compare to the amount of flour. For example, if a baking ratio uses half as much water as flour, then water would be assigned 50% in the ratio. If the water amount was one and a half times that of the flour, it would be assigned 150% in the ratio.

This means that the percent that represents the total yield will always be *greater than 100%*. While this may seem strange, it is very useful information, since it gives the relationship between the total yield and the specified amount of flour. For example, if the total yield represents 250%, it means that the total yield will be 2½ times the amount of flour used. This can help a baker determine how much flour to start with if he knows the total yield he is interested in producing, or vice versa.

To calculate ingredient quantities using the baker's percent:

1. Calculate a percent for each ingredient.

    ingredient's parts ÷ flour's parts = ingredient's percent

2. Calculate the amount of flour.

    known quantity ÷ corresponding percent = quantity of flour

3. Calculate ingredient quantities.

    quantity of flour × ingredient's percent = ingredient quantity

EXAMPLE 6.5.1 THE BAKER'S PERCENT

Use the baker's percent to change the part values in the 3-2-1 Pie Dough ratio (3 parts flour to 2 parts butter to 1 part water) into percents.

Ingredient's parts ÷ flour's parts = ingredient's percent
BUTTER: 2 ÷ 3 = 0.6666 = 66.66%
WATER: 1 ÷ 3 = 0.3333 = 33.33%

Divide each ingredient's part value by 3 (the number of parts of flour in the ratio) to calculate the percents.

A quick addition of those three percents shows that the total yield will be 200% of the amount of flour used:

	FLOUR	BUTTER	WATER	TOTAL
QUANTITY				
PERCENT	100%	66.66%	33.33%	200%

Since flour represents 3 parts and the ratio has 6 total parts, the percent for the total yield makes sense: the total yield will be twice—or 200% of—the amount of flour used. If you round the fractions in the percents for the butter and the water, it will result in a small discrepancy between the sum of the percentages for the ingredients and your total percentage. Using fractions will often result in more precise calculations, but it is usually safe to assume that if your ingredient percentages add up to a number such as 199.99%, you can round that total up to 200%.

Here is a side-by-side comparison of the parts in this ratio and their corresponding percents:

PARTS	PERCENTS
3-2-1 PIE DOUGH	3-2-1 PIE DOUGH
3 parts flour	100% flour
2 parts butter	66.66% butter
1 part water	33.33% water
6 parts total	200% total

EXAMPLE 6.5.2 THE BAKER'S PERCENT

If you use 15 pounds of flour to make 3-2-1 Pie Dough, how much of the other ingredients should you use? How much total pie dough will you produce?

	FLOUR	BUTTER	WATER	TOTAL
QUANTITY	15 #			
PERCENT	100%	66.66%	33.33%	200%

Enter the given information.

Quantity of flour × ingredient's percent = ingredient quantity
BUTTER: 15 # × 0.6666 = 10 #
WATER: 15 # × 0.3333 = 5 #

You already know the amount of flour (15 pounds). Multiply 15 pounds by each of the ingredients' percentages.

TOTAL: 15 # + 10 # + 5 # = 30 #
(also, 15 # × 2.00 = 30 #)

Add up the ingredient quantities to get the total yield.

	FLOUR	BUTTER	WATER	TOTAL
QUANTITY	15 #	10 #	5 #	30 #
PERCENT	100%	66.66%	33.33%	200%

The ingredient amounts add up to the required 30 pounds.

EXAMPLE 6.5.3 **THE BAKER'S PERCENT**

How much of each ingredient do you need to make 3 kilograms of 3-2-1 Pie Dough?

	FLOUR	BUTTER	WATER	TOTAL	
QUANTITY				3 kg	Enter the given information.
PERCENT	100%	66.66%	33.33%	200%	

Known quantity ÷ corresponding percent = quantity of flour
3 kg ÷ 200%
   = 3 kg ÷ 2.00
   = 1.5 kg

Divide the given amount by its percentage to calculate the amount of flour.

Quantity of flour × ingredient's percent = ingredient quantity
BUTTER: 1.5 kg × 0.6666 = 1 kg
WATER: 1.5 kg × 0.3333 = 0.5 kg

Multiply 1½ kilograms by each of the ingredients' percentages. (These calculated amounts were rounded slightly.)

	FLOUR	BUTTER	WATER	TOTAL	
QUANTITY	1.5 kg	1 kg	.5 kg	3 kg	The ingredient amounts add up to the required 3 kilograms.
PERCENT	100%	66.66%	33.33%	200%	

EXAMPLE 6.5.4 **THE BAKER'S PERCENT**

A cookie dough ratio is 100% cake flour, 66.66% butter, 33.33% sugar, and 16.66% eggs. How much cookie dough can you make with 12 ounces of pooled eggs?

	FLOUR	BUTTER	SUGAR	EGGS	TOTAL	
QUANTITY				12 oz		Enter the given information.
PERCENT	100%	66.66%	33.33%	16.66%	216.65%	

Known quantity ÷ corresponding percent = quantity of flour
12 oz ÷ 16.66%
   = 12 oz ÷ 0.1666
   = 72 oz

Divide the given quantity by its percentage to calculate the amount of flour. (This calculated amount was rounded slightly.)

Quantity of flour × ingredient's percent = ingredient quantity
BUTTER: 72 oz × 0.6666 = 48 oz
SUGAR: 72 oz × 0.3333 = 24 oz

Multiply 72 ounces by each of the ingredients' percentages. (These calculated amounts were rounded slightly.)

TOTAL: 72 oz + 48 oz + 24 oz + 12 oz = 156 oz
(also, 72 oz × 2.1666 = 156 oz)

Add up the ingredient quantities to get the total yield.

	FLOUR	BUTTER	SUGAR	EGGS	TOTAL
QUANTITY	72 oz	48 oz	24 oz	12 oz	156 oz
PERCENT	100%	66.66%	33.33%	16.66%	216.66%

PRACTICE PROBLEMS

For questions 1–3, express the ratio in baker's percent format. Round your percentages to the tenths place.

1. ## Basic Lean Bread Dough

   Makes 34.2 pounds

   20 # bread flour

   0.14 # yeast

   0.46 # salt

   13.6 # water

2. ## Biscuit Dough

   Makes 8 pounds

   2 # cake flour

   2 # all-purpose flour

   1 # butter

   ⅓ # shortening

   2⅔ # buttermilk

3. Sourdough

Makes 20 pounds

9.2 # bread flour

0.66 # whole wheat flour

6 # water

3.87 # white sour

0.27 # salt

For questions 4–6, fill in the missing information in the chart. Round all quantities to the hundredths place (2 decimal places) and round all percentages to the tenths place.

4. Parker House Rolls

INGREDIENT	WEIGHT	PERCENT
Bread flour		
Yeast, dry		0.9%
Salt		2.3%
Sugar		4.6%
Butter		8.8%
Milk		66.1%
TOTAL	50 #	

5. Brioche Dough

INGREDIENT	WEIGHT	PERCENT
Bread flour	6 #	
Eggs	2.4 #	
Salt	0.16 #	
Sugar		15%
Yeast, dry	0.07 #	
Milk, whole	1.39 #	
Butter	3 #	
TOTAL		

6. ## Pizza Dough

INGREDIENT	WEIGHT	PERCENT
Bread flour		
Yeast, dry		1%
Salt		2%
Sugar		1.5%
Olive oil	0.51 kg	
Water		59.5%
TOTAL	18 kg	168.8%

7. The ratio for French bread is 100% flour to 66% water to 2% salt to 1.5% yeast.

   a. How much French bread can you make with 6½ kilograms of flour?

b. How many grams of each ingredient do you need to make 2 kilograms of French bread?

c. Can you make 10 pounds of French bread using 2 ounces of yeast?

8. A ratio for corn tortilla dough consists of 94.8% masa harina (corn flour), 2.6% bread flour, 2.6% pastry flour, 1% salt, and 130.9% water.

   a. How many pounds of tortilla dough can you make with 12 ounces of masa harina?

   b. How many ounces of water are in each 4-ounce tortilla?

c. For a wholesale order you will need to produce 15 dozen 2½-ounce tortillas. How many pounds of each ingredient do you need?

9. A ratio for pizza dough consists of 100% bread flour, 1% dry yeast, 2% salt, 1.5% sugar, 4.8% olive oil, and 59.5% water.

a. How many kilograms of pizza dough can you make with 5½ kilograms of bread flour?

b. How many grams of yeast do you need for each kilogram of pizza dough?

c. For tonight's dinner service, you will need thirty-two 4-ounce pizza doughs. How many pounds of each ingredient will you need to make the correct amount of dough?

Appendix I

Additional Information on Units of Measure

Notes on Weight Measures

When measuring by weight, gravitational pull varies slightly depending on your altitude. The changes in atmospheric pressure that accompany changes in altitude can affect the weight of an ingredient. However, the differences from one location to another are negligible. According to the website How Many? (see web resources at the end of this appendix), a balance scale will eliminate any weight differences, as specific counterbalances are used when measuring.

Notes on Volume Measures

There is a system of dry volume measures and a system of liquid volume measures. Corresponding units in each system are different sizes. The chart below lists vessel size in cubic inches for both the liquid and dry volume scales.

U.S. DRY VOLUME	UNIT OF MEASURE	U. S. LIQUID VOLUME
CUBIC INCHES CONTAINED IN ONE UNIT		CUBIC INCHES CONTAINED IN ONE UNIT
2,150	bushel	N/A
537.6	peck	N/A
268.8	gallon	231
67.2	quart	57.75
33.6	pint	28.88
14.6	cup	14.65
8.4	gill (½ cup)	7.219

Notes on Volume-to-Weight Relationships for Water

METRIC RELATIONSHIPS

>1 liter = 1 kilogram = 1000 grams

>1 milliliter = 1 gram

U.S. CUSTOMARY RELATIONSHIPS

>1 gallon = 8 pounds 5 ounces, or 133 ounces

>1 fluid ounces = 1.039 (or 1.04) ounces

WEB RESOURCES FOR UNITS OF MEASURE

UNITED STATES DEPARTMENT OF COMMERCE

http://www.commerce.gov

NATIONAL INSTITUTE OF STANDARDS AND TECHNOLOGY

http://ts.nist.gov/WeightsAndMeasures/Publications/appxc.cfm

BUREAU INTERNATIONAL DES POIDS ET MESURES:

http://www.bipm.org/en/home

ONLINE MEASUREMENTS CONVERSION, CONVERSION TABLES, AND METRIC CONVERSION BY SERGEY GERSHTEIN AND ANNA GERSHTEIN

http://www.convert-me.com

HOW MANY? A DICTIONARY OF UNITS OF MEASUREMENT BY RUSS ROWLETT, DIRECTOR, CENTER FOR MATHEMATICS AND SCIENCE EDUCATION, UNIVERSITY OF NORTH CAROLINA AT CHAPEL HILL

http://www.unc.edu/~rowlett/units/index.html

http://www.unc.edu/~rowlett/units/custom.html

http://www.unc.edu/~rowlett/units/sipm.html

Appendix II
Volume Unit Equivalent Visual Memorization Aids

The charts below have proven useful for memorizing volume equivalents.

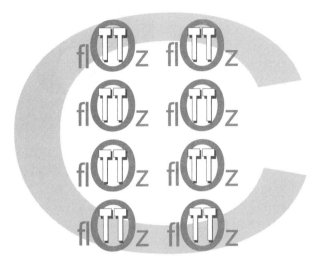

This chart can help you determine liquid volume equivalents involving units ranging from tablespoon to cup. For example, if you wanted to write an equivalent for the number of tablespoons in a cup, count the number of Ts (which represent tablespoons) in the C (which represents a cup). Since there are 16 Ts in the C, there are 16 tablespoons in a cup. You could also determine others such as 1 fluid ounce = 2 tablespoons or 1 cup = 8 fluid ounces. Even though teaspoons are not represented in this chart, knowing there are 3 teaspoons in 1 tablespoon can help you determine the number of teaspoons in a particular volume.

This chart involves liquid volume measures from 1 cup to 1 gallon. You can use this chart to figure out equivalents as you did above: by counting the number of smaller units contained in the larger unit.

This chart relates two dry volume units of measure: one bushel is equivalent to 4 pecks.

Appendix III
Changing Between Fractions, Decimals, and Percents

When working in a bakeshop or a kitchen, it is helpful to know how to change numbers between fraction form, decimal form, and percent form. Below are some procedures to help you do this. As with many aspects of mathematics, there are other valid procedures that will give you the same results as those described below. As long as you understand and can replicate the process you choose to follow, any suitable procedure will suffice.

Keep in mind that using one of these procedures does not change the quantity you have. It only rewrites the quantity in a different form. For example, writing a number as a percent (as described here) is different from using two numbers to *calculate* a percent.

1. **Starting with a fraction**

   A. **To change a fraction into a decimal,** divide the numerator by the denominator.

   EXAMPLE: Change $\dfrac{3}{16}$ into a decimal.

   $$\frac{3}{16} = 3 \div 16$$
   $$= 0.1875$$

   EXAMPLE: Change $\dfrac{7}{11}$ into a decimal.

   $$\frac{7}{11} = 7 \div 11$$
   $$= 0.\overline{63}$$

   A bar over a digit or digits (e.g., the 6 and 3 in this answer) means those digits repeat infinitely.

   B. **To change a fraction into a percent,** first change the fraction into a decimal, then move the decimal point two places to the right. Write the percent sign to the right of this new number.

   EXAMPLE: Change $\dfrac{5}{8}$ into a percent.

   $$\frac{5}{8} = 5 \div 8$$
   $$= 0.625$$
   $$= 62.5\%$$

   EXAMPLE: Change $\dfrac{7}{12}$ into a percent.

   $$\frac{7}{12} = 7 \div 12$$
   $$= 0.58\overline{3}$$
   $$= 58.\overline{3}\%$$

2. Starting with a decimal

A. **To change a decimal into a percent,** move the decimal point two places to the right and write the percent sign to the right of this new number.

EXAMPLE: Change 0.45 into a percent.

$$0.45 = 45\%$$

EXAMPLE: Change 0.7225 into a percent.

$$0.7225 = 72.25\%$$

B. **To change a (nonrepeating) decimal into a fraction,** write the digits in the decimal as the numerator of a fraction. The denominator is determined by the smallest place value in the original decimal. Reduce the fraction, if possible. (See "Reducing Fractions" at the end of this Appendix for assistance with this process.)

EXAMPLE: Change 0.35 into a fraction.

The smallest place value in this decimal is the hundredths place (where the 5 is), so the denominator is 100.

$$0.35 = \frac{35}{100}$$

$$= \frac{7}{20}$$

EXAMPLE: Change 0.312 into a fraction.

Since the 2 is in the thousandths place, the denominator is 1000.

$$0.312 = \frac{312}{1000}$$

$$= \frac{39}{125}$$

(Note: It is possible to change a repeating decimal into a fraction, but the procedure is beyond the scope of this appendix. The process often involves algebra and can get a bit tricky depending on where the repeating digits are in the decimal. Ask your instructor to show you a procedure he or she has successfully used.)

3. Starting with a percent

A. **To change a percent to a decimal,** drop the percent sign and move the decimal point two places to the left.

EXAMPLE: Change 81.3% into a decimal.

$$81.3\% = 0.813$$

EXAMPLE: Change 1.48% into a decimal.

$$1.48\% = 0.0148$$

B. **To change a percent to a fraction,** first change the percent into a decimal, and then change that decimal into a fraction (as described in Section 2B, above). Reduce the fraction, if possible.

EXAMPLE: Change 63.2% into a fraction.

$$63.2\% = 0.632$$

$$0.632 = \frac{632}{1000}$$

$$= \frac{79}{125}$$

EXAMPLE: Change 2.25% into a fraction.

$$2.25\% = 0.0225$$

$$0.0225 = \frac{225}{10000}$$

$$= \frac{9}{400}$$

C. **You can also change a percent into a fraction** by putting the digits in the percent over a denominator of 100. Reduce the fraction, if possible.

EXAMPLE: Change 18% into a fraction.

$$18\% = \frac{18}{100}$$

$$= \frac{9}{50}$$

If the percent has a decimal component, write the percent as a fraction, then move the decimal point in the numerator to the right until the numerator is a whole number. Add the same number of zeroes to the denominator as the number of places you moved the decimal point. Reduce the fraction, if possible.

EXAMPLE: Change 47.25% into a fraction.

$$47.25\% = \frac{47.25}{100}$$

$$= \frac{4725}{10000}$$

$$= \frac{189}{400}$$

Reducing Fractions

Reducing (or simplifying) a fraction means to write it as an equivalent fraction using smaller numbers in the numerator and the denominator. Frequently, you want to reduce a fraction to lowest terms; that is, you want to find an equivalent fraction with the smallest numerator and denominator.

To reduce a fraction, divide both the numerator and the denominator by a common factor. If you divide them by the greatest common factor, you will reduce the fraction to lowest terms.

EXAMPLE: Reduce $\dfrac{35}{100}$ to lowest terms.

The greatest common factor of 35 and 100 is 5, so divide the numerator and denominator by 5.

$$\frac{35}{100} = \frac{35 \div 5}{100 \div 5}$$

$$= \frac{7}{20}$$

If the greatest common factor is not readily apparent, divide the numerator and denominator by any common factor that you see. It may then be easier to see other common factors.

EXAMPLE: Reduce $\dfrac{225}{10000}$ to lowest terms.

$$\frac{225}{10000} = \frac{225 \div 5}{10000 \div 5}$$

$$= \frac{45}{2000}$$

Since 45 and 2000 have a common factor of 5, you can reduce the fraction further.

$$\frac{45}{2,000} = \frac{45 \div 5}{2,000 \div 5}$$

$$= \frac{9}{400}$$

You can also reduce a fraction by factoring the numerator and the denominator into prime factors and dividing out the common factors.

EXAMPLE: Reduce $\dfrac{40}{96}$ to lowest terms.

$$\frac{40}{96} = \frac{2 \times 2 \times 2 \times 5}{2 \times 2 \times 2 \times 2 \times 2 \times 3}$$

$$= \frac{5}{2 \times 2 \times 3}$$

$$= \frac{5}{12}$$

Appendix IV
The Butcher's Yield

The butcher's yield determines a breakdown of the various usable and unusable components of an animal and provides a system of allocating costs to these components. In the following class example, provided by chef Thomas Schneller at the Culinary Institute of America, a 12.7-pound center cut pork loin (purchased for $24.77) can be divided into components as follows:

COMPONENT	TRIM WEIGHT
Fat	0.0 #
Bones	1.2 #
Usable trim	1.2 #
Other (baby back ribs)	1.2 #
TOTAL TRIM WEIGHT	3.6 #
Total weight for the center cut pork loin	12.7 #
Less total trim weight	3.6 #
FABRICATED WEIGHT (BONELESS ROAST)	9.1 #

To calculate the yield percent, divide the fabricated weight by the AP weight:

fabricated weight ÷ AP weight = yield percent

$$9.1 \# \div 12.7 \# = 0.7165$$
$$= 71.65\%$$

You might be tempted to apportion the cost of each component based upon the percent of the AP weight that each component represents. However, not all of the components have equal value in the marketplace. Therefore, a value is assigned to each of the different components based upon their market value and these values are deducted from the AP cost, leaving the remaining (or net) cost of the desired cut.

COMPONENT	TRIM WEIGHT	×	TRIM PRICE / UNIT	=	TRIM VALUE
Fat	0.0 #	×	$0.00 / #	=	$0.00
Bones	1.2 #	×	$0.25 / #	=	$0.30
Usable trim	1.2 #	×	$1.20 / #	=	$1.44
Other (baby back ribs)	1.2 #	×	#3.50 / #	=	$4.20
TOTAL TRIM VALUE					$5.94

As-purchased cost for the center cut pork loin	$24.77
Less total trim value	$5.94
FABRICATED COST FOR THE BONELESS PORK ROAST	$18.83

To calculate the fabricated cost per pound, divide the fabricated cost by the fabricated weight:

fabricated cost ÷ fabricated quantity = fabricated cost per unit

$18.83 ÷ 9.1 # = $2.0692 / # (or $2.07 / #)

Appendix V
Information from *The Book of Yields*

This appendix contains selected information from *The Book of Yields* by Francis T. Lynch. Use this information as necessary to help you answer the practice problems in this book. If you use different relevant information than what was used to calculate the answers in the back of the book, your answers may vary slightly. If a question does not specify an ingredient in exactly the same way as it appears in this Appendix, use the closest available option.

DRY HERBS AND SPICES

ITEM	NUMBER OF TABLESPOONS PER OUNCE	NUMBER OF OUNCES PER TABLESPOON	NUMBER OF OUNCES PER CUP	NUMBER EACH PER OUNCE	NUMBER EACH PER TABLESPOON
BAY LEAF, WHOLE				130	
CHILE FLAKES, RED	5.90	0.169	2.71		
CINNAMON, GROUND	4.00	0.250	4.00		
CURRY POWDER	4.50	0.222	3.56		
NUTMEG, GROUND	4.25	0.235	3.76		
PEPPER, BLACK, CRACKED	4.00	0.250	4.00		
SALT, REGULAR	1.55	0.645	10.32		

FRESH HERBS

ITEM	OUNCES PER BUNCH OR PER AP UNIT	GARNISH LEAVES OR SPRIGS PER BUNCH	GARNISH LEAVES OR SPRIGS PER AP OUNCE	OUNCES OF STEMLESS LEAF PER BUNCH	WEIGHT YIELD PERCENT: STEMLESS LEAF PER BUNCH	OUNCE WEIGHT OF 1 TABLESPOON CHOPPED	YIELD: TABLESPOONS OF CHOPPED LEAF PER PURCHASED OUNCE	OUNCE WEIGHT OF 1 CUP CHOPPED
BASIL, SWEET	2.5	59	23.6	1.4	56.00%	0.088	6.4	1.408
CILANTRO	2.8	93	33	1.3	46.43%	0.093	5	1.486
OREGANO	1	40	40	0.78	78.00%	0.065	12	1.04
PARSLEY, ITALIAN	5.7	91	16	2.3	40.35%	0.113	3.51	1.8
ROSEMARY	1	22	22	0.8	80.00%	0.150	5.33	2.4
TARRAGON	1	48	48	0.8	80.00%	0.114	7	1.828

VEGETABLES

ITEM	AP UNIT	NUMBER OF MEASURES PER AP UNIT	MEASURE PER AP UNITS	TRIMMED/ CLEANED OUNCE WEIGHT OR COUNT PER AP UNIT	YIELD PERCENT	TRIMMED/ CLEANED OUNCE WEIGHT PER CUP	NUMBER OF TRIMMED/ CLEANED CUPS PER AP UNIT
ARTICHOKE HEARTS, MARINATED, DRAINED	jar	60	ounce	43	71.67%		
AVOCADOS, ½" DICE	each	7	ounce	5.5	78.6%	5.40	1.019
BEANS, GREEN, 1" CUT	pound	16	ounce	14.1	88.1%	3.90	3.615
BEETS, WHOLE, 2" DIAMETER	pound	16	ounce	10.56	66.0%		
BOK CHOY, REGULAR	head	24	ounce	21	87.5%		
BRUSSELS SPROUTS	pound	16	ounce	14.2	88.8%	3.20	4.438
BRUSSELS SPROUTS, MEDIUM, EACH	pound	20	each	20			
CARROTS, CHOPPED	pound	16	ounce	13	81.3%	4.90	2.653
CARROTS, DICED ⅓"–½"	pound	16	ounce	13	81.3%	5.00	2.600
CARROTS, GRATED	pound	16	ounce	13	81.3%	3.90	3.333
CARROTS, SLICED ¼"–⅙"	pound	16	ounce	13	81.3%	4.20	3.095
CAULIFLOWER, CUT 1" FLORETS	head	30	ounce	18	60.0%	4.70	3.830
CELERY, DICED ½"–⅓"	bunch	32	ounce	22	68.8%	4.00	5.500
CORN COB, FRESH NIBLETS	whole	1	each	5	29.0%	5.75	0.870
GARLIC, CHOPPED, FRESH	head	2.1	ounce	1.85	88.1%	4.80	0.402
GARLIC, CLOVES PER HEAD	head	2.1	ounce	12 cloves			
LETTUCE, BUTTER/ BIBB, CHOPPED	head	6	ounce	4.8	80.0%	1.95	2.462
LETTUCE, RED LEAF, CHOPPED	head	14	ounce	10.5	75.0%	1.95	5.385
LETTUCE, ROMAINE, CHOPPED	head	24	ounce	18	75.0%	2.00	9.000

ITEM NAME	AP UNIT	NUMBER OF MEASURES PER AP UNIT	MEASURE PER AP UNITS	TRIMMED/ CLEANED OUNCE WEIGHT OR COUNT PER AP UNIT	YIELD PERCENT	TRIMMED/ CLEANED OUNCE WEIGHT PER CUP	NUMBER OF TRIMMED/ CLEANED CUPS PER AP UNIT
MUSHROOMS, OYSTER, SLICED	basket	5.8	ounce	5.5	94.83%	2.10	2.619
ONIONS, BULB, ½" DICE	pound	16	ounce	14.5	90.6%	3.90	3.718
ONIONS, BULB, ¼" DICE	pound	16	ounce	14.5	90.6%	4.45	3.750
ONIONS, BULB, SLICED	pound	16	ounce	14.5	90.6%	3.00	4.833
ONIONS, EACH LARGE	each	13.7	ounce	12.5	91.2%		
ONIONS, GREEN, CHOPPED	bunch	3.5	ounce	2.9	82.9%	2.00	1.450
PEAS, SNAP	pound	16	ounce	15	93.8%	2.20	6.818
PEPPERS, GREEN, CHOPPED	pound	16	ounce	13	81.3%	5.20	2.500
PEPPERS, RED, CHOPPED	pound	16	ounce	13.5	84.4%	4.50	3.000
PEPPERS, RED, JULIENNE	pound	16	ounce	13.5	84.4%	3.60	3.750
POTATOES, PEELED, DICED	pound	16	ounce	12.5	78.1%	5.00	2.500
RADISHES, DAIKON	each	16	ounce	14	87.5%		
SQUASH, BUT-TERNUT, CUBED	pound	16	ounce	13.5	84.4%	4.60	2.935
SQUASH, HUBBARD, CUBED	pound	16	ounce	11.4	71.3%	4.10	2.780
SQUASH, SPAGHETTI	pound	16	ounce	11	68.8%		
SQUASH, ZUCCHINI, SLICED	pound	16	ounce	15	93.8%	3.80	3.947
TOMATOES, GRAPE	pint	11.2	ounce	82 each	98.00%	4.85	2.310
TOMATOES, PEELED, SEEDED, CHOPPED	pound	16	ounce	12.55	78.4%	5.90	2.127
TOMATOES, ROMA, DICED	pound	16	ounce	15	93.8%	5.70	2.632
TOMATOES, ROMA, SLICED	pound	16	ounce	15	93.8%	4.20	3.571

FRUIT

ITEM	AP UNIT	NUMBER OF MEASURES PER AP UNIT	MEASURE PER AP UNIT	TRIMMED/ CLEANED OUNCE WEIGHT OR COUNT PER AP UNIT	YIELD PERCENT	TRIMMED/ CLEANED OUNCE WEIGHT PER CUP	TRIMMED/ CLEANED CUPS PER AP UNIT
APPLES, FUJI, 88 COUNT, PEELED, CORED, SLICED	pound	16	ounce	11.91	74.44%	4.1	2.905
APPLES, GOLDEN DELICIOUS, 80 COUNT, PEELED, CORED, SLICED	pound	16	ounce	14.85	92.81%	3.73	3.981
APPLES, GRANNY SMITH, 88 COUNT, PEELED, CORED, SLICED	pound	16	ounce	11.82	73.88%	3.73	3.169
APPLES, MACINTOSH, 88 COUNT, PEELED, CORED, SLICED	pound	16	ounce	11.56	72.25%	3.88	2.979
APPLES, RED DELICIOUS, 80 COUNT, PEELED, CORED, SLICED	pound	16	ounce	14.38	89.88%	4.2	3.424
BANANAS, SLICED	pound	16	ounce	10.6	66.3%	5.29	2.00
GRAPEFRUIT	each	13.3	ounce	7	52.6%	7.4	0.95
KIWIFRUIT, SLICED	pound	16	ounce	13.5	84.4%	6.2	2.18
LEMON JUICE, YIELD 1 POUND	pound	16	ounce	6.62	41.4%	8.3	0.80
LEMONS, 165 COUNT WHOLE	pound	16	ounce	4 each			
LIME JUICE, YIELD 1 EACH	each	3.4	ounce	1.44	42.4%	8.3	0.17
MELON, CANTALOUPE, CUBED	pound	16	ounce	9.3	58.1%	5.65	1.65
MELON, WATERMELON, CUBED	pound	16	ounce	7.9	49.4%	5.36	1.47
ORANGE JUICE, YIELD 1 POUND, 72 COUNT	pound	16	ounce	6.01	37.6%	8.3	0.72
ORANGE JUICE, YIELD 1 EACH, 72 COUNT	each	8.5	ounce	3.2	37.6%	8.3	0.39
PEACHES, SLICED	pound	16	ounce	12.5	78.1%	6	2.08
PEARS, BOSC, 100 COUNT, PEELED, CORED, SLICED	pound	16	ounce	14.24	89.0%	4.98	2.859

ITEM	AP UNIT	NUMBER OF MEASURES PER AP UNIT	MEASURE PER AP UNIT	TRIMMED/ CLEANED OUNCE WEIGHT OR COUNT PER AP UNIT	YIELD PERCENT	TRIMMED/ CLEANED OUNCE WEIGHT PER CUP	TRIMMED/ CLEANED CUPS PER AP UNIT
RAISINS, NOT PACKED	pound	16	ounce	16	100.0%	5.1	3.14
RAISINS, PACKED DOWN	pound	16	ounce	16	100.0%	5.8	2.76
RASPBERRIES	pound	16	ounce	15.3	95.6%	4.3	3.56
STRAWBERRIES, SLICED	pound	16	ounce	14.7	91.9%	5.85	2.51
STRAWBERRIES, WHOLE, MEDIUM	pound	16	ounce	24 whole			

CANNED FOODS WEIGHT-TO-VOLUME

ITEM	TOTAL OUNCES PER #10 CAN	NET OR DRAINED WEIGHT IN OUNCES	DRAINED WEIGHT YIELD PERCENTAGE	OUNCES PER SINGLE CUP	OUNCES PER QUART	OUNCES PER HALF GALLON
BEETS, DICED (³⁄₈"), IN WATER	107.6	72.4	67.29%	5.3	21.8	48.25
CHERRIES, DARK SWEET, PITTED, IN HEAVY SYRUP	112.9	67.9	60.14%	5.9	25.9	54.05
GARBANZO BEANS, WHOLE, IN WATER	111.3	68.5	61.55%	5.65	23.05	48.4
PEARS, DICED, IN LIGHT SYRUP	108.8	61.4	56.43%	6.95	31.9	65
TOMATOES, CRUSHED, IN JUICE	101.55	101.55	100%*	8.58	35.15	70
TOMATOES, DICED, IN JUICE	108.5	67.05	61.8%	7.15	29.55	67.05

*The last three columns list drained weights unless noted by an asterisk.

DRY LEGUMES

ITEM	RAW: OUNCES PER CUP	RAW: CUPS PER POUND	COOKED: OUNCES PER CUP	1 CUP RAW YIELDS THIS NUMBER OF CUPS COOKED	1 POUND RAW YIELDS THIS NUMBER OF CUPS COOKED	1 POUND RAW YIELDS THIS NUMBER OF POUNDS COOKED	RAW TO COOKED WEIGHT PERCENT INCREASE
BLACK BEANS (TURTLE)	6.49	2.5	6.52	3.00	7.4	3.0	301%
GARBANZO BEANS	6.45	2.48	5.6	2.56	6.35	2.22	222%
KIDNEY BEANS	6.49	2.5	6.24	2.75	6.8	2.6	264%
LENTILS	6.77	2.4	6.98	3.00	7.1	3.1	309%
WHITE BEANS	7.13	2.2	6.31	2.75	6.2	2.4	243%

NUTS AND SEEDS

ITEM	OUNCES PER CUP	CUPS PER POUND	OUNCES PER PINT	PINTS PER POUND	POUNDS PER PINT
ALMONDS, SLIVERED	3.80	4.2	7.6	2.1	0.48
COCONUT, PACKAGED, SHREDDED	2.50	6.4	5.0	3.2	0.31
HAZELNUTS, CHOPPED	4.00	4.0	8.0	2.0	0.50
PECANS, CHOPPED	4.20	3.8	8.4	1.9	0.53
PINE NUTS, WHOLE, SHELLED	4.70	3.4	9.4	1.7	0.59
SESAME SEEDS, BLACK, ROASTED	4.05	3.95	8.1	1.98	0.51

FLOUR

ITEM	OUNCES PER CUP	CUPS PER POUND	OUNCES PER PINT	PINTS PER POUND	POUNDS PER PINT
FLOUR, ALL-PURPOSE	4.60	3.48	9.2	1.74	0.57
FLOUR, BREAD	4.80	3.3	9.6	1.7	0.60
FLOUR, CAKE	3.90	4.1	7.8	2.1	0.49
FLOUR, MASA (CORN)	4.15	3.9	8.3	1.9	0.52
FLOUR, PASTRY	4.25	3.8	8.5	1.9	0.53

SWEETENERS

ITEM	OUNCES PER CUP	CUPS PER POUND	OUNCES PER PINT	PINTS PER POUND	POUNDS PER PINT
GRANULATED SUGAR	7.10	2.25	14.20	1.127	0.89
HONEY	12.00	1.33	24.00	0.667	1.50
MOLASSES	11.60	1.38	23.20	0.690	1.45
POWDERED SUGAR, SIFTED	3.60	4.44	7.20	2.220	0.45
POWDERED SUGAR, UNSIFTED	4.35	3.68	8.70	1.839	0.54

SPECIAL BAKING ITEMS

ITEM	OUNCES PER CUP	CUPS PER POUND	OUNCES PER PINT	PINTS PER POUND	POUNDS PER PINT
BAKING POWDER	6.90	2.3	13.8	1.16	0.86
BAKING SODA	8.40	1.9	16.8	0.95	1.05
SALT, KOSHER, FLAKE	9.41	1.7	18.8	0.85	1.18
SALT, TABLE GRIND	10.32	1.6	20.6	0.78	1.29
YEAST, DRY ACTIVE	6.00	2.7	12.0	1.33	0.75

FATS AND OILS

ITEM	OUNCES PER CUP	CUPS PER POUND	FLUID OUNCES PER CUP
BUTTER	8.00	2.00	8
MARGARINE	8.00	2.00	8
OIL, VEGETABLE	7.70	2.08	8
SHORTENING	7.25	2.21	8

CONDIMENTS

ITEM	OUNCES PER TABLESPOON	TABLESPOONS PER OUNCE	TEASPOONS PER OUNCE	OUNCES PER CUP
HOISIN SAUCE	0.61	1.63	4.90	9.80
KETCHUP, 33% SOLIDS	0.60	1.67	5.00	9.60
MAYONNAISE, WHOLE EGG	0.48	2.11	6.32	7.60
PLUM SAUCE	0.63	1.58	4.75	10.10
SESAME TAHINI	0.55	1.81	5.42	8.85

DAIRY PRODUCTS

ITEM	OUNCES PER CUP	CUPS PER POUND	OUNCES PER PINT	PINTS PER POUND	POUNDS PER PINT
BLUE CHEESE, CRUMBLED	4.75	3.368	9.500	1.68	0.59
MILK, WHOLE (4%)	8.55	1.87	17.1	0.94	1.07
MILK, SWEETENED CONDENSED	10.80	1.481	21.600	0.74	1.35
SOUR CREAM	8.54	1.874	17.080	0.94	1.07

EGGS

SIZE OF EGGS	JUMBO	EXTRA-LARGE	LARGE	MEDIUM	SMALL
SHELLED OUNCE WEIGHT EACH	2.3	2.05	1.76	1.55	1.30

- Whites constitute 66.66%, yolks, 33.33% (or two-thirds white, one-third yolk).
- Yield of 1 large egg, shelled: 1.174 ounces white and 0.586 ounce yolk (roughly: 1.2 and 0.6).
- 1 dozen large eggs yields about 21 ounces pooled eggs, or 14 ounces whites and 7 ounces yolks.
- 1 quart of pooled eggs equals 19.44 large eggs or 22 medium eggs.
- 1 pound of pooled (shelled) eggs equals 9 large eggs (1.86 cups).

All material from *The Book of Yields* by Francis T. Lynch copyright 2008 by John Wiley & Sons, Inc. Reprinted with permission of John Wiley & Sons, Inc.

Answers to Practice Problems

CHAPTER 1

1.1 (page 5)

1. A
2. C
3. B
4. C
5. C
6. B
7. D
8.
   a. 1 quart = 4 cups
   b. 1 kilogram = 1000 grams
   c. 1 gallon = 4 quarts
   d. 1 tablespoon = 3 teaspoons
   e. 1 cup = 8 fluid ounces
   f. 1 pint = 2 cups
   g. 1 pound = 453.6 grams
   h. 1 liter = 33.8 fluid ounces

   i. 1 cup = 16 tablespoons
   j. 1 kilogram = 2.205 pounds
9.
   a. iii. ½ kilogram
   b. v. 10 milliliters
   c. ii. ½ pound
   d. i. ½ liter
   e. iv. 10 grams
   f. vi. 10 ounces

10.

Butter, cubed	approximately ½ kg
Brown sugar, light	approximately ½ kg
Sugar, granulated	approximately 120 g
Honey	approximately 360 g
Heavy cream	approximately 120 mL
Pecans	approximately 1 kg

1.2 (page 13)

1. 0.25 C
2. No, you don't have enough: 960 milliliters is approximately equivalent to 2.03 pints.
3. 1.81 C
4. 5.16 G
5. 17.01 kg
6. 7.84 times
7. 27.27 loaves
8. 3 qt
9. 4 oz
10. When the exact number of servings is not a whole number, both the rounded answer and the exact answer have been given.

    a. $\dfrac{1.5\,G}{1} \times \dfrac{128\,fl\,oz}{1\,G} = 192\,fl\,oz\,;\,48\,servings$

    b. $\dfrac{2\,G}{1} \times \dfrac{16\,C}{1\,G} = 32\,C\,;\,64\,servings$

    c. $\dfrac{1.625\,\#}{1} \times \dfrac{16\,oz}{1\,\#} = 26\,oz\,;\,34\,(34.6666)\,servings$

    d. $\dfrac{2\,qt}{1} \times \dfrac{4\,C}{1\,qt} \times \dfrac{16\,T}{1\,C} = 128\,T\,;\,64\,servings$

    e. $\dfrac{1\,pt}{1} \times \dfrac{2\,C}{1\,pt} = 2\,C\,;\,6\,servings$

    f. $\dfrac{1.5\,L}{1} \times \dfrac{33.8\,fl\,oz}{1\,L} = 50.7\,fl\,oz\,;\,16\,(16.9)\,servings$

    g. $\dfrac{1\,L}{1} \times \dfrac{1{,}000\,mL}{1\,L} = 1000\,mL\,;\,20\,servings$

    h. $\dfrac{375\,mL}{1} \times \dfrac{1\,L}{1{,}000\,mL} \times \dfrac{33.8\,fl\,oz}{1\,L} = 12.675\,fl\,oz\,;\,12\,(12.675)\,servings$

    i. $\dfrac{2.5\,kg}{1} \times \dfrac{2.205\,\#}{1\,kg} \times \dfrac{16\,oz}{1\,\#} = 88.2\,oz\,;\,14\,(14.7)\,servings$

    j. $\dfrac{1.75\,kg}{1} \times \dfrac{1000\,g}{1\,kg} = 1750\,g\,;\,14\,(14.8305)\,servings$

    k. $\dfrac{2.75\,\#}{1} \times \dfrac{453.6\,g}{1\,\#} = 1247.4\,g\,;\,24\,(24.948)\,servings$

l. $\dfrac{3\,\#}{1}\times\dfrac{16\,oz}{1\,\#}=48\,oz;\ 12\ \text{servings}$

m. $\dfrac{5\,kg}{1}\times\dfrac{1000\,g}{1\,kg}=5000\,g;\ 20\ \text{servings}$

11. Water   1.36 kg
   Yeast   567 g
   Flour, bread   9.52 kg
   Cottage cheese, low-fat   5.44 kg
   Sugar, granulated 0.51 kg
   Onions, minced   170 g
   Butter   0.68 kg
   Salt   170 g
   Dill, chopped   113 g
   Baking soda   113 g
   Eggs, large   0.68 kg
   Horseradish   21 g

12. Flour, bread   6.24 #
   Yeast, instant dry 1.52 oz
   Milk, whole   0.63 G
   Honey   3.00 oz

   Salt   2.01 oz
   Raisins   3.24 #
   Butter   0.25 #
   Egg yolks 1 ea

13. Milk   0.375 G
   Flour, AP 0.045 bag
   Oil   0.375 qt
   Butter   3.75 #
   Almonds, slivered 1.5 #
   Trout filets   22.5 #
   Lemon juice   0.9375 qt
   Parsley, dried   1.3333 jars

14. Water   1.5183 G
   Sugar   1.2127 bags
   Salt   0.0569 box
   Lemon juice   1.9012 pt
   Lemon zest   2.9629 oz
   Cornstarch   1.1243 boxes
   Egg yolks 2 dozen
   Butter   0.7495 #

1.3 (page 25)

1. Olive oil 0.31 C
   Pancetta 0.94 #
   Onion   0.70 #
   Garlic   2.63 oz
   Spinach 9.38 #
   Salt   2.58 oz
   Black pepper   0.83 oz
   Parmesan   0.70 #
   Nutmeg 0.20 oz

2. Flour   0.20 kg
   Baking powder   8 g
   Salt   6 g
   Eggs   302 g
   Egg yolks 200 g
   Vanilla extract   5 mL
   Butter   0.45 kg
   Sugar   0.40 kg
   Cornmeal   0.18 kg

3.

	INGREDIENT	VOLUME-TO-WEIGHT EQUIVALENT	NUMBER OF OUNCES IN 1 CUP	NUMBER OF FLUID OUNCES IN 1 CUP
a.	Rosemary, chopped fresh	1 T = 0.15 oz	$\dfrac{1C}{1}\times\dfrac{16\,T}{1\,C}\times\dfrac{0.15\,oz}{1\,T}=2.4\,oz$	8 fl oz
b.	Flour, spelt	1 pt = 7.8 oz	$\dfrac{1C}{1}\times\dfrac{1\,pt}{2\,C}\times\dfrac{7.8\,oz}{1\,pt}=3.9\,oz$	8 fl oz
c.	Pecans, chopped	3.8 C = 1 #	$\dfrac{1C}{1}\times\dfrac{1\,\#}{3.8\,C}\times\dfrac{16\,oz}{1\,\#}=4.21\,oz$	8 fl oz
d.	Nutmeg, ground	4.25 T = 1 oz	$\dfrac{1C}{1}\times\dfrac{16\,T}{1\,C}\times\dfrac{1\,oz}{4.25\,T}=3.76\,oz$	8 fl oz

4.

	INGREDIENT	VOLUME-TO-WEIGHT EQUIVALENT	NUMBER OF CUPS THAT 8 OUNCES WOULD FILL	NUMBER OF CUPS THAT 8 FLUID OUNCES WOULD FILL
a.	Honey	1 C = 12 oz	$\dfrac{8\text{ oz}}{1} \times \dfrac{1\text{ C}}{12\text{ oz}} = \dfrac{2}{3}\text{ C}$	1 C
b.	Lime juice	1 C = 8.3 oz	$\dfrac{8\text{ oz}}{1} \times \dfrac{1\text{ C}}{8.3\text{ oz}} = 0.96\text{ C}$	1 C
c.	Carrots, 1/3″ dice	1 C = 5 oz	$\dfrac{8\text{ oz}}{1} \times \dfrac{1\text{ C}}{5\text{ oz}} = 1.6\text{ C}$	1 C
d.	Chile flakes, red	1 C = 2.71 oz	$\dfrac{8\text{ oz}}{1} \times \dfrac{1\text{ C}}{2.71\text{ oz}} = 2.95\text{ C}$	1 C

5. 3.36 oz
6. 2 C
7. 1½ qt
8. 3.13 #
9. Yes (to make 75 tarts, you would need approximately 4.25 kg of hazelnuts)
10. 72.27 #
11. 3½ C
12. 1½ oz
13. 27 recipes
14. 26.65 g
15. 1.34 #
16. 7.01 oz
17. 4.29 pt
18. a. The sous chef assumed that 1 cup of molasses weighs 8 ounces.
    b. 8.7 oz
19. a. The extern forgot that 1 tablespoon is equivalent to ½ fluid ounce, not ½ ounce.
    b. 0.44 oz

20. Flour   6.90 #
    Baking powder   0.11 #
    Baking soda   0.07 #
    Salt   0.04 #
    Sugar   2.00 #
    Butter   1.5 #
    Sour cream   6.41 #
    Milk   1.60 #

21. Butter   28 g
    Sugar, granulated   126 g
    Egg yolks   66 g
    Flour   33 g
    Salt   6 g
    Milk   414 mL
    Vanilla extract   5 mL
    Orange juice   59 mL
    Orange zest   5 g
    Egg whites   333 g
    Sugar, powdered   10 g

CHAPTER 2

2.1 (page 40)

1. B
2. Increasing a recipe means using (and producing) larger quantities than the original recipe calls for. Thus, when you calculate a scaling factor in such a situation, you are dividing a larger number (your desired quantity) by a smaller number (the original recipe quantity). This will give you an answer that is a number greater than 1.
3. 72%
4. 250%
5. If you rounded a scaling factor of 3.4 down to 3, the scaled recipe would not yield a sufficient quantity. If you rounded it up to 4, the yield of the scaled recipe would be larger than necessary (and you may not have sufficient quantities of the ingredients).
6. 3.5 (or 3½)
7. 0.38
8. 4.17
9. 3.13
10. 3.8
11. 0.42
12. 1.51
13. 3.21
14. 2.11
15. 1.42
16. 0.43
17. 23.44
18. 0.4 (or ⅖)
19. 0.31
20. 2.25 (or 2¼)
21. 2.63
22. 0.31
23. 4.38
24. 1.86
25. No, you don't have enough. To make 50 tarts, you would need 4.6875 # of chopped leeks.

2.2 (page 47)

1. a. increasing
   b. 8
   c. 2 #
2. a. decreasing
   b. 0.39
   c. 3.12 oz
3. a. increasing
   b. 1.8
   c. 0.34 C
4. a. decreasing
   b. 0.25
   c. 3 oz
5. a. decreasing
   b. 0.19
   c. 2.28 T
6. a. increasing
   b. 8.89
   c. 1.97 #
7. a. increasing
   b. 4.26
   c. 36 fl oz
8. a. increasing
   b. 2.96
   c. 15.56 fl oz
9. 28 limes (the exact answer is 28.13 limes)
10. 10.58 oz
11. 5.4 #
12. 14.4 oz
13. 25 #

2.3 (page 57)

1. a. increasing
   b. 3.13
   c. 21.91 oz
2. a. decreasing
   b. 0.5 (or ½)
   c. 1½ T
3. a. decreasing
   b. 0.63
   c. 19 wedges (the exact answer is 18.9 wedges)
4. a. increasing
   b. 1.67 (or 1⅔)
   c. 0.72 oz

5. a. decreasing
   b. 0.59
   c. 3.54 oz
6. 2 oz
7. 6 eggs (the exact answer is 5.92 eggs)

8. 6.38 L
9. 210 mL
10. 2 #
11. 3.34 #

2.4 (page 69)

1. a. 7
   b. Shredded coconut   9.8437 #
      Sugar   4.6593 #
      Condensed milk   3 cans
2. a. 2.7
   b. Beets   20.25 #
      Sugar   1.7718 #
      Orange juice   0.3796 qt
      Chicken stock 2.7 qt
      Red wine vinegar   0.5062 C
      Butter   0.7593 #

   c. 111
3. a. 0.4
   b. Water   4.8587 #
      Sugar   2.4255 #
      Salt   0.0370 #
      Lemon juice   0.7605 pt
      Lemon zest   0.0740 #
      Cornstarch   0.4497 #
      Egg yolks   0.3516 #
      Butter   0.2998 #

CHAPTER 3

3.1 (page 77)

1. 86.45%
2. 65.62%
3. 59.38%
4. 70.36%
5. 84%
6. 45.50%
7. 83.34%

8. 60%
9. 45%
10. 71.87%
11. 94.48%
12. 82.67%
13. 62.5%
14. 71.42%
15. 65.98%

3.2 (page 84)

1. 78%
2. 92.24%
3. 19.0258 bunches
4. 128.32 oz
5. 81.792 oz
6. 1.875 bunches
7. 2.5 cases
8. 216 oz
9. 34.818 oz
10. 8.8345 C
11. 1.1851 oz
12. 10 heads (the exact answer is 9.7292 heads)
13. 4.4609 oz

14. 3 radishes (the exact answer is 2.5714 radishes)
15. 33.3 oz
16. Red; the yield is 84.4%, compared to 81.3% for green bell peppers
17. Largest: spaghetti (yield of 68.8%); smallest: butternut (yield of 84.4%)
18. 8 oranges (the exact answer is 7.7909 oranges)
19. 2.5060 #
20. No (it can be expected to yield only 197.6 oz)
21. Yes (they should yield 192 oz)
22. Your extern achieved a yield of 88.95%, so he probably fabricated Red Delicious. (Macintosh apples have a yield of approximately 72.25%.)

3.3 (page 93)

1. a. yes
    b. no
    c. yes
    d. no
    e. yes
2. a. yes
    b. yes
    c. yes
    d. no
    e. no

3. The first quantity listed is the revised recipe quantity; the second is the AP quantity.
    a. 1 #, 1 #
    b. 1.2 bu, 2.7272 bu
    c. 3 #, 3 #
    d. 2 bu, 2 bu
    e. 2.8461 ea, 5.4732 ea
4. a. 17 servings (the exact answer is 17.5522)
    b. 21 servings (the exact answer is 21.8666)
    c. 48 servings
    d. 7 servings (the exact answer is 7.02)
    e. 12 servings (the exact answer is 12.5054)

CHAPTER 4

4.1 (page 98)

1. 74 servings (the exact answer is 74.88 servings)
2. 3 oz (the exact answer is 3.0143 oz)
3. 4 oz (the exact answer is 4.104 oz)
4. 94 portions (the exact answer is 94.848 portions)
5. 49 portions (the exact answer is 49.592 portions)
6. Yes, since 10 heads is enough for 30 servings.
7. 184 servings (the exact answer is 184.32 servings)
8. 268 portions (the exact answer is 268.8 portions)
9. 68 muffins (the exact answer is 68.9381 muffins)
10. 2.0341 oz
11. 127 garnishes (the exact answer is 127.2727 garnishes)
12. 72 servings
13. 108 salads
14. 4 days (the exact answer is 4.6875 days)
15. 42 servings
16. 3 each (the exact answer is 3.0147 each)
17. 256 servings
18. 69 servings (the exact answer is 69.5826 servings)

4.2 (page 108)

1. 62½ avocados
2. 1.9208 onions
3. 5 cases (the exact answer is 4.6641 cases)
4. 5 bunches
5. 100 peppers
6. 5 bunches (the exact answer is 4.8074 bunches)
7. 42.9864 #
8. 2.4390 pt
9. 5 cases (the exact answer is 4.3985 cases)
10. 3 cases (the exact answer is 2.1428 cases)
11. 29.1666 #
12. 50 #
13. 6 cases (the exact answer is 5.9635 cases)
14. 8 zucchinis

1.

INGREDIENT	RECIPE QUANTITY	REVISED RECIPE QUANTITY	YIELD	AP QUANTITY
Mangoes, diced	2 #	2.2857 ea	68.8%	3.3222 ea
Red peppers, diced	2 ea	1.25 #		1.25 #
Lime juice, fresh	½ C	1.2205 ea	42.4%	2.8785 ea
Chili powder	½ oz	0.0312 #	100%	0.0312 #
Cilantro, chopped	1 bu	1 bu		1 bu

2.

INGREDIENT	RECIPE QUANTITY	REVISED RECIPE QUANTITY	YIELD	AP QUANTITY
Acorn squash	6 qt	6.9 #	75.6%	9.1269 #
Olive oil	6 T	0.0937 qt	100%	0.0937 qt
Onion, ¼" dice	9 C	2.5031 #	90.6%	2.7628 #
Salt, kosher flake	2 T	0.0452 box	100%	0.0452 box
Red peppers, chopped	12 ea	7.5 #		7.5 #
Garlic cloves	24 ea	0.2625 #		0.2625 #
Yogurt	3 C	0.75 qt	100%	0.75 qt
Cotija, crumbled	6 C	1.575 #	100%	1.575 #

3.

INGREDIENT	RECIPE QUANTITY	REVISED RECIPE QUANTITY	YIELD	AP QUANTITY
Butter	3 C	1.5 #	100%	1.5 #
Shallots	1 C	0.325 #	90.6%	0.3587 #
Scallions, chopped	1 C	0.5714 bu	82.9%	0.6892 bu
Chicken breasts (6 oz ea)	48 ea	18 #		18 #
Chicken broth	6 pt	3 qt	100%	3 qt
White wine	1½ qt	1.8934 bottles	100%	1.8934 bottles
Sour cream	3 C	1.5 pt	100%	1.5 pt
Spinach, stemmed	2 G	1.2 bags	65.6%	1.8292 bags
Parmesan, grated, fresh	5 C	0.9375 #	100%	0.9375 #
Salt, kosher flake	1 T	0.0226 box	100%	0.0226 box
Black pepper, cracked	⅓ C	0.1111 jar	100%	0.1111 jar

4.

INGREDIENT	RECIPE QUANTITY	REVISED RECIPE QUANTITY	YIELD	AP QUANTITY
Carrots, sliced	1½ #	1.5 #	81.3%	1.8450 #
Pickled ginger, minced	2 oz	0.125 #	100%	0.125 #
Black sesame seeds	2 T	0.0316 #	100%	0.0316 #
Scallions, thinly sliced	¾ bu	0.75 bu		0.75 bu
Sesame oil	4 t	0.0657 btl	100%	0.0657 btl

5.

INGREDIENT	RECIPE QUANTITY	REVISED RECIPE QUANTITY	YIELD	AP QUANTITY
Salt pork	12 oz	0.75 #	100%	0.75 #
Butter	10 oz	0.625 #	100%	0.625 #
Onion, small dice	2 #	2 #	90.6%	2.2075 #
Celery, small dice	12 oz	0.375 bu	68.8%	0.5450 bu
Red pepper, small dice	2¼ #	2.25 #	84.4%	2.6658 #
Flour, all-purpose	4¾ C	1.3656 #	100%	1.3656 #
Chicken stock	2½ G	2.5 G	100%	2.5 G
Corn niblets, fresh	8 #	0.6274 dozen	29%	2.1634 dozen
Potatoes, peeled and diced	10 #	0.2 bag	78.1%	0.2560 bag
Bay leaves	4 ea	0.0051 jar		0.0051 jar
Half-and-half	6 pt	1.5 ½ G	100%	1.5 ½ G
Tabasco sauce	¼ C	0.3333 bottle	100%	0.3333 bottle
Worcestershire sauce	2 T	0.125 bottle	100%	0.125 bottle
Salt, kosher flake	3 T	0.0678 box	100%	0.0678 box
Black pepper, cracked	1 T	0.0208 jar	100%	0.0208 jar

Lobster Salad with Beets, Mango, Avocado, and Orange Dressing

INGREDIENT	SCALED RECIPE QUANTITY	REVISED SCALED RECIPE QUANTITY	YIELD	AP QUANTITY
Lobster meat, cooked and sliced	9 #	9 #	100%	9 #
Red beets, cooked, peeled and sliced	72 oz	4.5 #	66%	6.8181 #
Mangoes, sliced	18 ea	18 ea		18 ea
Avocados, sliced	24 ea	24 ea		24 ea
Tomatoes, peeled, seeded and sliced	30 oz	1.875 #	78.4%	2.3915 #
Salt, regular	6 t	1.29 oz	100%	1.29 oz

Orange Dressing

INGREDIENT	SCALED RECIPE QUANTITY	REVISED SCALED RECIPE QUANTITY	YIELD	AP QUANTITY
Olive oil	40 fl oz	1.1834 L	100%	1.1834 L
Orange juice, fresh	20 fl oz	2.4411 ea	37.6%	6.4922 ea
Vanilla extract	3⅓ t	0.0347 btl	100%	0.0347 btl
Black pepper, cracked	1⅔ t	0.1388 oz	100%	0.1388 oz
Salt, regular	6⅔ t	1.4333 oz	100%	1.4333 oz

Crêpes Suzette

INGREDIENT	SCALED RECIPE QUANTITY	REVISED SCALED RECIPE QUANTITY	YIELD	AP QUANTITY
Sugar, granulated	340 g	0.7495 #	100%	0.7495 #
Butter, cubed	1360 g	2.9982 #	100%	2.9982 #
Orange juice, fresh	720 mL	2.9704 ea	37.6%	7.9 ea
Grand Marnier	720 mL	0.96 btl	100%	0.96 btl
Brandy	720 mL	0.48 btl	100%	0.48 btl

Dessert Crêpes

INGREDIENT	SCALED RECIPE QUANTITY	REVISED SCALED RECIPE QUANTITY	YIELD	AP QUANTITY
Eggs	24 ea	2 dozen		2 dozen
Heavy cream	2880 mL	6.084 pt	100%	6.084 pt
Milk, whole	1362 mL	0.3596 G	100%	0.3596 G
Butter, melted	84 g	0.1851 #	100%	0.1851 #
Flour, all-purpose	1362 g	3.0026 #	100%	3.0026 #
Confectioners' sugar	306 g	0.6746 #	100%	0.6746 #
Salt, regular	30 g	1.0582 oz	100%	1.0582 oz
Vanilla extract	48 mL	0.1014 btl	100%	0.1014 btl

Grocery List for Orange Growers of America Luncheon

Makes 48 servings

INGREDIENT	AP QUANTITY FOR LOBSTER SALAD	AP QUANTITY FOR ORANGE DRESSING	AP QUANTITY FOR CRÊPES SUZETTE	AP QUANTITY FOR DESSERT CRÊPES	TOTAL AP QUANTITY
Avocados	24 ea				24 ea
Beets	6.8181 #				6.8181 #
Black pepper, cracked		0.1388 oz			0.1388 oz
Brandy			0.48 btl		0.48 btl
Butter			2.9982 #	0.1851 #	3.1833 #
Confectioners' sugar				0.6746 #	0.6746 #
Eggs				2 dozen	2 dozen
Flour, all-purpose				3.0026 #	3.0026 #
Grand Marnier			0.96 btl		0.96 btl
Heavy cream				6.084 pt	6.084 pt
Lobster	9 #				9 #
Mangoes	18 ea				18 ea
Milk, whole				0.3596 G	0.3596 G
Olive oil		1.1834 L			1.1834 L
Orange juice, fresh		6.4922 ea	7.9 ea		14.3922 ea
Salt, regular	1.29 oz	1.4333 oz		1.0582 oz	3.7815 oz
Sugar, granulated			0.7495 #		0.7495 #
Tomatoes	2.3915 #				2.3915 #
Vanilla extract		0.0347 btl		0.1014 btl	0.1361 btl

CHAPTER 5

5.1 (page 133)

1. a. $1.1468 / C
    b. $0.1433 / fl oz
2. a. $0.273 / #
    b. $0.6019 / kg
3. a. $0.4118 / oz
    b. $14.5309 / kg
4. a. $1.72 / bu
    b. $0.86 / # (using 1 bunch = 32 oz)
5. a. $0.225 / oz
    b. $2.70 / C (using 1 C = 12 oz)

6. a. $0.0177 / g
    b. $2.3646 / C (using 1 C = 4.7 oz)
7. a. $1.35 / bu
    b. $0.54 / oz (using 1 bu = 2.5 oz)
8. a. $0.3411 / oz
    b. $1.6202 / C (using 1 C = 4.75 oz)
9. a. $0.0071 / mL
    b. $0.2112 / fl oz
10. a. $1.94 / can
    b. $0.194 / oz
    c. $2.0952 / C (using 1 C = 10.8 oz)

5.2 (page 145)

1. $1.38
2. $6.97
3. $0.88
4. $3.89
5. $8.95
6. $0.94
7. $0.07
8. $1.73
9. $3.73
10. $0.88
11. $0.26
12. $2.05
13. $3.80
14. $31.62
15. $0.32

16. $8.52
17. $6.46
18. $2.91
19. $6.71
20. $0.71
21. $0.44
22. $2.64
23. a. $1.00 + $1.3875 + $0.4464 + $11.1595
        = $13.9932 ———→$14.00
    b. $1.75
    c. $0.4375
24. a. $0.4487 + $0.1239 + $1.3474 + $3.8807
        + $0.0065 = $5.8072 ———→$5.81
    b. $0.3873
    c. $0.2904

5.3 (page 159)

1. a. 25%
    b. 33.94%
    c. 26.73%
    d. $9.48
    e. $9.74
    f. $15.37
2. 21.53%
3. 15.50%
4. $2.72
5. $3.65
6. $985.46
7. $1,310.13
8. C
9. C

10. D
11. A
12. $13.51
13. $8.39
14. 16.8%
15. 20.54%
16. It would decrease by 1.71% (to 19.29%)
17. It would increase by 1.81% (to 41.81%)
18. It would increase by 1.19% (from 25.97% to 27.16%)
19. It would increase by 2.34% (from 14.70% to 17.04%)
20. It would decrease by 1.13% (from 32.12% to 30.99%)
21. It would decrease by 2.52% (from 13.83% to 11.31%)
22. Total ingredient costs: $931.84, total sales: $3763.95; overall food cost percent = 24.75%

For questions 1–7, you may calculate slightly different ingredient costs, depending on if (and how) you round either your revised recipe quantities or your AP quantities on the recipe costing form.

1. Beef $12.0526
   Onions $0.4635
   Garlic $0.1135
   Vegetable oil $0.16
   Beef stock $0.9375
   Tomato purée $2.4137
   Jalapeños $0.1330
   Chili powder $0.6437
   Cumin $0.6602
   Kidney beans $0.295
   Salt $0.0059
   Total recipe cost = $17.88, cost per portion = $1.192, selling price = $4.77

2. Chicken breasts $10.125
   Yogurt $2.76
   Cayenne pepper $0.0097
   Iceberg lettuce $1.62
   Shallots $0.1587
   Olive oil $0.4659
   Gin $2.7329
   Grapes $1.2111
   Chicken stock $0.3125
   Corn syrup $0.3396
   Thyme $0.1374
   Cornstarch $0.0176
   Total recipe cost = $19.90, cost per portion = $1.6583, selling price = $8.30

3. Pizza dough $1.00
   Olive oil $0.2697
   Basil $0.0669
   Oregano $0.1709
   Tomatoes $0.8725
   Mozzarella $3.7235
   Parmesan $0.4954
   Black pepper $0.0498
   Garlic $0.0367
   Total recipe cost = $6.69, cost per portion = $0.669, selling price = $2.68

4. Flour $2.139
   Baking powder $0.1832
   Baking soda $0.0400
   Salt $0.0201
   Sugar $1.2220
   Butter $3.075
   Sour cream $9.54
   Milk $0.7856
   Total recipe cost = $17.01, cost per portion = $0.2362, selling price = $1.97

5. Onion $0.3406
   Red pepper $5.2110
   Green pepper $1.4643
   Carrots $0.4758
   Celery $1.1266
   Garlic $0.0567
   Sesame oil $0.0727
   Soy sauce $1.7499
   Five-spice powder $0.0526
   Sesame seeds $0.0386
   Green onions $0.8965
   Total recipe cost = $11.49, cost per portion = $1.149, food cost percent = 12.83%

6. Flour $7.05
   Butter $20.50
   Shortening $14.1333
   Salt $0.2557
   Total recipe cost = $41.94, cost per portion = $0.4368

7. Apples, Macintosh $0.825
   Apples, Granny Smith $0.81
   Sugar $0.2295
   Lemon juice $0.1256
   Flour $0.0193
   Cinnamon $0.0549
   Crumb topping $1.50
   Pie dough $0.4368
   Total recipe cost = $4.01, cost per portion = $0.5012, food cost percent = 15.42%

8. 0.3125 #

9. 0.6625 #

10. 0.2875 oz

11. Bananas

12.	0.5882 #	24.	0.5291 oz
13.	3.2845 ea	25.	9.7%
14.	5.1939 ea	26.	0.0375 #
15.	$0.0187 / oz	27.	2.7496 #
16.	$0.04 / fl oz	28.	$0.0574 / fl oz
17.	$0.48	29.	$0.0098 / mL
18.	$0.2756	30.	$1.1760
19.	$0.5235	31.	$0.0714
20.	$0.2808	32.	$0.0260
21.	$2.75	33.	$1.8416
22.	15.23%	34.	14.16%
23.	2.0105 oz	35.	$15.35

36. ## RECIPE COSTING FORM

Menu item   Halibut Steaks Provençal   Date _____

Number of portions   4   Size _____

Cost per portion $4.6075   Selling price $11.82   Food cost %   39%

RECIPE QUANTITY		REVISED RECIPE QUANTITY (IN PURCHASING UNIT)	QUANTITY TO PURCHASE		TOTAL COST	
Ingredient	Quantity	Revised Quantity	Yield %	AP Quantity	AP Cost	Ingredient Cost
Halibut steaks	24 oz	1.5 #	100%	1.5 #	$10.85 / #	$16.275
Onion, minced	¾ C	3 oz	90.6%	3.3112 oz	$0.05 / oz	$0.1655
Garlic cloves, minced	4 ea	0.0437 #		0.0437 #	$1.28 / #	$0.0559
Plum tomatoes, peeled and seeded	1¼ #	1.25 #	78.4%	1.5943 #	$1.09 / #	$1.7378
Olive oil	2 T	0.0295 L	100%	0.0295 L	$6.50 / L	$0.1917
					TOTAL RECIPE COST	$18.43

37.

RECIPE COSTING FORM

Menu item ___Asian Noodle Soup___   Date _____

Number of portions ___8___   Size _____

Cost per portion ___$0.4913___   Selling price ___$6.95___   Food cost % ___7%___

RECIPE QUANTITY		REVISED RECIPE QUANTITY (IN PURCHASING UNIT)	QUANTITY TO PURCHASE		TOTAL COST	
Ingredient	Quantity	Revised Quantity	Yield %	AP Quantity	AP Cost	Ingredient Cost
Buckwheat noodles	175 g	0.35 box	100%	0.35 box	$2.00 / box	$0.70
Chicken broth	2 L	0.5281 G	100%	0.5281 G	$2.19 / G	$1.1565
Lemongrass, trimmed and crushed	100 g	0.2204 #	65%	0.3391 #	$3.58 / #	$1.2142
Cilantro	½ bu	0.5 bu		0.5 bu	$1.50 / bu	$0.75
Chile flakes	5 g	0.0293 jar	100%	0.0293 jar	$3.95 / jar	$0.1137
					TOTAL RECIPE COST	**$3.93**

38.

RECIPE COSTING FORM

Menu item ___Berry Coulis___   Date _____

Number of portions ___24___   Size _____

Cost per portion ___$0.2541___   Selling price ___$1.16___   Food cost % ___22%___

RECIPE QUANTITY		REVISED RECIPE QUANTITY (IN PURCHASING UNIT)	QUANTITY TO PURCHASE		TOTAL COST	
Ingredient	Quantity	Revised Quantity	Yield %	AP Quantity	AP Cost	Ingredient Cost
Raspberries, cleaned	1 qt	2 pt	95.6%	2.0920 pt	$1.95 / pt	$4.0794
Strawberries, hulled and sliced	½ #	0.3418 qt	91.9%	0.3719 qt	$3.00 / qt	$1.1157
Sugar, granulated	12 oz	0.75 #	100%	0.75 #	$2.04 / 5 #	$0.306
Lemons, juiced	2 ea	2 ea		2 ea	$0.25 / ea	$0.50
Vanilla	1 t	4.9309 mL	100%	4.9309 mL	$6.00 / 300 mL	$0.0986
					TOTAL RECIPE COST	**$6.10**

39. RECIPE COSTING FORM

Menu item __Butternut Squash Soup__   Date _____

Number of portions __6__   Size _____

Cost per portion __$0.4016__   Selling price __$3.35__   Food cost % __12%__

RECIPE QUANTITY		REVISED RECIPE QUANTITY (IN PURCHASING UNIT)	QUANTITY TO PURCHASE		TOTAL COST	
Ingredient	Quantity	Revised Quantity	Yield %	AP Quantity	AP Cost	Ingredient Cost
Onion, large, diced	1 ea	0.8562 #		0.8562 #	$0.69 / #	$0.5908
Butternut squash, peeled and cubed	3½ C	1.0062 #	84.4%	1.1919 #	$0.46 / #	$0.5482
Chicken stock	1 qt	0.25 G	100%	0.25 G	$2.00 / G	$0.50
Salt, kosher flake	2 t	0.392 oz	100%	0.392 oz	$1.00 / 26 oz	$0.015
Heavy cream	1 C	0.25 qt	100%	0.25 qt	$3.00 / qt	$0.75
					TOTAL RECIPE COST	**$2.41**

1. **RECIPE COSTING FORM**

Menu item	Halibut Steaks Provençal	Date	
Number of portions	4	Portion size	
Cost per portion	$4.6850 Selling price $11.81	Food cost percent	39.00%

RECIPE QUANTITY			REVISED RECIPE QUANTITY		QUANTITY TO PURCHASE			AP COST			INGREDIENT COST
Ingredient	Quantity	Unit	Quantity	Unit	Yield %	APQ	Unit	APC	No.	Unit	
Halibut steaks	24.00	oz	1.5000	#	100.00%	1.5000	#	$10.85	1	#	$16.2750
Onion	0.75	C	3.0000	oz	90.60%	3.3113	oz	$0.05	1	oz	$0.1655
Garlic cloves	4.00	ea	0.0437	#	100.00%	0.0437	#	$1.08	1	#	$0.0471
Plum tomatoes	1.25	#	1.2500	#	78.40%	1.5944	#	$1.29	1	#	$2.0567
Olive oil	2.00	T	0.0295	L	100.00%	0.0295	L	$6.50	1	L	$0.1917
				0	0.00%	0.0000	0				$0.0000
				0	0.00%	0.0000	0				$0.0000
				0	0.00%	0.0000	0				$0.0000
				0	0.00%	0.0000	0				$0.0000
				0	0.00%	0.0000	0				$0.0000
				0	0.00%	0.0000	0				$0.0000
				0	0.00%	0.0000	0				$0.0000
				0	0.00%	0.0000	0				$0.0000
				0	0.00%	0.0000	0				$0.0000
									TOTAL RECIPE COST		$18.74

2. **RECIPE COSTING FORM**

Menu item — Asian Noodle Soup

Date —

Number of portions — 8

Portion size —

Cost per portion — $0.4925

Selling price — $6.95

Food cost percent — 7.09%

RECIPE QUANTITY			REVISED RECIPE QUANTITY		QUANTITY TO PURCHASE			AP COST			INGREDIENT COST
Ingredient	Quantity	Unit	Quantity	Unit	Yield %	APQ	Unit	APC	No.	Unit	
Buckwheat noodles	175.00	g	0.3500	box	100.00%	0.3500	box	$2.00	1	box	$0.7000
Chicken broth	2.00	L	0.5281	G	100.00%	0.5281	G	$2.19	1	G	$1.1565
Lemongrass	100.00	g	0.2204	#	65.00%	0.3391	#	$3.58	1	#	$1.2138
Cilantro	0.50	bu	0.5000	bu	100.00%	0.5000	bu	$1.50	1	bu	$0.7500
Chili flakes	5.00	g	0.1763	oz	100.00%	0.1763	oz	$3.95	6	oz	$0.1160
				0	0.00%	0.0000	0				$0.0000
				0	0.00%	0.0000	0				$0.0000
				0	0.00%	0.0000	0				$0.0000
				0	0.00%	0.0000	0				$0.0000
				0	0.00%	0.0000	0				$0.0000
				0	0.00%	0.0000	0				$0.0000
				0	0.00%	0.0000	0				$0.0000
				0	0.00%	0.0000	0				$0.0000
				0	0.00%	0.0000	0				$0.0000
									TOTAL RECIPE COST		$3.94

3. **RECIPE COSTING FORM**

Menu item	Berry Coulis	Date	
Number of portions	24	Portion size	
Cost per portion	$0.2542	Selling price $1.16	Food cost percent 22.00%

RECIPE QUANTITY			REVISED RECIPE QUANTITY		QUANTITY TO PURCHASE			AP COST			INGREDIENT COST
Ingredient	Quantity	Unit	Quantity	Unit	Yield %	APQ	Unit	APC	No.	Unit	
Raspberries	1.00	qt	2.0000	pt	95.60%	2.0921	pt	$1.95	1	pt	$4.0794
Strawberries	0.50	#	0.3418	qt	91.90%	0.3719	qt	$3.00	1	qt	$1.1157
Sugar, granulated	12.00	oz	0.7500	#	100.00%	0.7500	#	$2.04	5	#	$0.3060
Lemons	2.00	ea	2.0000	ea	100.00%	2.0000	ea	$0.25	1	ea	$0.5000
Vanilla	1.00	t	4.9309	mL	100.00%	4.9309	mL	$6.00	300	mL	$0.0986
				0	0.00%	0.0000	0				$0.0000
				0	0.00%	0.0000	0				$0.0000
				0	0.00%	0.0000	0				$0.0000
				0	0.00%	0.0000	0				$0.0000
				0	0.00%	0.0000	0				$0.0000
				0	0.00%	0.0000	0				$0.0000
				0	0.00%	0.0000	0				$0.0000
				0	0.00%	0.0000	0				$0.0000
				0	0.00%	0.0000	0				$0.0000
							TOTAL RECIPE COST				$6.10

4. RECIPE COSTING FORM

Menu item: **Butternut Squash Soup**   Date: _____

Number of portions: **6**   Portion size: _____

Cost per portion: **$0.4017**   Selling price: **$3.35**   Food cost percent: **12.00%**

RECIPE QUANTITY			REVISED RECIPE QUANTITY		QUANTITY TO PURCHASE			AP COST			INGREDIENT COST
Ingredient	Quantity	Unit	Quantity	Unit	Yield %	APQ	Unit	APC	No.	Unit	
Onion	1.00	ea	0.8562	#	100.00%	0.8562	#	$0.69	1	#	$0.5907
Butternut squash	3.50	C	1.0060	#	84.40%	1.1919	#	$0.46	1	#	$0.5482
Chicken stock	1.00	qt	0.2500	G	100.00%	0.2500	G	$2.00	1	G	$0.5000
Kosher salt	2.00	t	0.3920	oz	100.00%	0.3920	oz	$1.00	26	oz	$0.0150
Heavy cream	1.00	C	0.2500	qt	100.00%	0.2500	qt	$3.00	1	qt	$0.7500
				0	0.00%	0.0000	0				$0.0000
				0	0.00%	0.0000	0				$0.0000
				0	0.00%	0.0000	0				$0.0000
				0	0.00%	0.0000	0				$0.0000
				0	0.00%	0.0000	0				$0.0000
				0	0.00%	0.0000	0				$0.0000
				0	0.00%	0.0000	0				$0.0000
				0	0.00%	0.0000	0				$0.0000
				0	0.00%	0.0000	0				$0.0000
				0	0.00%	0.0000	0				$0.0000
									TOTAL RECIPE COST		**$2.41**

5.6 (page 207)

1. Option A ($0.0378 / fl oz, compared to $0.047 / fl oz for option B)
2. Option B ($2.9995 / #, compared to $3.5102 / # for option A)
3. Option B ($4.50 / G, compared to $10 / G for option A)
4. Option A ($0.4453 / fl oz, compared to $0.4659 / fl oz for option B and $0.4806 / fl oz for option C)
5. $2.3021 / #
6. $7.8228 / #
7. $1.4814 / #
8. $0.7285 / oz
9. $0.0161 / oz
10. Option A ($3.5211 / #, compared to $3.99 / # for option B)
11. Option B ($1.9569 / #, compared to $2.09 / # for option A)
12. Option B ($0.1539 / oz, compared to $0.2087 / oz for option A)
13. Option B ($0.0667 / fl oz, compared to $0.0883 / fl oz for option A)
14. Option C ($0.1843 / oz, compared with $0.4111 / oz for option A and $0.2778 / oz for option B)

15. Option C ($0.0406 / oz, compared with $0.0599 / oz for option A and $0.0636 / oz for option B)

16. The ingredient costs listed below are the cheaper option for each ingredient.

White wine	$1.3412 (option B)	
Crème de cassis	$2.493 (option B)	
Orange juice	$0.0527 (option A)	
Strawberry jam	$0.1644 (option B)	
Red plums	$1.5026 (option B)	
Basil	$0.6249 (option B)	
Red grapes	$2.2037 (option B)	
Sweet cherries	$2.6736 (option B)	
Strawberries	$1.6453 (option B)	
Crème fraiche	$2.69 (option A)	

Lowest total recipe cost = $15.40

CHAPTER 6

6.1 (page 217)

1. Possible answers include:
   A recipe calls for specific ingredient amounts; a ratio only gives a general formula.
   A recipe does not have to use the same units to measure all of the ingredients; a ratio most often will, once it is adapted to a specific situation.
   A recipe produces a specific yield; a ratio does not, by itself, produce any specific amount.

2. Possible answers include:
   A ratio can be adapted to work with any desired ingredient quantities or any desired yield.
   A ratio is often easy to remember (compared to remembering a recipe).
   A ratio is a tried-and-true formula that you are sure will work correctly, if you use it appropriately.
   A ratio allows for creativity based on knowledge of a standard formula.

3. Not all ingredients have the same volume-to-weight equivalent. The relationship between the volumes of two ingredients may not translate into the same weight relationship.

4. Convert all ingredient quantities into the same unit of measure, then determine the relationship between those quantities.

5. The ingredient quantities will not work out when measured by volume, since the volume-to-weight equivalents are not the same for all three of the ingredients in the ratio.

6. a. Since the egg, butter, and flour amounts are in the correct ratio (relatively speaking), change the amount of water to 1 pound 4 ounces (the same as the egg).
   b. 1½ # egg, ¾ # butter, ¾ # flour

7. a. Since the total weight of the flour is 1½ pounds, the recipe should call for the equivalent of 1 pound of egg, or 9 eggs.
   b. Change the recipe so it calls for 9 eggs, or so it calls for 3 pounds total of flour (most likely, by calling for 1 pound of each type of flour).

8. Possible ratios include 2½ : 1 : 1 : 1 : ½ or 5 : 2 : 2 : 2 : 1.

9. Possible ratios include 3 : 2¼ : 2 : ¾, 6 : 4½ : 4 : 1½, or 12 : 9 : 8 : 3.

10. After converting all the ingredient quantities into volume, the ratio is 4.91 : 2.5 : 0.98 : 1 : 1. A reasonable adjustment is to make the ratio 5 : 2½ : 1 : 1 : 1.

11. 3 : 1 : 2

6.2 (page 225)

1. a. 30 #
   b. 13.245 #
2. a. 36
   b. 1⅓ kg fat, ⅔ kg sugar
3. a. 6 qt (or an equivalent volume)
   b. 10
4. a. 4½ L
   b. 15 L
5. a. 41 oz
   b. 7.5337 #

6. a. 240 oz watermelon, 144 oz blueberries, 96 oz sliced peaches, 96 oz halved strawberries (or equivalent weights)
   b. 7.41 #
7. a. 2.8 kg
   b. 3.5714 kg
8. a. 3½ cups
   b. 4.225 ea
9. a. 2.25 oz
   b. 50 bagels
10. a. 24 servings
    b. 7.9788 #

6.3 (page 234)

1. a. 4 fl oz vodka, 2⅔ fl oz triple sec, 1⅓ fl oz cranberry juice
   b. 10.0986 bottles
2. a. 4.8 G cranberry juice, 3.2 G club soda, 1.6 G ginger ale, 1.6 G orange juice, 0.8 G orange slices
   b. 6.4 fl oz
3. a. 0.5853 # (or an equivalent weight)
   b. 28.05 # brown sugar, 21.04 # kosher salt, 14.02 # chili powder, 5.26 # granulated garlic, 3.51 # black pepper
4. a. 5.44 #
   b. 3.2778 #
5. a. 8.1845 # rolled oats, 3.2738 # almonds, 3.2738 # raisins, 2.4553 # banana chips
   b. No (to make 30 # of trail mix, you would need 14.2857 # of rolled oats)

6. a. 0.5443 bu
   b. 5.4888 ea
7. a. 2.7 # poppy seeds, 1.8 # sesame seeds, 0.9 # dried garlic, 0.9 # onion flakes, 0.45 # kosher salt
   b. 5.67 g poppy seeds, 3.78 g sesame seeds, 1.89 g dried garlic, 1.89 g onion flakes, 0.945 g kosher salt
8. a. 2.4 qt vodka, 2.4 qt cream of coconut, 1.8 qt heavy cream, 1.2 qt Kahlúa, 1.2 qt Irish cream liqueur
   b. 31 (the exact answer is 31.6875)
9. a. 5 kg water, 5 kg eggs, 2.5 kg butter, 2.5 kg flour
   b. 3.1372 dozen
10. a. 2 #
    b. 1.1037 # onion, 0.615 # carrot, 0.7267 # celery

6.4 (page 243)

1. 60% flour : 40% egg
2. 66⅔% liquid : 33⅓% egg
3. 40% liquid : 40% egg : 20% flour
4. 47% water : 47% bones : 6% mirepoix
5. 66⅔% milk or cream : 16⅔% egg yolks : 16⅔% sugar
6. 37½% milk : 28.1% flour : 25% egg : 9.4% butter
7. a. 30 g
   b. 6.4 oz

8. a. 200 mL triple sec, 100 mL cranberry juice
   b. 2½ fl oz vodka, 1⅔ fl oz triple sec, 0.83 fl oz cranberry juice
9. a. 166⅔ g water, 166⅔ g eggs, 83⅓ g butter, 83⅓ g flour
   b. 10.2 oz
10. a. 2¼ C oil, ¾ C acid
    b. 9 fl oz
11. a. 1½ pt
    b. 2.8 pt

1. 100% bread flour, 0.7% yeast, 2.3% salt, 68% water
2. 50% cake flour, 50% all-purpose flour, 25% butter, 8⅓% shortening, 66⅔% buttermilk
3. 93.3% bread flour, 6.7% whole wheat flour, 60.9% water, 39.2% white sour, 2.7% salt

4. # Parker House Rolls

INGREDIENT	WEIGHT	PERCENT
Bread flour	27.37 #	100%
Yeast, dry	0.25 #	0.9%
Salt	0.63 #	2.3%
Sugar	1.26 #	4.6%
Butter	2.41 #	8.8%
Milk, whole	18.09 #	66.1%
TOTAL	50 #	182.7%

5. # Brioche Dough

INGREDIENT	WEIGHT	PERCENT
Bread flour	6 #	100%
Eggs	2.4 #	40%
Salt	0.16 #	2.7%
Sugar	0.9 #	15%
Yeast, dry	0.07 #	1.2%
Milk, whole	1.39 #	23.2%
Butter	3 #	50%
TOTAL	13.92 #	232.1%

6. Pizza Dough

INGREDIENT	WEIGHT	PERCENT
Bread flour	10.66 kg	100%
Yeast, dry	0.11 kg	1%
Salt	0.21 kg	2%
Sugar	0.16 kg	1.5%
Olive oil	0.51 kg	4.8%
Water	6.34 kg	59.5%
TOTAL	18 kg	168.8%

7.　a.　11.02 kg
　　b.　1179.9 g flour, 778.7 g water, 23.6 g salt, 17.7 g yeast
　　c.　Yes (you only need 1.416 oz of yeast to make 10 # of French bread)
8.　a.　1.83 #
　　b.　2.26 oz
　　c.　11.5 # masa harina, 0.32 # bread flour, 0.32 # pastry flour, 0.12 # salt, 15.87 # water
9.　a.　9.28 kg
　　b.　5.92 g
　　c.　4.74 # bread flour, 0.05 # dry yeast, 0.09 # salt, 0.07 # sugar, 0.23 # olive oil, 2.82 # water

Glossary of Terms

AS-PURCHASED (AP) COST PER UNIT The cost of one purchased unit (e.g., the cost of 1 pound) of product

AS-PURCHASED (AP) QUANTITY The quantity of product purchased from a vendor or supplier

AVOIRDUPOIS Weight measure based on the U.S. 16-ounce pound

BAKER'S PERCENT A type of ratio where flour is assigned 100% and the other ingredients' percentages indicate their relationship to the amount of flour used

CONSTRAINING INGREDIENT An ingredient quantity that sets the limit for a recipe's yield

COST OF AN INGREDIENT The amount of money spent to buy the necessary amount of an ingredient for a recipe

COST PER PORTION The amount of money spent on the ingredient quantities used to make one portion of a menu item

COST OF SALES The amount of money spent on the ingredient quantities purchased during a specified time period used to produce menu items sold during that time period

COST OF SALES PERCENT The quotient of cost of sales and total sales, expressed as a percent

COUNT A number of objects

DIMENSIONAL ANALYSIS The process of unit conversion using unit fractions

EDIBLE PORTION (EP) QUANTITY The amount of usable product left over after performing a preparation process on an as-purchased quantity

EDIBLE PORTION (EP) COST PER UNIT The cost, including the cost of the waste, of one usable unit of product (e.g., the cost of one pound of fabricated product)

EQUIVALENT A quantity that is the same as another quantity

FABRICATION/FABRICATE To make by art or skill and labor; construct

FOOD COST The cost per portion

FOOD COST PERCENT The percent of a menu item's selling price that is represented by the cost per portion for that item; the percent of a menu item's selling price that covers the cost of the raw ingredients

GROSS PROFIT The difference between a menu item's selling price and its cost per portion; the amount of money left over from a menu item's selling price after the raw ingredients for that item have been paid for; the difference between sales and cost of goods sold

KITCHEN RATIO The relationship between two or more quantities expressed in the same unit

MIXED MEASUREMENT A measurement that is expressed in two units of measure (e.g., 3 # 2 oz or 1 T plus 1 t)

PART SIZE The quantity represented by one part in a ratio

PAR STOCK The minimum necessary on-hand quantities of all ingredients

PORTION (SERVING) SIZE The amount served to one person, either of a dish or of a single ingredient

RATIO The relationship between two quantities expressed in the same unit

RECIPE YIELD The amount of product produced by a recipe

SCALING FACTOR The number used to increase or decrease both the yield of a recipe and the ingredient quantities used to make that adjusted recipe

SELLING PRICE The amount of money charged to a customer for a menu item (also called menu price)

STANDARD COST A forecasted cost for a particular food item or items

STANDARD RECIPE A recipe that is used for consistent production in the foodservice industry

STANDARD UNIT OF MEASURE An authorized or approved unit of weight or measure

SUBRECIPE A recipe that is a component of another recipe

SYSTÈME INTERNATIONAL D'UNITÉS (SI) The system of measurement that measures volume using liters (and other units based on the liter) and measures weight using grams (and other units based on the gram)

TARE To zero a scale; to reset a scale's display so it reads zero

TRIM LOSS QUANTITY The amount of waste generated during a specific preparation process

UNIT CONVERSION The process of rewriting a quantity in a different unit of measure

U.S. CUSTOMARY SYSTEM The system of measurement that measures weight using pounds and ounces and measures volume using teaspoons, tablespoons, cups, pints, quarts, gallons, pecks, and bushels

VOLUME The amount of space that an object or substance occupies

WEIGHT The heaviness or mass of an object or substance

YIELD PERCENT The percent of a purchased quantity that is usable for a specific purpose

YIELD TEST A kitchen test used to determine the percent of a quantity that is usable for a specific purpose

References

Bureau International des Poids et Mesures, http://www.bipm.org.

Culinary Institute of America (2004). *Baking and Pastry: Mastering the Art and Craft.* Hoboken, NJ: John Wiley & Sons.

Culinary Institute of America (2004). *Baking at Home with the Culinary Institute of America.* Hoboken, NJ: John Wiley & Sons.

Culinary Institute of America (2003). *Cooking at Home with the Culinary Institute of America.* Hoboken, NJ: John Wiley & Sons.

Culinary Institute of America (2004). *Gourmet Meals in Minutes.* New York: Lebhar-Friedman.

Culinary Institute of America (2006). *The Professional Chef,* 8th ed. Hoboken, NJ: John Wiley & Sons.

Culinary Institute of America (2007). *Techniques of Healthy Cooking,* 3rd ed. Hoboken, NJ: John Wiley & Sons.

Culinary Institute of America (2007). *Vegetables.* New York: Lebhar-Friedman.

Gershtein S., Gershtein A. (1996–2005). Convert-Me [online measurements conversion, conversion tables, metric conversion]. Retrieved from: http://www.convert-me.com.

Katzen, M. (2000). *The New Moosewood Cookbook. Berkeley, CA: Ten Speed Press.*

Lynch, F. T. (2010). *The Book of Yields,* 8th ed. Hoboken, NJ: John Wiley & Sons.

National Institute of Standards and Technology, http://ts.nist.gov/WeightsAnd Measures/Publications.appxc.cfm

Rowlett, R. (July 11, 2005). How Many? A Dictionary of Units of Measurement. Retrieved from: http://www.unc.edu/~rowlett/units/index.html; http://www.unc.edu/~rowlett/units/custom.html; http://www.unc.edu/~rowlett/units/sipm.html.

Ruhlman, M. (2009). *Ratio: The Simple Codes Behind the Craft of Everyday Cooking.* New York: Scribner.

Traunfeld, J. (2000). *The Herbfarm Cookbook.* New York: Scribner.

United States Department of Commerce, http://www.commerce.gov; http://ts.nist .gov/WeightsAndMeasures/Publications/appxc.cfm.

Index

Note: Numbers in italics indicate photo pages.

A

abbreviations
for measures of volume, 4
for measures of weight, 2
all-purpose flour, volume-to-weight equivalent, 22
answers to practice problems, 277–300
AP (as-purchased) cost per unit. *See* as-purchased (AP) cost per unit
AP (as-purchased) quantity. *See* as-purchased (AP) quantity appendices, 259–276
Appendix I: Additional Information on Units of Measure, 259–260
Appendix II: Volume Unit Equivalent Visual Memorization Aids, 261–262
Appendix III: Changing Between Fractions, Decimals, and Percents, 263–266
Appendix IV: The Butcher's Yield, 267–268
Appendix V: Information from *The Book of Yields*, 269–276
as-purchased (AP) cost per unit
comparing, when waste is a factor, 201–202
comparing, when waste is not a factor, 200–201
definition of, 139
in recipe costing, 139
as-purchased (AP) quantity(ies)
calculating, 82–90
calculating for a recipe, 112–118
calculating by using portion size or recipe quantities, 104–111
calculating total cost of recipe, 143
definition of, 74
grocery list, role in creating, 119
in recipe costing, 139
recipe quantities that compensate for waste, 91–94
avoirdupois, definition of, 2

B

baker's percent, 241, 248–257
Baking at Home with the CIA, 26, 64, 65, 66
balance scale, 3, *3*

Book of Yields, The, 22, 24, 40, 47, 76, 82, 83, 96, 101, 107, 117, 196, 203, 204, 205, 206, 269, 276
information from, 269–276
bridge method, 9
bushel, 4
butcher's yield, 204, 267–268
butter, volume-to-weight equivalent, 22
buying products, factors to consider, 201, 202

C

canned foods weight-to-volume, yield of, 273
cheddar, grated, volume-to-weight equivalent, 22
chili powder, volume-to-weight equivalent, 22
compaction's effect on weight of substance when measured by volume, 24
comparative costing, 200–212
constraining ingredient, 39
scaling a recipe based on, 56
conversion, unit. *See* unit conversion
converting
between weight and volume, 21
units of measure within weight or within volume, 8–20
Cooking at Home with the CIA, 25, 34, 116
cooking and math, similarities between, viii
corn niblets, volume-to-weight equivalent, 22
cost of an ingredient
calculating, when waste is a factor, 140–142
calculating, when waste is not a factor, 139–140
comparing, 204
definition of, 139
factors causing fluctuation, 192
food cost percent and, 158
labor's impact on, 206
cost per portion
definition of, 143–144
effect on food cost percent, 156–158
food cost percent and, 158
cost of sales percent, definition of, 156
count, definition of, 91, 92
Culinary Institute of America, The, 7, 17, 18, 19, 20, 21, 23, 25, 26, 34, 63, 64, 65, 66, 71, 72, 116, 118, 119, 123, 124, 125, 127, 128
cup, 4–5, 9

W

waste
    and AP costs per unit, 200–202
    and cost of an ingredient, 139–142
    recipe quantities that compensate for, 91–92
water, volume-to-weight relationships for, 259
Web resources for units of measures, 260
weighing ingredients, 232
weight
    as accurate method to measure ingredients,
        24
    definition of, 2
    density's effect on, *22*
    measuring by, 2–3
    recipe quantities that compensate for, 91–92
    of substance when measured by volume, factors
        affecting, 23–24
    and volume, converting between, 21
weight equivalents, commonly used, 9

weight measures, notes on, 259
weight ratio versus volume ratio, *215*

Y

yield, butcher's, 204, 267–268
yield, desired
    calculating based on scaling factor, 47
    scaling recipes based on, 46–47
yield percent, 73–94, 112, 119
    calculating, 73–81
    definition of, 74
    exceptions to the rule, 92
    fabrication and, 76, 83–84, 91
    in 2-in-1 recipe costing form (Excel version), 194
yield test
    definition of, 76
    factors affecting results of, 76

Z

zero. *See* tare